TRANSFORMING CITIES

Transforming Cities examines the profound changes that have characterised cities of the advanced capitalist societies in the final decades of the twentieth century. It analyses ways in which relationships of contest, conflict and co-operation are realised in and through the social and spatial forms of contemporary urban life. In particular, this book focuses on the impact of economic restructuring and changing forms of urban governance on patterns of urban deprivation and social exclusion. It contends that these processes are creating new patterns of social division and new forms of regulation and control.

Contributors analyse innovative strategies of urban regeneration, the shift from Fordist to post-Fordist cities, new patterns of possession and dispossession in urban spaces, the production of cultural representations and city images, the evolution of novel forms of political power, emerging patterns of policing and surveillance, the development of partnerships between public and private agencies, the mobilisation of resistance by urban residents and implications for the empowerment of communities and individuals.

Nick Jewson is Senior Lecturer in the Department of Sociology at the University of Leicester and **Susanne MacGregor** is Head of the School of Sociology and Social Policy at Middlesex University.

TRANSFORMING CITIES

contested governance and new spatial divisions

Edited by
NICK JEWSON and
SUSANNE MACGREGOR

LONDON AND NEW YORK

First published 1997
by Routledge
11 New Fetter Lane, London EC4P 4EE

Simultaneously published in the USA and Canada
by Routledge
29 West 35th Street, New York, NY 10001

Typeset in Baskerville by Solidus (Bristol) Limited
Printed and bound in Great Britain by
TJ International Ltd, Padstow, Cornwall

British Library Cataloguing in Publication Data
A catalogue record for this book is available from the British Library

Library of Congress Cataloging in Publication Data
Transforming cities : contested governance and new spatial divisions /
edited by Nick Jewson and Susanne MacGregor.
p.   cm.
"Derived from papers delivered at the British Sociological
Association Annual Conference for 1995"—P. 1.
Includes bibliographical references and index.
1. Sociology, Urban—Great Britain.   2. Cities and towns—Great
Britain.   I. Jewson, Nick.   II. MacGregor, Susanne.
HT133.T74   1997
307.76′0941—dc20   96-29377
CIP

ISBN 0-415-14603-8 (hbk)
ISBN 0-415-14604-6 (pbk)

CONTENTS

TABLES

CONTRIBUTORS

Wendy Ball is currently a researcher in the School of Law at the University of Warwick. She worked previously as a Research Fellow with the Centre for Research in Ethnic Relations, University of Warwick, and as a lecturer in Sociology and Adult Continuing Education. Her research and teaching interests are in educational policy-making, race and gender. She is co-editor of *Race and Local Politics* (with John Solomos, Macmillan 1990).

Mike Beazley is Lecturer in Black Country Planning at the Centre for Urban and Regional Studies at the University of Birmingham. He has a long-standing interest in how the development process impacts on low income communities. His experience includes five years spent in Vancouver conducting his doctoral research on public involvement in urban mega-project planning processes.

James A. Beckford is Professor of Sociology at the University of Warwick and a Vice-President of the International Sociological Association. His current research is concerned with civic religion, chaplaincies and the relationship between religion and politics. His main publications include *The Trumpet of Prophecy: A Sociological Analysis of Jehovah's Witnesses* (Basil Blackwell 1975), *Cult Controversies: The Societal Response to Religious Movements* (Tavistock 1985) and *Religion and Advanced Industrial Society* (Routledge 1989).

Chris Collinge is Lecturer in the Centre for Urban and Regional Studies at the University of Birmingham. His fields of research include the development of local and regional economies and economic policies, the politics and management of subnational government in the UK and Europe. Before joining CURS he was Research Fellow at the Cranfield School of Management.

Mike Danson is Professor in Economics in the Department of Economics at the University of Paisley. He has researched extensively on urban and regional economies and policies, writing in particular on the development and underdevelopment of the Scottish economy.

Janet Foster is Lecturer in Criminology at the University of Cambridge, Institute of Criminology. Her main areas of research interest are crime, community, urban sociology and qualitative methodology. She has conducted research for the Home Office on 'difficult to let' housing estates. In addition to numerous articles and research reports, her publications include *Villains: Crime and Community in the Inner City* (Routledge 1990) and *Cultures in Conflict, Worlds in Collision* (UCL Press 1996).

Mike Geddes is Research Manager and Principal Research Fellow at the Local Government Centre, Warwick Business School, University of Warwick. He has experienced, practised and researched urban and regional policy in both central and local government. His research interests include local strategies for industrial change, poverty and social exclusion, and the future of local public services. He is co-editor of the journal *Local Economy*.

Stephen Hall is Lecturer in the Centre for Urban and Regional Studies at the University of Birmingham. His research interests include comparative urban policy, local economic development and urban governance.

David Harvey is Professor of Human Geography at Johns Hopkins University. Among his best known books are *Social Justice and the City* (Edward Arnold 1973), *The Limits to Capital* (Basil Blackwell 1982), *Consciousness and the Urban Experience* (Basil Blackwell 1985), *The Urbanisation of Capital* (Basil Blackwell 1985) and *The Condition of Postmodernity* (Basil Blackwell 1989).

Gordon Hughes is Principal Lecturer in Social Policy and Sociology at Nene College, Northampton. Since October 1995 he has been on a three-year secondment to the Open University. He is co-ordinator of the Social Policy Research Group and course leader of the MA Policy Studies. His current research interests are in multi-agency strategies of crime prevention, community consultation with the police and modes of inspection across the public sector.

Bob Jessop is Professor of Sociology at Lancaster University. He is best known for his research on state theory, Thatcherism, the regulation approach and welfare states. He has recently finished a research project on economic and political policies in post-socialism and is currently writing up an ESRC-funded project on local governance. His numerous books include *Thatcherism: A Tale of Two Nations* (Polity 1988), *Regulation Theory & The Transition to Post-Fordism* (Polity 1990) and *The Politics of Flexibility: Restructuring State and Industry in Britain, Germany and Scandinavia* (co-editor, Edward Elgar 1991).

Nick Jewson is Director of the Ethnicity Research Centre, and Senior Lecturer in Sociology, at the University of Leicester. He has researched widely in the fields of ethnicity and employment, equal opportunities policies and programmes, changing labour markets, community relations, and the sociology of health and health care. Among his recent publications are *Formal Equal Opportunities Policies and Employment Best Practice* (with David Mason, Department for Education and Employment 1995) and *Homeworkers in Britain* (with Alan Felstead, HMSO 1996).

John Lea is Professor of Criminology at Middlesex University. His numerous publications include *What is to be done About Law and Order* (with Jock Young, Pluto Press 1993) and *Losing the Fight Against Crime* (with Jock Young and Richard Kinsey, Basil Blackwell 1986).

Patrick Loftman is a Senior Lecturer at the Built Environment Development Centre at the University of Central England. He has conducted extensive research, and published widely, on urban regeneration issues and the way in which they impact on disadvantaged communities.

Susanne MacGregor is Professor and Head of the School of Sociology and Social Policy at Middlesex University. She has conducted a wide range of research on urban problems and urban policy and is the author of *The Politics of Poverty* (Routledge 1981), *Tackling the Inner Cities* (edited with Ben Pimlott, Clarendon Press 1991) and *The Other City: People and Politics in New York and London* (co-edited with Arthur Lipow, Humanities 1995), and numerous other books, articles, essays and reports.

Rosemary Mellor is Senior Lecturer in the Department of Sociology at the University of Manchester. Currently, her research interests are focused on urban change in the UK and Russia. Her numerous publications include *Urban Sociology in an Urbanised Society* (Routledge & Kegan Paul 1977).

Gerry Mooney is Senior Lecturer in Sociology and Social Policy in the Department of Applied Social Studies at the University of Paisley. He has written widely on urban studies and is currently researching the spatial distribution of poverty and social exclusion on Clydeside and the changing representation of peripheral estates.

Jayne Mooney is Lecturer in the School of Sociology and Social Policy at Middlesex University. Her research interests include violence against women, methodology, deprivation and crime. Her publications include *The Miranda Crime and Community Survey* (Middlesex University Centre for Criminology 1993) and *The Hidden Figure: Domestic Violence in North London* (Islington Council 1993).

Robert Moore is the Eleanore Rathbone Professor of Sociology at the University of Liverpool. His main areas of research interest and academic publication comprise 'race' relations, urban development, poverty and deprivation. He has been involved in the Third European Poverty Programme in Liverpool. Among his best-known books are *Race Community & Conflict* (with John Rex, OUP 1967), *Slamming the Door* (with Tina Wallace, Robertson 1975) and *Racism & Black Resistance in Britain* (Pluto Press 1975).

Brendan Nevin is a Lecturer at the Centre for Urban and Regional Studies at the University of Birmingham. For the past ten years he has worked in Birmingham, the Black Country and Glasgow on urban issues which affect disadvantaged communities.

Peter Ratcliffe is Senior Lecturer in Sociology at the University of Warwick. He has written widely both in and at the interfaces between sociology, social statistics, social policy and social geography. Since the 1970s his work has been mainly focused on issues of 'race' and ethnicity. His main publications are *Colonial Migrants in a British City: A Class Analysis* (co-editor, Routledge & Kegan Paul 1979), *Racism and Reaction: A Profile of Handsworth* (Routledge & Kegan Paul 1981), *Ethnic Discrimination: Comparative Perspectives* (University of Uppsala 1992), *'Race', Ethnicity and Nation: International Perspectives on Social Conflict* (editor, UCL Press 1994) and *Social Geography and Ethnicity in Britain: Geographical Spread, Spatial Concentration and Internal Migration* (HMSO 1996).

Mike Sheaff is a Senior Lecturer in the Department of Sociology at the University of Plymouth. He completed his doctorate on industrial and business studies at the University of Warwick. His research interests are focused on the sociology of work and the sociology of health. He is a Plymouth City counsellor and Chair of the Plymouth City Council Anti-Poverty Committee.

ACKNOWLEDGEMENTS

The editors would like to offer their thanks to all the contributors to this volume for their generous co-operation. The chapters are based upon papers delivered at the British Sociological Association Annual Conference for 1995, Contested Cities: Social Process & Spatial Forms. We should like to thank the staff and students of the Department of Sociology at the University of Leicester for their invaluable support in running the Conference, especially James Fulcher. We owe a particular debt of gratitude to Robert Ash, both for his contribution to the Conference and for the excellent work he has done in the production of the text of this book. We should also like to thank Ian Goodchild who played a crucial role in dealing with copy editing and other queries.

NJ/SM
January 1997

TRANSFORMING CITIES

Social exclusion and the reinvention of partnership

Nick Jewson and Susanne MacGregor

THE THEMES OF THE VOLUME

This collection of essays focuses on aspects of the profound transformations that have characterised cities of the advanced capitalist societies in the final decades of the twentieth century. It analyses ways in which relationships of contest, conflict and co-operation are realised in and through the social and spatial forms of contemporary urban life. These processes, it is contended, are creating new patterns of social division and new forms of regulation and control. More specifically, contributors analyse innovative strategies of urban regeneration, the shift from Fordist to post-Fordist cities, new patterns of possession and dispossession in urban spaces, the production of cultural representations and city images, the evolution of novel forms of political power, emerging patterns of policing and surveillance, the development of partnerships between public and private agencies, the mobilisation of resistance by urban residents and implications for the empowerment of communities and individuals. Taken together, the essays give an account of the impact of economic restructuring and changing forms of urban governance on patterns of urban deprivation and social exclusion.

The chapters are all derived from papers delivered at the British Sociological Association Annual Conference for 1995, which was organised around the theme 'Contested Cities: Social Process and Spatial Forms'. The study of urban sociology has recently undergone its own revival – rescued from, on the one hand, overspecialisation and mundane description and, on the other, theoretical paradigms that denied sociological significance to the city as a social form. Renewed vigour and conviction among scholars are evidenced in the liveliness of the BSA conference on which this volume is based, increased publications in the field and moves towards new overarching theoretical syntheses. The chapters that follow offer, then, a distinctive approach, seeing change through the critical eye of sociology.

The ways urban spaces are generated in social relationships, and the ways social relations take distinct spatial forms in cities, are key processes which it is the task of urban sociology to analyse. In this perspective, cities are conceived not merely as sites or arenas of social interaction but as built spatial entities which incorporate and constitute the constraints and opportunities of a wide range of social relationships. This theme is introduced by David Harvey in the first chapter in this volume – expressed in the notion of 'framing cities' – and is sustained in the chapters which follow.

The chapters offer remarkably topical discussions of cities and urban policies in the 1990s whilst, at the same time, locating current trends in a broader context. They reflect the more sceptical approach which now characterises academic and policy debates about cities, as the after-effects of the excesses of the 1980s become only too apparent. They also link macro and micro level analyses. Middle range and grand theorisations are complemented by careful investigations of particular cities. They also bring together writing and research which have tended to be compartmentalised; for example, discussions of local government have been separated from discussions of leisure and pleasure, crime and policing and other social processes. When the sociological imagination focuses on the city itself as a social and spatial form, more holistic analyses emerge.

A FRAMEWORK OF ISSUES

The renewal of theoretical and empirical work in urban sociology has been brought about by a recognition of the significance of cities within the forms and dynamics of western capitalism. A transformation of capitalism – and, thus, simultaneously a transformation of cities – has been taking place in the second half of the twentieth century. These changes have generated a series of crises and conflicts, including the decline of manufacturing and the growth of unemployment, polarisation between the socially excluded and the better-off (although increasingly insecure) middle classes, increasing disillusion and dissatisfaction with traditional political parties and political classes, the deleterious environmental impacts of current systems of production and distribution, and the failure of available ideologies (both welfare statism and neo-liberalism) to come up with effective policy solutions (Jacobs 1992: 8). The interrelated processes entailed in these changes, and their associated social divisions, provide a framework of issues for the investigation of urban forms and relationships – and, hence, for the chapters in this volume.

Restructuring employment and restructuring cities

An increasingly flexible and deregulated labour market characterises the 1990s as companies have responded to technological innovation and global competitiveness. There has been a significant decline in the proportion of people employed in full-time and permanent jobs whilst the numbers of those working part-time, on short-term contracts and in self-employment have grown. Women now make up nearly half of the employed workforce. Subcontracting, out-sourcing and so-called 'non-standard' forms of employment have become integral features of labour markets. The services sector has waxed while manufacturing has waned. Pursuit of economies of scale has been replaced by an emphasis on small-batch production and niche marketing of goods and services. In many contexts large-scale, hierarchical organisations have given way to small and medium-sized enterprises with flatter managerial structures. 'The demand for workers in skilled high technology based occupations as well as in low paid and labour intensive sectors such as hotels, catering and retail distribution looks set to grow' (Taylor 1996: 208). The impact on urban forms of such transformations in labour markets and labour processes has given rise to the notion of a post-Fordist city. Such a city is characterised by a regime of flexible accumulation that creates new spatial and social relationships (cf. Harvey 1989a; Savage and Warde 1993).

Awareness of these trends has been added to prior concerns about the decline of cities which dominated the 1970s. The symptoms of decline noted then were loss of population, loss of employment, fiscal problems resulting from the erosion of the tax base, disproportionate numbers of poor households concentrated in poor areas (characterised especially in the USA by housing abandonment, arson, vandalism, high crime rates, drug dealing, and dependence on welfare), and a concentration of minority ethnic groups in separate areas of the city. The gloomy prognoses which derive from these accounts were challenged in the 1980s by views which heralded the revival of city centres, sometimes focused around cultural institutions, the arts, leisure and consumption activities (Bianchini 1989 and 1990). Yet alongside these booming developments, in other areas there has remained decline, distress, disparity of income and lifestyle and divergence of values and opportunities. New kinds of low-paid, insecure and low-status jobs are generated by the demands of tourists, gentrifiers, concert-goers, conference delegates and other affluent urban consumers. Landscapes of consumption and of devastation exist side by side, and in intimate relation with one another (Zukin 1991).

Globalisation, post-Fordist cities and social exclusion

The restructuring of urban employment relations has been a global process, generating new international divisions and connections between capital, labour and resources. Of central importance has been, as a result of financial deregulation and the explosive growth of electronic communications, the speedy movement of money within and between world markets. There has been a world-wide social and spatial reorganisation of economic activities and a restructuring of capital, resulting in new functions for financial markets and challenges to established political institutional 'containers', such as the nation-state (Sassen 1994). This has led to a reordering of the significance and influence of cities across the face of the planet. New patterns of wealth and poverty, dispersal and centralisation, control and subordination have been created. Profound shocks have been felt in all parts of the world and many human lives disrupted, posing particular difficulties of adaptation for western societies, coming as they did after a uniquely stable period of steady economic growth in the decades following the Second World War.

A key characteristic of this transformation is its pattern of uneven development. Massey insists that the concept of uneven development refers 'to more than the fact that there are more jobs in some places than others, or even that there are better jobs in some places than others' (Massey 1994: 86). She stresses that an important element of uneven development is the spatial structuring of the relations of production in capitalist societies – unequal relationships which imply positions of dominance and subordination (ibid.: 87) – and that analysis is incomplete without recognition of this spatial ordering. On the ground, this results in some regions/countries/cities monopolising control functions, while other regions/countries/cities are locked into subordinate roles. The key point is that 'the overlapping and interweaving of all these spatial structures is the basis for a spatial division of labour' (ibid.: 90). Thus, for example, the picture of Britain described by Massey is one where the North remains dominated by branch-plant structures, with an increasing proportion of these being responsible to headquarters outside the UK. Along with this have gone other changes which impact on local economies and local social relations, especially increasing subcontracting, casualisation and contracting out (hollowing out of core functions). These transformations, she argues, have exacerbated the north–south divide: '[n]orth and south are locked in very different ways into *international* spatial structures and the international division of labour' (ibid.: 97). She continues:

> The economy of London and the south-east is in many ways more in competition with and linked to other international metropolitan regions and world cities than it is with the rest of the UK ... In contrast, the factories of the north are linked into, and in competition with, similar factories in similar regions in Europe, and also to some extent in the Third World.
>
> (Massey 1994: 97)

Within cities, polarisation of the labour market is also evidenced in increasing spatial segregation.

It has become commonplace to describe these transformations in terms of processes conveniently, if misleadingly, labelled as 'globalisation'. More sceptical writers have challenged the sweeping nature of this analysis – and the pessimistic conclusions that seem to follow for political action. Authors such as Will Hutton (1995) and Paul Hirst and Grahame Thompson (1996) have argued that the role of the nation-state, while altered, has not been eroded to the extent that the globalisation argument would imply. Hirst and Thompson argue that '[g]lobalisation has become a fashionable concept in the social sciences, a core dictum in the prescriptions of management gurus and a catchphrase for journalists and politicians of every stripe' (Hirst and Thompson 1996: 1). They offer instead a 'scepticism about global economic processes and optimism about the possibilities of control of the international economy and of the viability of national political strategies' (ibid.). The term 'international' is used deliberately by these writers rather than 'global' to indicate that 'most companies trade from their bases in distinct national economies' (ibid.: 185).

Nevertheless, competition between localities for inward investment has increased, with cities and regions seeking to project themselves on a global stage in order to attract capital investment. This, in turn, often entails creating a distinctive civic image that, it is hoped, will establish the city as an attractive niche for some aspect of transnational economic operations. Such images may emphasise environmental features, educational and cultural institutions, scientific prowess, historical heritage, attitudes of residents, and so on. City boosters may feel that investment in prestige projects, cultural spectacles or international events will help foster a positive image, resulting in competition between urban localities to build conference centres, sponsor tourist attractions and host sporting contests (cf. Harvey 1989a; Biancini 1991; Mulgan 1990). In these circumstances the ambience and style of the city become economic assets. Some cities have long established advantages in this regard; others have to be more creative in inventing, or re-presenting (King 1996), their charms.

In post-Fordist cities there is at the same time a growing concern with a phenomenon now labelled 'social exclusion' – a new name for the old problem of poverty. This concern has, to a significant degree, been stimulated by fear of rebellion and disorder. The dominant discourse in contemporary politics now focuses on issues of social integration and disintegration. The upbeat account of transformation has been challenged by those who draw attention to increasing inequality and poverty in contemporary societies. Post-Fordism has been accompanied by de-industrialisation, the growth of unemployment (particularly long-term unemployment), and social exclusion. Social exclusion involves detachment from social and political participation and from the labour market. These tensions are crystallised in contemporary cities, as social divisions are compounded by spatial segregation. Sociology's traditional task, of employing careful investigation to draw attention to the dark side of progress, becomes of renewed importance.

There is growing concern that policy responses to these enormous challenges are inadequate. One in three children in Britain lives in poverty, 14 million people are on low incomes (4.5 million of whom are in work) and welfare expenditure itself is at a historic high point. Across Europe some 20 million people are unemployed. Yet there is marked reluctance among political parties to talk of redistributive social policies. In many countries – including Germany, France and the UK – there is growing uncertainty about the possibility of retaining welfare state arrangements. Indeed, social exclusion may itself be the result of the restructuring and dismantling of the welfare state, reflecting transformations in forms of urban and national governance. According to Lord Dahrendorf, there should be three principal objectives of current policies: prosperity, civility and liberty. The challenge for contemporary cities is whether they will be able to square the circle – attain all three in equal measure. In particular, with regard to social exclusion, the urgent tasks are to retrieve the excluded and to prevent future exclusion.

The development of appropriate policies requires better understanding of the social processes which lead to social exclusion – and here social scientists may make a contribution. Research is needed that demonstrates the dynamics through which people gain access to opportunities, or are denied them. A structural analysis would show how poverty is inherent in cities rather than being accidental or self-inflicted. The revival of interest in social networks is welcome here in helping to analyse these social processes and showing how different processes operate in different arenas. Profiling and mapping techniques can give publicity to social trends, and give a picture of the landscape of social exclusion, but these techniques are only as good as the data they utilise and need to be approached with care. Poverty is a socio-spatial phenomenon and research and theory must make this central to their accounts.

Governance, control and urban policies

Governance can be defined as 'the control of an activity by some means such that a range of defined outcomes is attained' (Hirst and Thompson 1996: 184). As such, governance is not just the province of the state and may include a wide range of activities. It has been argued, however, that there is now an urgent need to redesign public policy and social provision in the light of the massive transformations characterising late twentieth-century capitalism:

> Today ... [w]e live in an era of breathtaking change. We live in a global marketplace, which puts enormous competitive pressure on our economic institutions. We live in an information society, in which people get access to information almost as fast as their leaders do. We live in a knowledge-based economy, in which educated workers bridle at commands and demand autonomy. We live in an age of niche markets, in which customers have become accustomed to high quality and extensive choice. In this environment, bureaucratic institutions developed during the industrial era – public *and* private – increasingly fail us.
>
> (Osborne and Gaebler 1993: 15)

In the context of social change and the fear of disintegration, the dominant questions surround the possibility of coherent and integrated governance, the knitting together of the myriad of agencies involved in the governing process and the salience of democratic processes. A distinctive and central element in modern politics remains the claim of the state to exclusive control of a definite territory (Hirst and Thompson 1996: 170). However, transformations in international economic relationships and enhanced vigour of locally based social movements have, to some degree, challenged this claim. Hirst and Thompson hint that in the post-Fordist age, governance may come to parallel features of the former shape of politics in the Middle Ages, where 'political authorities and other forms of functionally specific governance (religious communities and guilds for example) had existed in complex and overlapping forms that made parallel and often competing claims to the same area' (ibid.: 171). The new political world is one of 'complexity and multiplicity of levels of types of governance' (ibid.: 183).

In these circumstances, identifying and explaining relationships between government and non-governmental forces in policy formulation and implementation becomes of renewed interest and importance. Osborne and Gaebler (1992) argue, in their influential and best-selling book, that the 'one-size-fits-all' approach to government and services no longer works, nor is it what people want. They see this as an opportunity to reinvent government, through allowing an entrepreneurial spirit to transform the public sector. The redistributive and public investment projects of welfare states have also been challenged by constraints from international financial markets, limiting the interventions available to national governments. Privatisation, deregulation and the growth of market-based services have further reduced the role of direct state provision and fostered the notion of the 'enabling state' (Cochrane 1993).

Some commentators have seen in this a reduction of the scope of national governments to one more akin to local government. Local governments 'cannot make war or peace; they cannot issue passports or forbid outsiders from entering their territory; they cannot issue currency; and they cannot control imports or erect tariff walls' (Peterson 1981: 4). What has for a long time been true of city politics also becomes the case for national politics; that is, public policies can only be explained by looking at their place within the larger socio-economic and political context. So, ironically, in this new era much can be learnt by national governments from studying what happens at the city level.

In the context of changing forms of governance, the redefinition of poverty as social exclusion reflects a perception that the political problem is one of unruly social categories, unacceptable behaviours and no-go areas. For example, in a wide-ranging discussion of drugs policy in American cities, Elliott Currie has outlined the implications of a punitive response to a 'collapsing economy and an increasingly depriving and fragmented society' (Currie 1993: 161). He argues that: 'The overuse of incarceration may strengthen the links between street and prison and help to cement users' and dealers' identity as members of an oppositional drug culture' (ibid.). Social exclusion may produce a variety of responses: opposition (through crime, terrorism or milder forms of political protest); retreat and apathy ('welfare dependence', mental illness); or separatism (Farrakhan-like social movements). Crucially, the growth of such responses challenges the very legitimacy and effectiveness of governance and demands a political response from the included.

The partnership approach to governance

At the same time as an increasingly entrepreneurial form of government has taken hold, entailing new styles of management and accounting for public finance, there has arisen a new approach to governance; that is, 'partnership'. The reasons for the promotion of partnership to the top of the political agenda have much to do with the economic restructuring of local economies and deep-seated changes in the machinery of government at both local and national levels (Bailey *et al.* 1995). Stoker has observed:

> While significant differences persist from country to country, it is clear that the need for some form of public–private co-operation exists in all advanced societies. Growing competition between cities for investment, and the role of business interests in local decision making have increasingly shaped the urban terrain. Decentralisation and shifting responsibilities within the state, increased financial constraints, and the development of privatised services utilising both profit and non-profit organisations have also created additional complexities for local governments. Urban governments are increasingly working through and alongside other interests.
>
> (Stoker 1996: 269)

Partnership is increasingly seen 'not only as an essential adjunct of policy but as the most important foundation of the government's strategy towards urban areas' (Bailey *et al.* 1995: 1).

The explanation advanced by Bailey *et al.* for the growth of partnership approaches emphasises the end of the post-war consensus; Thatcherism, with its stress on deregulation, the role of the free market and privatisation; reactions to the effects of Thatcherism in the form of riots, protests and rising crime; and the questioning of neo-liberalism by some business leaders influenced by notions of corporate social responsibility. However, socially responsible business leaders are in limited supply and pressures to seek greater efficiency and profitability override other considerations. Indeed, the very pursuit of efficiency by individual enterprises is a cause of many of the social problems which public policy has to address. Companies and agencies externalise their costs by dumping the expenses of rationalisation or changing production methods – such as pollution, sickness and unemployment – onto the wider society. What may be rational for an individual company can be very irrational for the public and others affected.

From the mid-1980s, the loss of power and finance by local authorities, and the growth of 'quangos', resulted in a series of uncoordinated *ad hoc* initiatives, some of which were actually counterproductive. The local policy vacuum left by the withdrawal of the local state was increasingly filled by proponents of a partnership approach, equally attractive to local authorities and businesses trying to manufacture a new role for themselves.

Partnership represents a particular form of a new urban regime, emerging in remarkably similar forms in cities around the world. As defined by Keating, an urban regime is 'a set of arrangements through which policy decisions are made, encompassing formal structures and informal relationships among political and economic elites comprising the governing coalition' (Keating 1991: 7–8). Harvey sees these public–private partnerships as part of the new entrepreneurialism which reflects the transformation of urban governance in late capitalism (Harvey 1989b). Governance itself becomes speculative in execution and design, patterned by flexible specialisation. It is also a response to the impact of neo-liberalism on social life, a recognition of the need to deal with the problems of social disintegration and poverty which have accompanied deregulation and restructuring. Alarm about rising crime, urban riots and social discontent fuels fears that these conditions might give rise to political opposition, especially in the form of extreme social movements. The legitimacy of the political system is, thus, threatened by increasing social exclusion.

Partnership is an attractive concept to government, because it commits other interests to regeneration (such as the private sector and the local community), it diffuses responsibility for success or failure, and ensures that relatively low levels of public expenditure can be used to lever large amounts of private investment. Finally the debate and potential conflict about means and ends normally associated with such programmes is largely transferred to the agencies within the partnership and thus is relatively excluded from wider public debate (Bailey *et al.* 1995: 39).

Most literature on partnership in urban studies has concentrated on its role in encouraging cities to compete one with another. Less attention has been given to the innovative social policies which accompany, and are designed to be compatible with, the new economic policies. The key objective is to create a stable environment within which business can operate. The new policies absorb and implement management practices which have spread from the private sector into public life during this phase of capitalist transformation. Social provision and public policy can be seen to alter to match the general development of the social relations of production.

A key issue within this restructuring is whether a place will be allowed for democratic procedures. Integration is the key objective and this may be attained by various methods, of which the democratic form is only one. So a crucial question for the partnership approach is to what extent it can deliver accountability, along with a balancing of efficiency and equity. Without a firm base in democratic principles and practices, partnership could become a system for co-opting institutions into an extended system of repressive control (Cohen 1985; MacGregor 1995). Crucial questions, therefore, include: which interests, and which players, will be included in partnerships and which will be left outside? Who will be the leaders within partnerships? Whose agendas will prevail?

Chapters in this book indicate various ways in which attempts are being made to knit together members of partnerships, in the interests of effectiveness and integration. Moreover, partnerships may be directed towards the goal of harnessing and controlling competing players in the urban scene. There is abundant evidence that, when the state withdraws, a benevolent hidden hand of the market does not automatically take over. Indeed, one might go so far as to say there is no such thing as the market: there are only employers, political parties, tenants groups, trade unions, police forces, professional bodies, churches, local authorities – all making claims to decision-making about the allocation of resources within a given area. What partnership is about is the building of coalitions of interest, or alliances, among these groups in the name of the wider interest of the city as a whole. Within these constellations, there remains a key role for a public power – the national state and local government, for example, especially through the rule of law – to mediate between these plural groups.

There is a need for more detailed empirical studies of the place of partnerships within restructured urban institutions, organisations and relations. Regulation as a process needs to be studied using imaginative methods, 'pluralistic evaluation', perhaps, which will highlight the processes and texture of regulation, showing 'the socially embedded, socially regularised nature of class struggle' (Jessop 1995b: 310).

There is, of course, another sense in which the term 'partnership' may be used: that is, with respect to concepts of social partnership, which describe a settlement between government, employers and unions, working together to develop public policy. This continental European conception is rather different from that which has developed in British and American cities, where trade unions have been generally excluded from these arrangements. Interesting and innovative as such ideas may seem, in the British context they fly 'in the face of so much custom and practice and history in industrial relations that one has to wonder how successful' the promotion of such ideas may be (Robert Taylor, speaking at Unions 95 conference). Employers in Britain reject the concept and, according to Taylor, employers would not be influenced into a social partnership unless they had to operate 'in a legal and political climate where they have to co-operate, where they have to seek partnership' (ibid.). For this legislation would be needed.

THE CHAPTERS

The chapters are grouped into four sections. Part I, 'Framing the City', provides an overview and theorisations of transformations occurring in contemporary urban forms and ways of life.

David Harvey presents a perspective that identifies themes which are reflected in all the chapters which follow. He reminds us of the centrality of cities and urban social relations to the condition and prospects of the human species: the footprint of the city on the earth is now more massive than ever (cf. Girardet 1992). He makes the case for the importance of locating sociological studies in the city, the place where wider social processes are condensed, rarefied and exaggerated. Harvey sees 'the city' not as a mere site for contest but as the framework within which debate about the future can take place. He argues for placing concepts of the urban and of democracy at the centre of social and political theory. He goes on to explore the role of relationships within communities in the democratic process – in particular the conditions under which the 'militant particularism' of localised causes and campaigns can be generalised into more universal processes of struggle.

Bob Jessop also recognises the importance of 'state' and 'ideology' in the analytic framework to be applied to the city. Like Harvey, he argues for a revived awareness that people make their history but not in conditions of their own making. Jessop explores the interconnections between the re-imagining, and re-imaging, of local economies and the re-design of urban governance mechanisms. These he places in the context of developments in global economic and political interdependencies. He suggests that the effectiveness of entrepreneurial strategies rests upon a re-imagining of the city as an economic, political and cultural entity. This, in turn, is closely linked to the emergence of new forms of public–private partnerships and networks. Jessop argues that in newly dominant political arrangements, characterised by a hollowing out of the nation-state, social policy and human need have been subordinated to the demands of capital and business.

John Lea focuses on crime control, an issue often disregarded in regulation theory. He questions the historical accuracy of some representations of Fordism. He reminds us that the Keynesian Welfare State was itself productive of social disorder. This is an important antidote to current discussions, which can all too easily portray a golden age of Fordism and the welfare state. The assumption that the post-war years were characterised by effective incorporation and stability can lead to an exaggeration of the extent of current collapse. This, in turn, raises questions about the extent to which conflict and disorder are integral to the current situation and whether there is a crisis of control. Lea asks whether the concept 'post-Fordism' 'describes the emergence of a new, stable mode of development ... or ... simply grasps the symptoms of a deepening capitalist recession'.

Rosemary Mellor, in a particularly lucid account of changing regeneration strategies in Manchester, outlines the policy agendas which have emerged in this period. She examines the commodification of leisure as a strategy of urban renewal – in particular, the part played by an emerging heritage industry, cultural institutions and recreational attractions in successive waves of speculative development in the city during the 1980s and 1990s. Her chapter highlights the role of business leaders, various agencies and the local authority in the management of local partnerships. She also outlines the impact of these developments on the poor in the city and the emergence of new patterns of exclusion. Her account shows how circumstances within cities are tied in to wider processes of capitalist development but she also emphasises that they reflect the particularities of conurbations and regional economies as well as the strategies chosen by political elites.

A long-standing theme of urban sociology has been that of charting the lives of city residents and identifying their lived experience in the urban environment. This tradition has particularly sought to reveal, measure and highlight the plight of the poor and the oppressed, by means of generating and analysing qualitative and quantitative data. Part II, 'Mapping and Measuring City Life', comprises chapters that focus on specific aspects of division, poverty and inequality in contemporary cities, with particular reference to race, gender and class. Social and economic changes impact on different groups and cities in different ways. A key concern of these chapters is to map some of these changes and variations. The examples discussed here reflect wider trends in the development of mature capitalist societies while also illustrating the importance of national and local particularities, especially with respect to political arrangements. Individually and collectively, these chapters enable us to glimpse aspects of the complex and cross-cutting web of constraints and opportunities created by global and local urban processes, analysed in Part I of the book, in the lives of disadvantaged and marginalised urban residents.

The chapter by Gerry Mooney and Mike Danson opens with a review of theories of inequality, the 'dual city' and polarisation. While profound social and economic changes lie behind the transformation of cities, particular government policies have also played a significant part. These can be, and are, contested. The authors' case study of Glasgow illustrates the parallel development of regeneration processes with growing social and spatial divisions. However, they criticise the frequently used concept of the 'dual city'. They argue that evidence concerning the extent and growth of poverty in Glasgow questions the idea of a concentrated and well defined 'underclass' living in separate areas.

Peter Ratcliffe also questions conventional categories and concepts which have assumed a taken-for-granted character in much social analysis. He draws upon data derived from the 1991 Decennial Census to explore patterns of housing tenure and ownership among Britain's ethnic minority populations. His detailed and sophisticated analysis generates results that lead to a revision of much conventional wisdom about the location of ethnic minorities within housing markets. It also reveals how complex interrelationships between ethnicity, class, household formation and stage in the life cycle shape patterns of advantage and disadvantage.

Jayne Mooney's chapter also challenges commonplace understandings in her analysis of violence in the city. She draws upon the findings of the North London Domestic Violence Survey, conducted in the London Borough of Islington. In the same tradition of careful social investigation, she demonstrates the gendered nature of the incidence, location and experience of violence in the city. She formulates and comments upon a series of hypotheses that address the assumptions and assertions of four different theoretical schools: new administrative criminology, left realists, family violence theorists and radical feminists. Her empirical data enable her to evaluate key elements of each of these perspectives.

Similarly, Janet Foster questions another common assumption – that of the collapse of community in the city. It is frequently suggested that local authority and other publicly owned housing estates are particularly prone to a dearth of community ties and neighbourliness. Foster's chapter reports the findings of a research study, based on participant observation and interviews, on a 'difficult to let' estate in London. Many aspects of the estate might be expected to inhibit neighbourliness, including adverse aspects of the physical environment and the turn-over in the tenant population. Nevertheless Foster discerned established networks among residents – mediated by class, ethnicity and gender – providing practical services and emotional support.

Part III, 'New Forms of Regulation: Partnership and Empowerment', focuses on political developments. In analysing new forms of governance, it explores issues surrounding specific strategies of urban regulation and regeneration, including the notion of partnership. These chapters consider the extent to which such processes empower local communities and residents. A theme which comes through very clearly in these chapters is the consistency of the approach being adopted in different areas of public policy, illuminating with empirical material the theories developed in the earlier chapters by Harvey, Jessop, Lea and Mellor. Strikingly similar institutional arrangements and forms, expressed in analogous languages and rhetorics, are being deployed in different areas of urban governance. Although individual case studies report a degree of confusion or uncertainty within specific partnerships, when viewed comparatively a common pattern can be discerned in programmes concerned with health, poverty and policing. These similarities support the view that a distinctive mode of regulation is under construction.

Chris Collinge and Stephen Hall review the development of regime theory and the theory of hegemony. These are compared and then evaluated through the prism of a case study of urban governance in Birmingham. The authors describe the emerging shape of local governance as the 'networked, privatised local state form'. Their analysis describes the complex range of participants and alliances within partnerships. They also show how the growth of non-elected quangos and agencies, linked to private businesses and companies, undermines democratic accountability. They conclude that both neo-Marxist and neo-pluralist paradigms have much to offer and that theoretical analysis can be advanced by developing a dialogue between them.

Mike Sheaff examines the development of partnerships as responses to poverty and division. His chapter is based upon a study of programmes to promote health within some of the most deprived areas of Britain, located in the city of Plymouth. Urban environments have long been conceived as a prime site for intervention in the struggle against illness and disease. However, the terms of such interventions have also been a battleground; for example, are the sick to be seen as authors of their own misfortunes or as victims of their material and social circumstances? Sheaff shows how urban partnerships devoted to the promotion of health may put the emphasis on community empowerment or authoritarian discipline, personal responsibility or social reform, individual counselling or collective development. He refers to the rise of a new discourse of rights and duties around these themes of partnership and community. He warns that: 'The view that rights are contingent upon personal behaviour can evolve into a far uglier form of authoritarianism.'

Robert Moore's chapter focuses on poverty programmes in Liverpool, within the context of European policies and initiatives. He stresses, as do Mooney and Danson, that poverty is no longer a problem of the margins but is a core feature of contemporary society. He suggests that earlier forms of the local state often consisted of exclusionary coalitions. Those who were not well served included women, ethnic minority groups, the poor, the unemployed, the disabled, the different and the deviant. He sees some potential in the new forms of partnership which might bring in groups previously left outside, such as the voluntary sector and community representatives. However, his account of events in Liverpool raises questions about the circumstances under which it is possible to forge effective partnerships. His analysis highlights that communities are not homogeneous or unified entities; sometimes they contain rivalries, conflicts and disagreements that influence outcomes. In addition, deeply ingrained distrust of outside bodies on the part of historically disadvantaged and exploited local groups may also represent an obstacle.

These textured, locally based studies suggest that 'politics matters'. An underlying theme is that changing forms of governance present opportunities for resistance, innovation and participation, along with attempts at more effective social discipline. Gordon Hughes is especially critical of approaches which neglect the role of countervailing forces. His chapter reports on a study of changing strategies of policing and crime prevention in an English Midlands county. Hughes contends that what he calls 'radical totalitarianism' gives insufficient attention to empirical evidence and underestimates the scope for local resistance: 'the story which unfolds . . . is not a simple one of unified local resistance to centrally developed trends but nor is it one of supine obedience to the centralist agenda'. He emphasises, however, that the new arrangements are by-passing democratic structures of representative government.

Part IV, 'The Politics of Exclusion and Resistance', considers ways in which local communities and other groups of city dwellers seek to mobilise potential sources of support and create alternative identities. These chapters explore how, in the context of transformations in their lives, urban residents seek to shape the future of the cities they inhabit.

The chapter by Mike Beazley, Patrick Loftman and Brendan Nevin reviews responses to large-scale urban developments in Vancouver, San Francisco and Birmingham. Their analysis suggests that talk of public involvement has merely been a thin veneer over determinedly pro-growth policies, in which local political elites have colluded to drive forward urban development. Despite national and local differences, they tell a depressingly familiar tale across their three examples. They report that the needs of deprived communities are routinely neglected or swept aside in the face of massive regeneration projects, some of which are ostensibly devoted to alleviating poverty and social exclusion. They conclude that: 'The challenge to local democracy to represent more fully the needs and interests of socially excluded groups could hardly be a more vital one.'

Ethnic community identities may comprise one of the bases on which resistance is mobilised. However, growing ethnic difference in contemporary cities can, under certain circumstances, be a source of contention and conflict that threatens to overwhelm democratic processes. As Hindess has pointed out, 'bitterly divided communities cannot accept the logic of majority rule or tolerate the rights of minorities' (1992: 163). The chapter by Wendy Ball and James Beckford examines ways in which political activities within a large English city are, at least in part, shaped by ethno-religious community ties. They explore ways in which minority groups are incorporated into, or excluded from, the political process, focusing specifically on issues surrounding school-level education. The chapter illustrates some of the developing bases of community identity, and local political and cultural mobilisation, in contemporary cities.

Mike Geddes concludes the collection by giving further attention to the issue of exclusion from democratic processes. He stresses, as have others, that all the social changes described have presented severe tests for traditional patterns of political representation. However, like Robert Moore, he sees some grounds for optimism in the fact that 'the empowerment of local communities is now an accepted dimension of the partnership approach'. These new structures do undermine conventional local representative government but they also open up new political spaces, within which previously marginalised voices may be heard. While not offering a clear vision of an alternative to increasing surveillance and regulation, Geddes' chapter encourages attention to the development of new approaches which might encourage the survival and expansion of democratic forms.

Geddes' chapter thus brings the collection full circle to the issues raised in David Harvey's opening discussion. Harvey calls for transformations which will transcend particularities and encourage a negotiation of 'universalities through which to talk about how the cities of the future should be'. It is the hope of the editors of this collection that this volume can contribute to that 'long revolution'.

CONCLUSION

The chapters in this collection explore a number of dimensions, or meanings, of the theme 'transforming cities'. They analyse the direction of contemporary changes in the economic, political and cultural relationships and spaces that comprise cities. They identify and evaluate the policies and procedures of those who currently seek to shape and guide the transformation of cities. They examine the struggles which surround attempts, by various social groups and classes, to redefine or reinvent images of particular cities and of urban life in general. These issues, in turn, raise questions about what kinds of urban transformations are desirable and, crucially, what democratic forms facilitate popular participation in determining these ideals.

Part I

FRAMING THE CITY

1

CONTESTED CITIES

Social process and spatial form

David Harvey

At the beginning of this century, there were little more than a dozen or so cities in the world with more than a million people. They were all in the advanced capitalist countries and London, by far the largest of them, had just under 7 million. At the beginning of this century too, no more than 7 per cent of the world's population could reasonably be classified as 'urban'. By the year 2000 there may be as many as 500 cities with more than a million inhabitants. The largest of them (like Tokyo, São Paulo, Bombay and possibly Shanghai) will boast populations of more than 20 million, trailed by a score of cities, mostly in the so-called developing countries, with upwards of 10 million. Sometime early next century, if present trends continue, more than half of the world's population will be classified as urban rather than rural.

The twentieth century has been *the* century of urbanisation. There has been a massive reorganisation of the world's population, of its political and its institutional structures and of the very ecology of the earth.

These observations immediately suggest some fundamental questions. First, given these transformations, why is it that the urban so frequently disappears from our discussions of broader political–economic processes and social trends? Most of the writing about our recent history has failed to take into account this massive reorganisation and its consequences. The urban rarely appears as a salient category in our analyses. The crucial categories seem to be those of modernisation, modernity, post-modernity, capitalist and industrial society. So what has happened to the category 'urban'? This question is important because the qualities of urban living in the next century will define the qualities of life for the mass of humanity. And all political–economic processes we observe are mediated through the filter of urban organisation. Discussions of contemporary politics, for example, often proceed as if a concept like that of 'democracy' can remain unaffected by urban transformations when, plainly, there is a huge difference between democracy in ancient Athens and democracy in contemporary São Paulo.

If we think about the likely qualities of life in the next century by projecting forward current trends in our cities, most commentators would end up with a somewhat dystopian view. We are producing marginalisation, disempowerment, alienation, pollution and degradation. It might be said that this is nothing new and that, in the nineteenth century, conditions were even worse. In the past, however, urbanisation and the consequences of urbanisation were taken rather more seriously than they are today. In the late nineteenth century, the bourgeoisie at least had some notion that cities were important places and, therefore, that urban reform was necessary. This generated a bourgeois reform movement – from Birmingham to Chicago – which included figures such as Jane Addams, Octavia Hill, Charles Booth, Patrick Geddes, Ebenezer Howard and many others. All of these had some vision for the future and a clear grasp of the need for reform. The nineteenth century faced the difficulties of the urban in a very positive and powerful way. It blended socialist sentiments, anarchist ideas, notions of bourgeois reformism and social responsibility into a programmatic attempt to clean up the cities. The 'gas and water socialism' of the late nineteenth and early twentieth centuries did a great deal to improve the conditions of urban life for the mass of the population. There are many contemporary analysts who, armed with the insights of Foucault, will assert that these innovations were merely about social control, which indeed in part they were. But having acknowledged this point, I think we have also to recognise that a significant proportion of the population found itself living in better circumstances as a result. Moreover, inherent in these interventions was a visionary notion of an alternative city – a city beautiful with facilities and services that would, indeed, pacify alienated populations.

Some of that concern would be helpful to have back in our cities right now. In the past, capital regarded cities as important places which had to be efficiently organised and where social controls needed to operate in some sort of meaningful way. We now find that capital is no longer concerned about cities. Capital needs fewer workers and much of it can move all over the world, deserting problematic places and populations at will. As a result, the coalition between big capital and bourgeois reformism has disappeared. Moreover, the bourgeoisie itself seems to have lost much of its guilty conscience about cities. It has, I think, concluded there is little to fear from socialist revolution, and so has attenuated its engagement with reformism. Increasingly the wealthy seal themselves off in those fanciful, gated communities – which are being built all over the United States – that enable the bourgeoisie to cut themselves off from what their representatives call by the hateful term 'the underclass'. 'The underclass' is left inside the ghetto, along with drugs, Aids, epidemics of tuberculosis and much else. In this new politics, the poor no longer matter. The marginalisation of the poor is accompanied by a blasé indifference on the part of the rich and powerful.

This blasé indifference is a matter of great concern. Accordingly I would like to highlight some fundamental questions and beliefs about the role of the city in political, economic, social and ecological life. In defining that role, we are also formulating a notion of the kind of cities we would like to construct into the next century.

I would like to begin with a fundamental methodological question: what is the relationship between process and form? This relationship is contained in the title of this conference and I think it is worth while to think a little bit about it. In my own work – from the standpoint of historical, geographical materialism and very strongly in the dialectical tradition – one of the rules of engagement which I have always tried to follow is to say that process takes precedence over things. We should focus on processes rather than things and we should think of things as products of processes. From this standpoint, we have to ask some fundamental questions about the nature of the categories we use to describe the world. Most of the categories we use tend to be 'thing' categories. If instead we examine dynamics and processes, we may try to do so by conceiving them as relationships between pre-existing things. But if *things* too are not pre-existing, but are actually constituted in some way by a process, then you have to have a rather different vision. This transformation in our way of thought seems to me absolutely essential if we are going to get to the heart of what the city is about.

Tony Leeds, an urban anthropologist, towards the end of his life wrote this:

> In earlier years I thought of society ... as a structure of positions, roles, statuses, groups, institutions and so on, all given shape ... by the cultures on which they draw. Process I saw as 'forces', movement, connection, pressures, taking place in and among these loci or nodes of organisation, peopled by individuals. Although this still seems largely true to me, it has also come to seem a static view – more societal order than societal becoming ... Since it does not seem inherent in nature ... that these loci exist, it seems unacceptable simply to take them as axiomatic; rather we must search for ways to account for their appearances and forms. More and more, the problems of becoming ... have led me to look at society as continuous process out of which structure or order precipitates in the forms of the loci listed above.
>
> (Leeds 1994: 32)

This, then, is a conceptualisation in which process takes priority over things and which focuses on the way in which things get precipitated out of process.

Two terms or words deserve closer examination in our discussions. One is 'urbanisation' – which we can convert into the 'urban process' or the 'urbanising process' or the 'urbanisation process'. The other is a 'thing-type' word – 'the city'. It is important to consider the relationship between the urbanising process and this thing called the city. Now, from a dialectical standpoint, the relationship between process and thing becomes complicated because things, once constituted, have the habit of affecting the very processes which constituted them. The ways that particular 'thing-like structures' (such as political-administrative territories, built environments, fixed networks of social relations) precipitate out of fluid social processes and the fixed forms these things then assume have a powerful influence upon the way that social processes can operate. Moreover, different fixed forms have been precipitated out at different historical moments and assume qualities reflective of social processes at work in particular times and places. The result is an urban environment constituted as a palimpsest, a series of layers constituted and constructed at different historical moments all superimposed upon each other. The question then becomes how does the life *process* work in and around all of those *things* which have been constituted at different historical periods? How are new meanings given to them? How are new possibilities constructed? I suggest that attention to this relationship between process and form will help us understand why the urban has been neglected and, furthermore, will enable us to change completely the terms of the debate.

In this vein, I want to suggest that the reduction of the urban – or the portrayal of the city as a minor feature of social organisation – can only occur when particular assumptions are made about the nature of space and time or space/time. There are three different ways of understanding spatiality or space/time that are worth noting here. The first way is the absolute notion of space/time – attributable to Newton, Descartes and Kant – in which space and time are mere containers of social action. They are passive, neutral containers. These passive, neutral containers simply allow us to locate the action which is occurring. I would like to suggest that there is a parallel here with thinking that conceives of cities as passive, neutral containers of processes and contests. These ways of thinking focus on contestations occurring *within* the city – the city happens to be the mere *site* of a process of contestation (over gender, race, class or whatever). A radically different approach is one which sees the city not so much as a site of contestation but as something to be constructed and in which the contestation is over the construction, or *framing*, of the city itself. What would that imply about notions of space and time?

There is a well-known alternative to the absolute view of space/time: that is, the relative view attributed mainly to Einstein and worked on by others since. In this view, space and time, although they are still containers, are not neutral with respect to the processes they contain. Metrics of space and time can and do vary depending upon the nature of the processes under consideration. In geography, this idea has been adapted to think of different ways of measuring and mapping distances. Physical distance is different from distance measured in terms of the cost or time taken to move between points and in the last two cases the space described is not necessarily Euclidean. Different metrics yield different maps of the space–time co-ordinates within which social interaction occurs.

A third perspective on space/time that I have employed – indeed it was incorporated in *Social Justice in the City* more than twenty years ago – is a relational view. The relational view is primarily attributable to Leibnitz and is laid out in its most explicit form in the Leibnitz/Newton, Leibnitz/Clarke correspondence. This view is that space and time do not exist outside of process: process defines space/time. Each particular kind of process will define its own distinctive spatio-temporality. Our studies should, therefore, aim to explain the way in which different processes define spatio-temporality, and then, having defined that spatio-temporality, find themselves bound by its rules in certain kinds of ways. Moreover, our cities are constituted not by one but by multiple spatio-temporalities, producing multiple frameworks within which conflictual social processes are worked out.

From this standpoint, we have to take very seriously the notion which Giddens uses, and which most of us for a long time have argued for; namely, that space and time are not simply constituted *by* but are also constitutive *of* social processes. This is also true for the urban. The urban and the city are not simply constituted by social processes, they are constitutive of them. We have to understand that dialectic in order to appreciate how urbanisation is constructed and produces all of these thing-like configurations which we call cities – with political organisation, social organisation and physical structures. We have to appreciate better the centrality of that moment of urban construction, which is fundamental to how the social process operates. In exactly the same way, we have to take seriously the idea of that moment of construction of spatio-temporality, which then defines how the system itself will operate. From this standpoint, it is possible to reposition the urban as fundamental in contemporary debates. At the same time we transform our notion of urbanisation. We would abandon the view of the urban as simply a site or a container of social action in favour of the idea that it is, in itself, a set of conflictual heterogeneous processes which are producing spatio-temporalities as well as producing things, structures and permanencies in ways which constrain the nature of the social process. Social processes, in giving rise to things, create the things which then enhance the nature of those particular social processes.

One outcome may be that we find ourselves stuck for a very long time with a particular kind of social process. An example would be nuclear power. Once nuclear power stations exist all sorts of things follow. If a nuclear power station goes on the blink, can you imagine calling a town meeting to discuss democratically what to do about it? The answer is no, you can't. In these circumstances, we are immediately driven back to the realms of expert knowledge and expert decision-making. So a thing has been created which for as long as it lasts – which is going to be a very long time – is by its very nature going to be basically undemocratic in terms of the sort of social process that supports it. Here is a social process that has defined a certain spatio-temporality for the next 10,000 years, which in turn implies perpetuation of a certain kind of social order if it is not to unravel in highly destructive ways.

We have to be thinking in these kinds of terms about the nature of cities. What kinds of cities we create, how we create them, how flexible they are, how adjustable they can be: these are the questions we need to ask in order to understand better the relationship between process and thing. Our aim and objective should be to liberate emancipatory processes of social change. In so doing, however, we must understand that liberatory impulses and politics are always going to be contained and constrained by the nature of things which have been produced in the past.

This, then, is my first major point. We have to reconceptualise the urban as the production of space and the production of spatio-temporality, understood as a dialectical relationship between process and thing.

The second major point I would like to make concerns the currently widespread invocation of the word 'community'. It too entails an exploration of process/thing relationships. One of the aspects of much contemporary debate about the urban which I find particularly striking is the tendency when faced with all sorts of difficulties again and again to reach into this bag called 'community', on the assumption that 'community is going to save us all'. Community, endowed with salving powers, is perceived as capable of redeeming the mess which we are creating in our cities. This mode of thinking goes all the way from Prince Charles and the construction of urban villages through to communitarian philosophies that, it is believed, will save us from crass individualistic materialism.

There is here too an issue about the relationship between the thing called community and the processes which constitute it. What kinds of processes constitute community? Is a community, once constituted, going to liberate or imprison further social processes? A lot of community construction projects are, in the end, a recipe for isolation. They isolate groups from the city as a whole. They move them towards a fragmented notion of what the urban process is about. Here I find myself in agreement with Iris Marion Young when she says:

> Racism, ethnic chauvinism and class devaluation I suggest, grow partly from the desire for community ... Practically speaking, such mutual understanding can be approximatcd only within a homogeneous group that defines itself by common attributes. Such common identification, however, entails reference also to those excluded. In the dynamics of racism and ethnic chauvinism in the United States today, the positive identification of some groups is often achieved by first defining other groups as the other, the devalued, semihuman.
>
> (Young 1990: 321)

What, then, are the implications of current notions of community? In answer, I would like to propose a dialectical view of relationships between process and community.

I think it is important to acknowledge that a lot of community activism is absolutely fundamental to many forms of social struggle. As a form of mobilisation of power of people in place it can sometimes be extremely important and extremely useful. Community activism can simply be a way of containing discontent but it can also be a very important moment in more general mobilisation. In this context, we have to think about the construction of community not as an end in itself but as a moment in a process. Here I refer to critiques of the nineteenth-century thinking which I described earlier. There were two flaws in that thinking. The first was the belief that, somehow or other, the proper design of *things* would solve all of the problems in the social process. It was assumed that if you could just build your urban village, like Ebenezer Howard, or your Radiant City, like Le Corbusier, then the thing would have the power to keep the process forever in harmonious state. The problem of these thinkers was not that they had a totalising vision or subscribed to master narratives or indulged in master planning. Their problem was not that they had a conception of the city or the social process as a whole. Their problem was that they took this notion of thing and gave it power over the process. Their second flaw was that they did much the same with community. Much of the ideology that came out of Geddes and Ebenezer Howard was precisely about the construction of community. In particular, the construction of communities which were fixed and had certain qualities with respect to class and gender relations. Once again, the domination of *things* seems to me to be the fundamental flaw.

What then is the significance of community mobilisation? The concept I wish to use here is the one that Raymond Williams tentatively suggested, and which he then shrank away from, but which I want to resurrect. It is what Williams calls 'militant particularism'. This idea suggests that almost all radical movements have their origin in some place, with a particular set of issues which people are pursuing and following. The key issue is whether that militant particularism simply remains localised or whether, at some point or other, it spills over into some more universal construction. Williams suggested that the whole history of socialism had to be read as a series of militant particularisms which generated what he described as the extraordinary claim that there is an alternative kind of society, called socialist, which would be a universal kind of condition to which we could all reasonably aspire. In other words, in this view foundational values and beliefs were discovered in particular struggles and then translated onto a broader terrain of conflict. It seems to me that the notion of community, viewed in this way, can be a positive moment within a political process. However, it is only a positive moment if it ceases to be an end in itself, ceases to be a *thing* which is going to solve all of our problems, and starts to be a moment in this *process* of broader construction of a more universal set of values which are going to be about how the city is going to be as a whole.

The third major point I am going to make is this: until very recently there was almost no mention of cities in the ecological literature. Cities were always regarded as the high point of the pollution and plundering of planet Earth. The environment was equated with nature; it was certainly not the built environment of cities. There is something curious about ecological rhetoric here (although I am probably misrepresenting some of the current thinking because it is getting a bit more sophisticated). Ecological rhetoric is committed to a totalising perspective in the sense that, quite rightly, it perceives that everything relates to everything else. However, it has also failed to address the environment of cities and the 50 per cent of the world's population that are living in urban circumstances.

Why is it that we tend to think of the built environment of cities as somehow or other not being *the* environment? Where did that separation come from? Again it comes back to the notion that there is a thing called a city, which has various qualities and attributes, that is not part of a process. It seems to me that we have to think of environment and environmental modification as a fundamental process which we have always been engaged in and will always continue to be engaged in. The environmental modification process then has to be understood as producing certain kinds of structures and things, such as fields, forests and cities. That environmental modification process cannot be separated from the whole question of urban living. There is, it seems to me, nothing particularly anti-ecological about cities. Why should we think of them that way? When does the built, constructed environment end and 'the natural environment' begin? Where does society begin and nature end? Go and look in a field of wheat and say where nature begins and society ends. You can't do it.

Here too, then, there is a dichotomy which works its way through our thinking, which we have to challenge, in which the relationship between processes and things is fundamental. We have to pay serious attention to the nature of the ecological modification process, and understand it not as something which is simply resident in nature. For example, one of the major ecological variables at work in the world right now is money flow. Just think of what would happen to the ecosystems of the world if the money flow stopped. How many ecosystems of this world are actually supported by money flow? Vast areas of the world would undergo radical ecological change if the money supply or commodity exchange was suddenly cut off or stopped. Some radical ecologists appear to relish such an outcome, as a transformation back to some ecologically sustainable condition in which the alienation of self from nature can be overcome by human beings treading far more lightly on the surface of the earth. But I believe we must pursue a much more positive ecological politics. Ecological transformations are an inevitable facet of how human beings live their lives and construct their historical geographies. Urbanisation *is* an ecological process and we desperately need creative ways to think and act on that relation. Conversely, it is impossible to talk of ecological politics without concomitantly examining urban processes in all their complexity and fullness.

We have to move the urban, and the urbanising process, into a more central position in our debates and discussions about ecological, social, political and economic change. From this standpoint, there are a number of myths that we have to confront and contest.

The first myth is the simple idea that when we have got the economy right then we can spend money to get our cities right. This sort of thinking takes the view that cities are relatively unimportant: when we have got enough money and we have organised ourselves right then we can spend a little time fixing them up. From my perspective that is entirely the wrong way round. Getting things economically right in our cities is *the* path towards economic change and economic development, even to economic growth. To treat the cities as the secondary feature of this whole dynamic is essentially wrong.

The same is true with respect to social relations. We should not wait upon some great political revolution to tell us how to reorganise our cities in a socialist or eco-feminist or some other way. No, what we have to do is to work on the nature of the social relations in the cities. If there is going to be a revolution, it is going to be a long revolution, located within the urban process. That long revolution of social relations is going to have to comprise a steady working out, over a long period of time, of transformations. Here, I think again, community mobilisation and the transformation of militant particularism have a vital role to play, enabling us to find the universal concerns that exist within a realm of difference. There is a certain dialectic here of unity and difference, universal and particular, which has to be worked out. We should not retain the notion of community as particularity or difference. We have to transcend those particularities and look for a negotiation of universalities through which to talk about how the cities of the future should be.

The point is not to see cities as anti-ecological. Cities are fundamental ecological features in themselves and the processes that build cities are ecological processes. The world of ecology and that of cities are part and parcel of each other; what we have to do is link them together much more strongly, in a more programmatic way. It is only in those terms that we can really push towards a full understanding of the theme of this conference – 'contested cities'. This issue is not simply about contestation inside cities but more importantly concerns contests over the construction and framing of cities – especially what they are going to be in the future.

2

THE ENTREPRENEURIAL CITY

Re-imaging localities, redesigning economic governance, or restructuring capital?[1]

Bob Jessop

The principal forms, functions, and policy mechanisms of local and regional economic strategy in advanced western capitalist societies have undergone major changes during the last two decades. There have been major shifts in cities' roles as subjects, sites, and stakes in economic restructuring and securing structural competitiveness. These shifts are reflected in increased interest in, and emphasis on, the 'competition state'[2] at the national (and, at least in Europe, supranational) level and the 'entrepreneurial city' at both regional and local levels. The distinctive feature of 'competition states' and 'entrepreneurial cities' is their self-image as being proactive in promoting the competitiveness of their respective economic spaces in the face of intensified international (and also, for regions and cities, inter- and intra-regional) competition.[3] There is wide variety in understandings of the dynamics of such competition, sources of competitive advantage, and the most suitable strategies for securing such advantage. The timing and causes of these changes in understanding and policy also vary widely across nations, regions, and cities.

This chapter does not discuss specific cases.[4] Nor does it offer a much-needed typology of 'entrepreneurial' strategies or review their underlying views of competitiveness. Instead it examines four general aspects of recent changes affecting cities: (a) the re-imaging of local economies and/or their states in and through discourses about the 'entrepreneurial city'; (b) the link between this re-imaging and re-design of urban governance mechanisms; (c) the links between these twin changes and alleged trends towards globalisation and triadisation of the capitalist economy and the emerging primacy of geo-economics over geo-politics; and (d) the general structural context in which these interconnected changes in cities' overall economic role are occurring. Although my focus here is on their discursive aspects, these changes must also be related to material contradictions and tensions in existing forms of economic regulation and/or governance that help to sustain the resonance of the new discourses.[5] Moreover, although I note the seeming plausibility of these narratives, this does not mean that they are true (even if they are associated with 'truth effects') nor that changes in governance informed by them will be successful.

SOME THEORETICAL PRELIMINARIES

My approach to the topics mentioned in the introduction is shaped by three main theoretical currents: the French regulation approach, neo-Gramscian state theory, and critical discourse analysis. I consider the economy in an inclusive sense; that is, as an ensemble of socially embedded, socially regularised, and strategically selective[6] institutions, organisations, social forces, and activities organised around (or at least involved in) the self-valorisation of capital in and through regulation. This approach has important implications for the analysis of competitiveness in so far as it shifts attention from comparative to competitive advantage and also radically extends the economic and extra-economic factors which are relevant to the latter. This in turn extends the scope for entrepreneurship as applied to cities as well as firms (cf. Benko and Lipietz 1994; Best 1990; Castells and Hall 1993; Porter 1994; Sabel 1989). The state is also considered 'in its inclusive sense' (or, as Gramsci also put it, 'political society + civil society'). For present purposes it is considered as an ensemble of socially embedded, socially regularised, and strategically selective institutions, organisations, social forces, and activities involved in realising the 'collective will' of an imagined political community.[7] Two key theoretical implications of this approach are the problematic boundaries of the state apparatus and the dependence of state power on forces beyond the state in the narrow sense. This suggests in turn that the political sphere can be seen as the domain where attempts are made to (re-)define a 'collective will' and to (re-)articulate various mechanisms and practices of government *and governance* in pursuit of projects deemed to serve it.

This chapter also emphasises the constitutive role of discourse in all lived social relations. This has obvious implications for the re-imaging of economic spaces and local governance. Just as national states can be seen as but one specific form of imagined political community, so the 'national economy' is only one possible imagined space of economic activities. Accordingly, rather than seek objective criteria which identify the necessary boundaries of an economic space (on whatever territorial or functional scale), this issue is more fruitfully considered in terms of the imaginary constitution of the economy. This involves its discursive construction as a distinctive object (of analysis, regulation, governance, conquest, and/or other practices) with definite boundaries, economic and extra-economic conditions of existence, typical economic agents and extra-economic stakeholders, and an overall dynamic (cf. Barnes and Ledubur 1991; Daly 1993). Economies may be distinguished in different discourses for different purposes[8] and these discourses are always liable to contestation. Struggles to constitute specific economies as subjects, sites, and stakes of competition typically involve manipulation of power and knowledge in order to establish recognition of their boundaries and geometries.

Narrating the entrepreneurial city/region

A recent observation by Margaret Somers provides a useful entry point for making sense of changing urban and regional economic strategies from a discourse-analytic viewpoint. In a paper on ontological narrativity, she notes that

> it is through narrativity that we come to know, understand, and make sense of the social world, and it is through narratives and narrativity that we constitute our social identities ... all of us become to *be* who we *are* (however ephemeral, multiple, and changing) by being located or locating ourselves (usually unconsciously) in social narratives *rarely of our own making.*
> (Somers 1994: 606; emphasis in original. Cf. White 1987)

From this perspective, the current consensus on the need for 'entrepreneurial' cities can be interpreted as a product of convergent public narratives about the nature of key economic and political changes affecting post-war Europe and North America – narratives which have been persuasively (but not necessarily intentionally) combined to consolidate a limited but widely accepted set of diagnoses and prescriptions for the economic and political difficulties now confronting nations, regions, and cities and their respective populations. Like all narratives, these have three key elements: (a) a selective appropriation of past events and forces; (b) a temporal sequence with a beginning, middle, and end; (c) and a relational emplotment of the events and forces and their connection to some overarching structure which permits some causal and moral lessons to be drawn (cf. Ewick and Silbey 1995: 200). Thus we find selective narrations of past events and forces which generate a distinctive account of current economic, social, and political problems – the resolution of which is now deemed to require decisive changes in the purposes, organisation, and delivery of economic strategies focused on the urban and/or regional levels and infused with some kind of entrepreneurial spirit. The entrepreneurial city or region has been constructed through the intersection of diverse economic, political, and socio-cultural narratives which seek to give meaning to current problems by construing them in terms of past failures and future possibilities. These narratives are often connected with complementary discourses (both narrative and non-narrative in form) that are mobilised to contextualise these changes and reinforce calls for action. In sum, although the rise of the entrepreneurial city or region as subject, site, and stake in economic competitiveness was not pre-scripted in the overall dynamic of capitalism, nor has it been a pure accident or chance discovery. It has been constructed in and through public narratives.

The *appeal* of these narratives depends on their resonance with (and hence their capacity to re-interpret and mobilise) the personal (including shared) narratives of significant categories (or groups) of those who have been affected by the contingent development of the post-war economic and political order. For some, these personal narratives concern economic and social exclusion and experiences of unwanted market and/or state failures;

others may have experienced unwonted economic and social success which they ascribe to their own entrepreneurial talents, risk-taking, flexibility, or self-improvement. Such experiences provide an important field of discursive intervention for 'policy entrepreneurs' in the private and public domains. The *effectiveness* of these public narratives in promoting governmentalising or regularising practices which support the 'entrepreneurial' city depends in turn on their links to wider cultural and institutional formations which, in Somers's words, provide 'a web of interlocution' (1994: 614). In this context a central role is played by the discourses of the enterprise culture, enterprise society, innovative milieux, networks, strategic alliances, partnerships, governance, and so forth. And their overall *plausibility* depends on meta-narratives which reveal linkages between a wide range of interactions, organisations, and institutions and/or help to make sense of whole epochs (cf. Somers 1994: 619). The geo-economic meta-narratives of the crisis of Fordism and globalisation–triadisation have a key role here, as do geo-political narratives about the end of the Cold War, communist collapse, and the economic threats to national survival from East Asia.

Given this linkage between meta-narratives and personal stories and their mediation by institutional narratives, the 'entrepreneurial city' has proved to be plausibly emplotted and is currently the dominant response to urban problems. Indeed, as Eisenschitz and Gough (1993) argue, there is a marked convergence among major political currents in Britain on endogenous local economic development initiatives. In this context it should be noted, of course, that such 'bootstraps' strategies need not be neo-liberal in form or content. For many alternatives have been proposed: besides property-led or more general market-led initiatives dominated by business interests, we also find strategies which are more neo-corporatist, neo-statist, or even community-based in governance structure – albeit still more or less closely dependent for success on market forces. What these initiatives share is the entrepreneurial concern to create 'new combinations' of economic and/or extra-economic factors which will further urban and regional competitiveness.[9] Such 'new combinations' (or innovations) could aim to secure dynamic (or strong)[10] competitive advantages for a city (or region), or else to gain some static (or weak) comparative advantage. The former comprises economic, political, and social innovations intended to enhance productivity and other conditions of structural competitiveness;[11] the latter includes modifications in formal and substantive regulatory, facilitative, or supportive measures[12] aimed at capturing mobile investment (a deregulatory race to the bottom) as well as simple image-building measures with the same purpose (boosterism). Similar trends can be found elsewhere (e.g., Eisinger 1988; Ettlinger 1994; Fosler 1988; Gaffikin and Warf 1993; Harvey 1988; Hirsch *et al.* 1991; Keating 1993; Leitner 1989; Mayer 1994; Preteceille 1990; Przeworski 1986; Stewart and Stoker 1989; Stöhr 1989, 1990). The persuasiveness of this sort of entrepreneurial narrative is closely linked in turn to the parallel discursive constitution of specific sites of economic activity as 'natural' (commonsensical, taken-for-granted) units of economic management, regulation, or governance. In the post-war boom years the tendency was for this site to be seen as the national economy; more recently views of 'naturalness' have bifurcated in the direction of the global and local economies – subsequently synthesised in some strategic contexts in the idea of 'glocalisation'.

The rise of the entrepreneurial city or region in the geo-economic space of Atlantic Fordism clearly depends on quite specific narrative accounts of the crisis of its post-war mode of economic growth and its social mode of economic regulation. The plausibility of these narratives depends in turn on their resonance with personal narratives rooted in experience and more general meta-narratives about the significance of long-run economic and political changes. That these institutional and meta-narratives have such a powerful resonance at present does not mean, of course, that they should be taken at face value. All narratives are selective, appropriate some arguments, combine them in specific ways. It is important to consider what is left unstated or silent, what is repressed or suppressed in official discourse. Moreover, given that there are always various plausible narratives, one must also consider the differential capacities of their narrators to get their messages across and secure support for the specific lessons they entail. It is also important to consider how the plausibility of competing narratives is shaped by the structural biases and strategically selective operations of various public and private apparatuses of economic, political, and ideological domination. Public narratives do not compete for influence on an even playing field but are subject both to discursive and structural selectivities[13] as well as the need to establish some resonance with personal narratives. Such concerns take us well beyond a concern for narrativity, of course, into the many extra-discursive conditions of narrative appeal. A further set of important issues concerns the relevance of these various narratives to class, gender, and race; their implications for economic and social exclusion within cities and among regions; and their role in more general attempts to hegemonise public and private discourse in the interests of specific accumulation strategies or political projects. Unfortunately these issues cannot be addressed here (but see, for example, Bakshi *et al.* 1995; Beynon *et al.* 1989; Massey 1994; McDowell 1991; Pollert 1991).

Emplotting the rise of the entrepreneurial city

> Narratives are constellations of *relationships* (connected parts) embedded in *time and space,* constituted by *causal emplotment* ... It is emplotment that permits us to distinguish between narrative on the one hand, and chronicle or annales, on the other. In fact, it is emplotment that allows us to construct a *significant* network or configuration of relationships.
>
> (Somers 1994: 616–17)

The rise of the 'entrepreneurial city' has been variously emplotted. But two broad paradigms predominate: the geo-economic and geo-political – with the former, at least in this regard, being primary (cf. Altvater 1994; Luttwak 1990; Sum 1996).

Among the key themes in geo-economic meta-narratives are global-isation and/or internationalisation; the rise of new technologies; the crisis of the post-war mode of growth, its associated regional policies and growth pole strategies and characteristic mixed economy of welfare and social redistribution; the competitive threat posed by East Asian economies; and the increased salience of ecological problems whose scope does not coincide neatly with national boundaries. These economic, technological, and ecological factors are said both to have undermined the borders of the national state, thereby rendering it anachronistic, and to have exposed all national economies to greatly intensified global competition that is difficult to evade and thus exerts downward pressure on 'unproductive' public expenditure. The prime goals of post-war economic policy (full employ-ment, stable prices, economic growth, and a sustainable balance of payments) can no longer be delivered in and through the national state. This in turn undermines the national state's capacity to deliver redis-tributive social welfare and limit the degree of social exclusion. In this sense the post-war economic and political regime has failed and, if cities and regions are to escape the consequences of this failure, it is essential to modify economic strategies, economic institutions, modes of governance, and the form of state. These must be re-designed to prioritise 'wealth creation' in the face of international, inter-regional, and intra-regional competition since this is the prior condition of continued social redistribu-tion and welfare. Such narratives lead, *inter alia*, to the discovery of the entrepreneurial city as a new phenomenon and its presentation as inevitable on practical, if not normative, grounds. In turn this forecloses discussion and debate over alternative ways of defining and resolving current problems.

Key geo-political themes bearing on the 'competition state' and 'entre-preneurial city' include the end of the Cold War, the approach of the Pacific Century, and the rise of so-called 'tribal' identities. The Soviet communist collapse and the end of the Cold War are said to have replaced the struggle between capitalism and communism as competing world systems by struggles between competing versions of capitalism. Thus competition between national states is redefined in favour of civilian economic and technological issues rather than military concerns; and security discourses are reoriented towards environmental risks, sustainable development, and control over transnational migration flows. This is reflected in the reor-ientation of foreign policy towards technological, economic, and ecological issues and the increased salience of foreign affairs in many fields of domestic policy. Such changes help to explain the rise of the 'competition' state at supranational (e.g., European) and national levels. Moreover, for reasons suggested in the dominant geo-economic narratives about the changing forms of competition and the importance of structural com-petitiveness, this discursive reorientation also requires a more active, supply-side oriented role for regional and local states. In this sense geo-political factors are also mobilised by the central state to promote entrepreneurial cities and regions as key contributory elements in securing the international competitiveness of national economies. This is reinforced by reinvigorated 'tribal' identities which are oriented to regional rather than national identities. Furthermore, once the sovereign national state's traditional role in defence is downgraded, many of its other functions may also be displaced to other political levels. In short, given these changes in geo-politics as well as the increased importance of geo-economics, the 'region state' (Ohmae 1991) and/or 'transnational territory' (Sassen 1994) are said to become more important for many purposes than the national state (cf. Horsman and Marshall 1994; Kennedy 1993; Luttwak 1990).

RE-DESIGNING URBAN GOVERNANCE

On both geo-economic and geo-political grounds, the national state would seem, in Daniel Bell's now classic aphorism, too small to solve the big problems, and too big to solve the small problems, in today's world (Bell 1987). It is no longer so obviously the taken-for-granted primary actor in international or domestic politics. In turn this is prompting not only the expansion of supranational and subnational forms of govern*ment* but also the search for new forms of govern*ance* able to overcome the problems linked to pure market or hierarchical, bureaucratic solutions. Experiments with new forms of economic governance for the new urban regimes are intelligible in this context.

Post-war forms of urban government are often ill-equipped for pursuit of the new entrepreneurialism and are increasingly interpreted as part of the problem of poor economic performance. This is reflected in continuing experiments to find new, more appropriate forms of articulation of regulation and governance in response to narratives which ascribe part of the blame for failure and crisis on previous models of urban politics and local economies. This can be illustrated from a recent paper by Fosler, an American local economic development adviser. He refers, as do many others, to the emerging local economic development paradigm which emphasises the role of a reinvigorated, market-driven, private sector in securing economic growth in a Schumpeterian growth dynamic. But he also notes that this requires the development of institutions to shape and execute the state's responsibilities in this regard. Thus he writes that:

> the new institutional capacities include a conceptual reorientation of the economic role of governance; the ability to generate and apply knowledge across a broad range of policy areas; fashioning new mechanisms and approaches to leadership and decision-making; redesigning systems and strategies for getting results; and creating more effective means of performance assessment and accountability.
>
> (Fosler 1992: 4)

He also notes that the range of these new state responsibilities cannot be satisfactorily handled within a single state agency: there needs to be a range of agencies. Nor can they be satisfactorily handled by the state alone. Instead the strategic reorientation of the state requires that: (a) governance as an instrument of economic performance must combine a top-down, long-term strategic vision and bottom-up, market driven, performance-oriented action; and (b) a new generation of organisational intelligence and new mechanisms of organisational and agency co-ordination are developed which can display market features but also offer means of effective performance quality assessment and accountability. What is required, in short, is a strategy for institutional change (Fosler 1992: 9–13). These arguments illustrate the broad consensus which has emerged on the need for new institutional arrangements. But what precise forms of 're-inventing' and/or restructuring of local government are required to effect this change in governance is still unresolved (on re-inventing, see Osborne and Gaebler 1993). Some of the problems posed by the re-design of economic governance are considered in my concluding remarks.

CONTEXTUALISING THE ENTREPRENEURIAL CITY/REGION

One way to interpret the rise of 'entrepreneurial' cities and regions is to relate it to other contemporary societal trends. Here it is certainly worth noting how this phenomenon corresponds to and reinforces other changes in the organisation and exercise of economic and political power. As I have already indicated above some major geo-economic trends that help to contextualise 'entrepreneurial' cities and regions (see also Jessop 1993), the following comments focus on the broader political significance of the rise of such cities and regions.

The loss of taken-for-grantedness in the nature of the national economy and the national state is reflected in three often identified changes in the organisation of the national state's economic activities: (a) a shift from nationally determined, locally relayed, welfare-oriented measures of economic and social redistribution to (supra-)nationally facilitated, locally determined, wide-ranging supply-side intervention in the local and regional economy in its most inclusive, socially embedded, socially regulated sense; (b) a shift in economic governance mechanisms from the typical post-war bifurcation of market and state to new forms of network-based forms of policy co-ordination which cross-cut previous 'private–public' boundaries and involve 'key' economic players from local and regional as well as national and, increasingly, international economies; and (c) an associated shift from an allegedly Fordist, Keynesian, welfarist policy paradigm to one stressing flexibility, innovation, and entrepreneurship. It is these changes in their combination at the local or regional level that are often condensed into the contested concept of the 'entrepreneurial city'. I now consider them in more detail, noting their import for the changing nature of cities and regions.

First, there is a general trend towards *de-nationalisation of statehood.* This structural trend is reflected empirically in the 'hollowing out' of the national state apparatus with old and new state capacities being reorganised territorially and functionally on subnational, national, supranational, and trans-local levels. One aspect is the partial loss of *de jure* sovereignty by national states in certain respects as policy-making powers are transferred upwards to supranational bodies and their rules and decisions become binding on national states. This trend is especially clear in the European Union but is also visible under NAFTA and other intergovernmentally organised regional blocs. Another aspect is the decentralisation of authority to subordinate levels of territorial organisation and/or the development of transnational but interlocal policy-making.

Entrepreneurial cities or regions are significant in this context in two analytically distinct ways. On the one hand, there is the enhanced role of regional or local states in economic development and, on the other hand, the development of transnational linkages among regional or local authorities, involving what is sometimes called 'paradiplomacy' (Dommergues 1992) or 'intermestic' politics (Duchacek 1984). As the first aspect is amply covered elsewhere in the scholarly literature, I will focus on the second. Cities and regions now engage in their own forms of foreign economic policy in such diverse fields as industrial policy, research and development, technology transfer, market development, tourism development, labour markets, etc. Such activities meet the Schumpeterian criterion of 'entrepreneurial activity' to the extent that they seek 'new combinations' to derive strong and/or weak competitive advantages. In Europe the authorities and agencies involved operate supranationally at the EU level as well as transnationally and often bypass their national state when doing so, thereby reinforcing the tendency towards 'hollowing out'. In seeking to strengthen their political influence in these regards they also aim to develop a critical mass of diverse agencies involved in economic decentralisation at different administrative levels: the city, network of cities, administrative area, region, state, and the European Union level (cf. Dommergues 1992: 11–12). The European Commission itself has for some time been cultivating links with regional or local authorities as well as governance agencies to enhance its own power *vis-à-vis* national governments. It promotes the formation and consolidation of specific regions (including internal cross-border regions, 'virtual regions' based on similar interests rather than contiguity, and regions extending beyond the EU into Eastern and Central Europe) through its own direct interventions and its promotion of territorial and functional partnerships (cf. Murphy 1993; on virtual regions, see Boisier 1994). This can be seen in the 'Europe of the Regions' strategy in so far as the EU is currently allied with subnational regions in identifying possible economic and political spaces for a new political settlement based on subsidiarity rather than sovereignty. Although the funds available for such EC-sponsored activities are small compared with national resources (let alone compared with the magnitude of the problems involved), they have a major symbolic import and wield significant political (if not economic) leverage (cf. Tömmel 1992).

Second, there is a general structural trend towards the *de-statisation of political regimes.* This is reflected empirically in a shift from govern*ment* to govern*ance* on various territorial scales and across various functional domains. Governments have always relied on other agencies, of course, to aid them in realising state objectives or projecting state power beyond the formal state apparatus. At stake here is the reordering of the relationship between government and governance within the overall political system and, in conjunction with the first trend, major trans-territorial and international governance mechanisms at regional and local level. Thus this trend typically involves a movement away from the central role of official state apparatuses in securing state-sponsored economic and social projects and political hegemony towards an emphasis on partnerships between governmental, para-governmental, and non-governmental organisations in which the state apparatuses are often little more than *primus inter pares*. Although this trend typically involves a loss of decisional and operational autonomy by state apparatuses (at whatever level), it can also enhance their capacity to project state power and achieve state objectives by mobilising knowledge and power resources from influential non-governmental partners or stakeholders.

This trend is clear not only on the international and national level but also in the restructuring of regional or local governance. For example, local authorities in Britain are developing new initiatives for the promotion of endogenous economic development based on enhanced structural competitiveness at the same time as special purpose agencies have proliferated and there is growing separation between the commissioning and provision of local services (Clarke and Stewart 1994: 164–5). Likewise, turning from institutional arrangements to more substantive aspects of local politics, local states in Britain and elsewhere are becoming a partner, facilitator, and arbitrator in public–private consortia, growth coalitions, etc., and thereby losing their overall co-ordinating role for and on behalf of local community interests.

And, third, there is a general trend towards the *internationalisation of the national state* and its sub-governments. This apparently paradoxical tendency refers to the increased strategic significance of the international context of domestic state action and the latter's extension to a wide range of extra-territorial or transnational factors and processes. It involves a change, in short, in the overall balance of the state's strategic orientations. This is reflected in economic and social policy, for example, in so far as the prime object of economic and social intervention by the national state has changed from the well-balanced domestic performance of the 'national economy' to its overall 'international competitiveness' understood in very broad terms. This can be seen in the tendential shift from the Keynesian welfare concerns of post-war European national states to less state-centred Schumpeterian workfare concerns in an emerging 'post-national' political regime. These concerns are reflected in diverse policies to promote permanent innovation, an enterprise culture, and labour market flexibility as well as to subordinate social policy more generally to the perceived imperatives of international competition. Neo-liberalism is, to repeat, only one empirical manifestation of this trend.

Whilst this trend is very clear in the transformation of the national state, it also applies to local states. For these, too, must take account of the changing international context of their economic activities. This is reflected, *inter alia*, in the attempt to combine endogenous economic development with inward investment as well as to engage in export promotion and/or import substitution activities in a continually changing international economy. In addition, of course, intranational as well as international rivalries are involved in the inter-local competition for inward investment, reskilling, etc.

EXPLAINING THE RISE (AND FALL?) OF THE ENTREPRENEURIAL CITY

Clearly, in seeking to contextualise the re-imaging of the city and the re-design of urban governance, I have already begun to prepare an alternative (but not wholly dissimilar) narrative. The present section builds on this to provide a more general account of the discursive rise of the entrepreneurial city in two ways. The first involves expanding the account of the crisis of the national economy and national state; the second involves considering the possible competitive advantages of new forms of economic strategy and/or economic governance to the resolution of this crisis in the interests of capital. There is no obvious stopping point in regard to the first exercise and my expanded account is still far from complete. And the second exercise requires more detailed discussion of the limits of these strategies and governance mechanisms (and hence a discussion of possible causes of their subsequent fall) than can be given here. In both respects, therefore, the following comments must be seen as initial steps towards a research agenda rather than final conclusions.

Although most national economies have long been organised around major urban economies[14] and also integrated into pluri-national productive systems (such as colonial systems or Atlantic Fordism), the various urban and pluri-national economies associated with Atlantic Fordism were primarily managed in and through the national state. Thus, as objects of political management, the complex field of economic relations was handled as if it were divided into a series of relatively closed national economies. Urban and regional policy was primarily redistributive in character, pursued in a top-down manner, and concerned to equalise economic and social conditions within such national economies (cf. Chisholm 1990; Stöhr 1989). Likewise, international economic policy was oriented to co-operation to underwrite the smooth operation of national economies. In this sense the typical post-war national Keynesian Welfare State can be distinguished from preceding state forms, such as the mercantilist, liberal constitutional, or imperialist state; and also from emerging state forms oriented to the management of recently rediscovered or newly formed regional economies on various subnational and supranational scales, including localised cross-border linkages. Thus the post-war national economy and its associated national state emerged as a specific historical moment in the changing dynamic of economic 'reproduction–regulation'. It would be very interesting in another context to explore the narrative constitution of this state form.

With the continued internationalisation of Atlantic Fordist economies and the emergence of East Asian economies, however, it became harder to achieve the national economic objectives of the post-war Keynesian Welfare State. Efforts were initially made to secure these objectives through resort to planning and/or corporatist concertation of national economies as well as to increased central and local government intervention in managing crisis-induced uneven economic development in various cities and regions within a national economic context. The general tendency for these policies to fail further undermined the taken-for-grantedness of the national economy as an object of economic management and heightened the resonance of new narratives of international competitiveness, economic flexibility, entrepreneurialism, and decentralised forms of governance. This tendential shift was reinforced in so far as regional and local economies were increasingly seen to have their own specific problems which could be resolved neither through national macroeconomic policies nor through uniformly imposed mesoeconomic or microeconomic policies. This indicated the need for new measures to restructure capital in regard to these newly significant economic spaces. In turn, this prompted demands for specifically tailored and targeted urban and regional policies to be implemented from below, with or without national or supranational sponsorship or facilitation. Another major phenomenon accompanying the economic crisis of Atlantic Fordism was the emergence of new social movements with strong roots in crisis-prone cities. These movements also helped, often unwittingly, to create the conditions for the emergence of the 'entrepreneurial' city or region. Thus, in some cases, the preferred means to roll back the state has been active sponsorship of the so-called 'third sector' (located between market and state) alongside other forms of decentralised public–private partnerships; in others, the central state has simply passed the buck to local government by requiring localities to solve their own problems by involving as many different local stakeholders and partners as possible.

It is this increasing pluralisation that helps to explain the recent growth in experiments with different forms of governance in 'entrepreneurial' cities and regions. In broad terms governance can be defined in contradistinction to both the market and the state as a form of co-ordination involving the self-organisation of inter-organisational relations. The most general case for this shift away from pure market exchange and government hierarchy can be couched in terms of the evolutionary advantage[15] of the self-organising logic of inter-organisational relations where a plurality of interdependent but autonomous organisations, each controlling important resources, need to co-ordinate their actions to produce a joint outcome which is deemed mutually beneficial. The complex problems of economic regeneration in a turbulent environment mean that market solutions and formal, rational–legal solutions are deemed inadequate. In this sense the current expansion of networks at the expense of markets and hierarchies, and of governance at the expense of government, is not just a pendular swing in some regular succession of dominant modes of policy-making. Instead there has been a shift in the institutional centre of gravity (or 'institutional attractor') around which policy cycles operate due to real qualitative shifts in the basic problems which current regularising or governmentalising policies must address. For, given the major transition from Fordism to post-Fordism (linked additionally to new technologies, internationalisation, and regionalisation), there is increased importance attached to micro-level governance and the supply side. Analogous trends are prompted by the crisis of the national state – with a proliferation of cross-border and multi-tier problems which can no longer be contained or controlled by individual national states nor resolved in and through neo-realist anarchy.

CONCLUDING REMARKS

The theoretical approach adopted here involves two related claims. First, there is a close link between economic strategies and economic discourses since it is only in and through the latter's mediation that problems are identified, policies pursued, and crises resolved. Second, an essential element of the regularisation of economic activities within a given accumulation regime is an effective mode of meta-governance; that is, a specific articulation of government and governance mechanisms able to (re-)regularise functional and territorial aspects of the imagined economy in question. Both claims concern the restructuring of capital as well as the re-design of urban regimes. It is in this context, I suggest, that we can begin to make sense of the twin facts that: (a) the city is being re-imagined – or re-imaged – as an economic, political, and cultural entity which must seek to undertake entrepreneurial activities to enhance its competitiveness; and that (b) this re-imag(in)ing is closely linked to the re-design of governance mechanisms involving the city – especially through new forms of public–private partnership and networks. This is evident in the wide range of self-presentational material emitted by cities and/or agencies involved in their governance. Rather than being competing accounts of what is happening in the contemporary city, therefore, the re-design of governance appears as an integral part of the re-imaging of the city as well as of the restructuring of capital. This also implies that the failure of such re-designed forms of governance has adverse consequences for the image of the 'entrepreneurial city' and its continued ability to compete in the 'global marketplace'. In this regard it is important to note that, following the narrative of market failures used to justify the Keynesian Welfare State and the narrative of state failures used to justify the revival and extension of governance, one can begin to see the emergence of problems of governance failure. For many current proposals intended to create and consolidate 'entrepreneurial' cities and regions lack the governance mechanisms needed to permit their effective implementation. Too often their main (if not sole) material existence takes such forms as consultants' reports, outline proposals, non-binding agreements, glossy brochures, more or less regular conferences, meetings, or seminars, cultural exchanges, databases, and information centres. In other cases there has been a proliferation of small-scale partnerships with limited co-ordination, insufficient resources, and, often, conflicting goals. There is greater emphasis on civic boosterism and deregulatory place-marketing than on public–private partnerships seriously oriented to structural competitiveness in a post-Fordist age and able to consolidate the socially embedded, socially regulated conditions for dynamic competitive advantage. It is in this context that the issue of variant forms of capitalism (and their associated forms of governance) is returning to haunt the neo-liberal approach to regional and local economic development in Britain.

NOTES

1 The present chapter arises from an ESRC research project on local governance, grant number L311253032. It has benefited from discussions with colleagues and students at Lancaster University, and with participants in the ESRC programme on local governance. The usual disclaimers apply.

2 A term introduced by Cerny (1990).

3 Elsewhere I describe this shift as the transition from the Keynesian welfare to the Schumpeterian workfare state (Jessop 1993, 1994). I refer here to 'entrepreneurial cities' because this term has entered lay accounts and is more readily related to narrative and discursive questions.

4 Editorial constraints prevent inclusion here of case material on Britain. Results from my ESRC-sponsored research on the Thames Gateway and Greater Manchester will be published elsewhere.

5 I have attempted this elsewhere (Jessop 1993, 1995a).

6 In a regulationist context, strategic selectivity refers to the differential impact of the core structural (including spatio-temporal) features of a labour process, an accumulation regime, or a mode of regulation on the relative capacity of particular forces organised in particular ways to successfully pursue a specific economic strategy over a given time horizon and economic space, acting alone or in combination with other forces and in the face of competition, rivalry, or opposition from yet other forces. Cf. on the state, Jessop (1990: 260) and *passim.*

7 Anderson (1991) regards nations as 'imagined' communities; states, regions, cities, etc., are likewise 'imagined' entities.

8 For example, there are marked differences between positive and negative place-marketing, depending whether the aim is to attract inward private investment or to mobilise public funds for urban regeneration.

9 Entrepreneurship, according to Schumpeter, an emblematic thinker for contemporary capitalism, involves 'new combinations' to create new business opportunities.

10 Here I draw on Cox's distinction between 'strong' and 'weak' competition: the former refers to potentially positive-sum attempts to improve the structural competitiveness of a region through innovation, the latter to essentially zero-sum attempts to secure the reallocation of existing resources at the expense of other regions. Whereas weak competition is socially disembedding, strong competition involves the territorialisation of economic activity (cf. Cox 1995: 218).

11 For a discussion of the concept of structural competitiveness and its dimensions, see Jessop *et al.* (1993).

12 These terms are defined in Jessop (1982: 245–55).

13 On discursive selectivity, see Hay (1996); on structural selectivity, see Jessop (1990).

14 See especially Jacobs (1984).

15 This evolutionary advantage should be understood in Schumpeterian terms: the capacity to innovate and learn in a changing environment.

3

POST-FORDISM AND CRIMINALITY

John Lea

INTRODUCTION

The aim of this chapter is to bring some aspects of the recent debate on the
transition from 'Fordism' to 'post-Fordism' to bear on the issues of criminality
and crime control. The latter is an area generally ignored by recent debates in
social theory about the dynamics of contemporary social change. 'Fordism'
and Regulation Theory in general derive from studies of the labour process
and capital accumulation. Notable attempts to extend the analysis to the level
of the state (Jessop 1990, 1994b) have generally focused on welfare and social
policy. If it is useful to speak of a transition to the 'post-Fordist welfare state'
(Burrows and Loader 1994), it may be possible to identify similar dynamics at
work in the area of criminal justice and crime control. In what follows I shall
firstly elaborate a model of the classic Keynesian Welfare State (KWS) in the
context of the expanding post-war economy and explore some of its
implications for crime and crime control. Secondly, I shall identify some
problems and instabilities in the classic welfare state model in the area of
crime and crime control, which might be identified as contradictions to be
resolved by any transition to a new form of economy, state, social structure.
Finally I shall attempt to examine some of those changes and developments as
they are identified by post-Fordism and critically assess their implications for
crime and crime control.

THE POST-WAR BOOM AND THE CLASSIC WELFARE STATE

The period of post-war stable economic expansion is conventionally
defined as the period from 1950 until the early 1970s. The characterisation
of this period as Fordist refers to the development of a mass consumption
market adequate to expanding production through rising labour productivity and mass production line systems as pioneered by Henry Ford.
Market demand was stabilised through rising wages negotiated by well-
organised but 'responsible' trade unions, Keynesian demand management,
and the welfare state as a set of universal social rights to minimum income,
housing, health and education. But Fordism was more than simply a set of
economic arrangements. 'Post-war Fordism has to be seen ... less as a mere
system of mass production and more as a total way of life. Mass production
meant standardisation of the product as well as mass consumption; and that
meant a whole new aesthetic and a commodification of culture' (Harvey

1989a: 135–6). An integral part of Fordism concerned social homogenisation around common patterns of consumption and lifestyle. Rising wages, it was widely believed, were accompanied by a narrowing of income inequalities (Crosland 1956) and a meeting of working-class and middle-class lifestyles around nuclear-family-oriented consumption patterns displacing older identities based on work, class cohesion and community. Old class conflicts would fade as the technical solution of social and economic problems heralded the 'end of ideology' while work was simply a means of income for individuals to 'maintain their relatively prosperous and rising standard of living and for their inclination towards a family centred style of living' (Goldthorpe *et al.* 1968: 150).

The implications of such an ideal typical state of affairs for crime and crime control are clear. Firstly, the elimination of major social inequalities would enable democratic criminal law and criminal justice agencies to serve all sections of society alike. A new popular consensus around crime control could parallel that around universalist social welfare rights. The consolidation of shared values through mass consumption, mass education and social mobility would, in turn, standardise sensitivities to violence, concepts of harm and victimisation, around those deployed by criminal law and criminal justice agencies. One example of the dynamics of such a process could be identified at the level of the new suburban 'neighbourhood' which would articulate middle-class notions of space in which 'interpersonal relations are unnecessary at the street level and the command over space does not have to be assured through continuous appropriation' (Harvey 1987: 271–2). Middle-class lifestyles appropriate space through mobility – cars and telephones – by contrast with the traditional working-class community where

> Exchange values are scarce, and so the pursuit of use values for daily survival is central to social action ... The result is an often intense attachment to place and 'turf' and an exact sense of boundaries because it is only through active appropriation that control over space is assured.
>
> (Harvey 1987: 271–2)

For the traditional working class the defence of local space was a defence of networks of mutual aid and direct appropriation of use values – often involving local 'criminal' economies. Thus while the traditional community was hostile to outsiders – the police in particular – as a threat to the direct domination of space,[1] the middle class, being concerned simply with external threats to property and the 'tone' of the neighbourhood view the state 'as basically beneficial and controllable, assuring security and helping keep undesirables out, except in unusual circumstances (the location of "noxious" facilities, the construction of highways etc.)' (Harvey 1987). Thus Fordism and the welfare state would complete that long process of penetration of the police into working-class communities, begun during the second half of the last century (Brogden 1982; Cohen 1979; Storch 1976), and establish a consensual basis for the criminal justice system, and for societal reactions to crime.

Meanwhile the elimination of poverty and bad housing would remove the main source of crime. Urban renewal would gradually eliminate the traditional working-class community with its own moral economy of offenders and victims – in which concrete communal knowledge of events (e.g., shared notions of legitimate and illegitimate violence in specific situations) could provide alternative descriptions and solutions to those provided by criminal law and its agencies. The persistence of generalised juvenile delinquency in older working-class areas, for example, was to be seen as rooted in the nature of traditional working-class culture. This was the interpretation of the juvenile crime problem which had been followed by Mays (1954) and other British studies. 'The evidence of all the English studies appears strongly supportive of ... [the] ... theory that the bulk of delinquency represents straightforward adolescent conformity to the expectations of lower class culture' (Downes 1966: 113). In this way delinquency could be seen as an essentially residual problem, a question of areas of economic and social structure which had yet to be incorporated into Fordism and the consequent cultural homogenisation around consumption and family-oriented norms. Once these communities had been reconstructed then residual working-class criminality would assimilate to a middle-class experience of crime as consisting overwhelmingly of disruptions to normal social interaction by mainly marginalised or isolated individuals. Whether such pathology needed to be dealt with by welfare, medical treatment, or punishment was largely a technical matter upon which experts could decide (Wootton 1959). The important point was that the systematic social bases of crime had been removed and all that was left were individuals. That the juridical legal subject presupposed free will while the welfare client was assumed to lack it was less important than that they were both varieties of the individualisation of social problems.

Such a view of the effects of Fordism and the KWS is of course simply the extrapolation of one tendency. There was indeed a relative consensus around criminal justice and crime control during the 1950s and early 1960s, as witnessed by the relative paucity of legislation in the area and social survey findings indicative of a cross-class consensus concerning generally positive attitudes to the police (Reiner 1992). Crime, although it began its exponential rise from the mid-1950s, was low by present standards. The social stabilisation and cohesion of Fordist welfare state society was to some extent reflected in the proportionate decline of incarceration in the face of non-supervisory and non-disciplinary – in the Foucauldian sense – forms of penality such as fines and community service. As Bottoms remarked:

> The implication would be that the penal project of the classical reformers failed at the end of the eighteenth century because it did not in itself produce order ... and there was insufficient social control exercised elsewhere in society to make the classical juridical project possible. In modern states, however, such power does exist, and so the schemes of classical penality render themselves as more realistic possibilities, at least for some crimes and some offenders.
>
> (Bottoms 1983: 195–6)

Fordism and the KWS were, in other words, the main agencies of the social control which made possible an extension of the classical juridical project. For Bottoms non-custodial penality is not to be seen as 'spreading the net' of disciplinary power (see Cohen 1985) since Fordism and the KWS have already completed this task – although as we shall see, in contradictory ways.

CONTRADICTIONS OF THE FORDIST WELFARE STATE

As Bob Jessop has noted (1994a), talk of 'post'-Fordism presupposes an identification of contradictions within Fordism that produce, and are resolved by, the transition. In fact there are two problems. It is firstly necessary to consider the extent to which Fordism was an accurate characterisation of British society during a substantial part of the post-war period.[2] At the level of economic development, the declining performance of the British, relative to other capitalist economies, is well known and the weak performance of the Fordist mass production industries has been noted (Overbeek 1990). Jessop considers that Britain only achieved a 'flawed Fordism' which ultimately has affected the ability to move to a successful post-Fordism (1990, 1994b). The tendencies to homogenisation in terms of class structure, income distribution and consumption patterns were shown, by the early 1960s, to have been grossly exaggerated (Titmuss 1962; Nicholson 1967).

However, it became clear that Fordism itself contained some important fissile tendencies at the level of economic and social organisation. The expansion of mass production industries generally involved the movement of skilled workers out of the older industrial and inner city areas. The remaining poor were decreasingly situated in cohesive working-class communities, with their networks of social support, and more in polarised isolated housing estates where they had been 'left behind' as more skilled elements of the working class had moved out of the area. The experience of poverty was increasingly one of isolation and individualisation. Paradoxically, rising crime was one result of the breakdown of the very traditional working-class communities whose indigenous criminality had attracted the attention of sociologists like Mays (1954). An obsession with alleged criminogenic features of these communities glossed over the fact that while they may have sanctioned elements of social crime – such as pilferage from work or shoplifting – they also exercised control over many forms of interpersonal violence and victimisation.[3] Indeed the very process of incorporation of such communities into a Fordist culture heightened criminogenic tendencies. While mass production and consumption failed to consolidate social homogenisation in terms of income and class, the diffusion of a Fordist culture and expectations of mass consumption was more successful and resulted in an increase in relative deprivation.

Fordism, in other words, achieved an 'Americanisation' of mass culture, the criminogenic effects of which had been previously studied in some detail by American subcultural theorists (Merton 1957; Cloward and Ohlin 1960; Cohen 1955) grappling with the earlier development of Fordism in

North America. In Robert Merton's classic formulation, anomie as a source of criminal and deviant behaviour became an inbuilt structural contradiction in Fordist culture in which 'a system of cultural values extols, virtually above all else, certain *common* success-goals *for the population at large* which the social structure rigorously restricts or completely closes access to approved modes of reaching' (Merton 1957: 146). Meanwhile, in his review of British subcultural studies, David Downes had noted the paradoxical effects of the incorporation of 'traditional' communities with their more insulated field of aspirations (Runciman 1965), into the mass-consumption-oriented (Fordist) culture. He noted that

> the very measures proposed to cut down on delinquency might seem to aim at promoting status-consciousness and – by inference – status frustration, thus providing the necessary base for the emergence of delinquent motivations on 'American' lines. By breaking down working class conservatism, the main force for aspiration-control would be removed.
>
> (Downes 1966: 268)

As post-war capitalist expansion began to decline with the resultant growth in poverty – which could only now be conceptualised as relative deprivation or inequality (Townsend 1979) – it is hardly surprising that crime continued to rise.[4]

There is a second area in which the development of the KWS introduced problems and conflicts in the area of crime and its control. I refer to what might be termed the 'widening and deepening' of criminality. In the work of Habermas (1976, 1987), for example, the welfare state is seen to exercise simultaneously a stabilising and destabilising effect on social relations. This is because

> while the welfare state guarantees are intended to serve the goal of social integration, they nevertheless promote the disintegration of life-relations when these are separated, through legalised social intervention, from the consensual mechanisms that co-ordinate action and are transferred over to media such as power and money.
>
> (Habermas 1987: 364)

Thus the welfare state, particularly the KWS, aimed at social integration through the granting of social rights. Even where these rights aimed at preserving traditional family structures, by displacing taken-for-granted consensus – for example, around patriarchal family values – to political and economic structures of rights and welfare provision, they enabled the politicisation and critical questioning of such values. This process, in Habermas's view, lies behind the development of new social movements. These can be of two types, 'offensive' and 'defensive' (Ray 1993). The former aims at the repoliticisation and reclamation of the life-world through the discursive justification of values, while the latter attempts to restore traditional authority in the only form that it can now be re-imposed; that is, conservative political ideology. The feminist movement is the obvious example of the first and the New Right of the second.

As far as crime is concerned there are two implications. Firstly, legal relations and criminal justice intervention can follow on the heels of welfare and social rights. Once the relations of family members are de-traditionalised, then hidden areas of family violence can be opened up as relations between offenders and victims as legal subjects, and the stronger intervention of criminal justice agencies, demanded. In such a context, at least a proportion of violence by men to women or children, in family situations can be seen as individualised attempts to restore traditional unspoken authority relations, while conservative social movements attempt the same through political channels. In this sense the personal is political and crime is politics. The KWS not only failed to solve the traditional class problems of poverty and inequality, but the shifting of identity formation from work to consumption, celebrated by the theorists of homogenisation and 'civic privatism' (Almond and Verba 1965) as a form of depoliticisation, had the contrary result of widening social conflict from 'class' to the private sphere. Criminal justice itself becomes politicised in a double process. Key social relations of the private sphere are deconstructed as relations between offenders and victims, while, simultaneously, the latter become blurred such that the distinct identity of the offender and the victim, as required by the criminal law and the process of criminal justice, fade into a 'continuum of violence' (Kelly 1988).

A final set of issues concerned the relationship between the criminal justice system and the welfare state as alternative strategies for guaranteeing rights and dealing with social problems. Firstly, the very presence of the welfare state further contributes to the 'denaturalisation' of crime by establishing a tactical division of labour between welfare and criminal justice agencies about who should deal with particular problems and individuals (Pitch 1995). This leads to competition between 'welfare' and 'justice', and their associated bureaucracies, over who should deal with a particular set of problems – as in the case of juvenile delinquency, drugs, etc. The consequence is further politicisation of criminal justice – as in movements for 'back to justice'. The competition with welfare leads to a tension within criminal justice between a formal legitimacy based on due process and the rule of law and one based on output criteria of effectiveness in dealing with social problems. As Foucault remarked, concerning the way in which characteristically modern institutions aimed at regulation and surveillance displace those based on law and right:

> I do not mean to say that law fades into the background or that institutions of justice tend to disappear, but rather that the law operates more and more as a norm, and the judicial institution is increasingly incorporated into a continuum of apparatuses (medical, administrative and so on) whose functions are for the most part regulatory.
>
> (Foucault 1979: 144)

Thus criminal justice institutions such as police and prison systems start to look increasingly 'inefficient' in solving the problems of crime. Highly politicised 'offensive' social movements demanding a return to traditional notions of punishment and responsibility run into growing cynicism about the effectiveness of criminal justice as a solution to social problems. Even Conservative Home Secretaries succumb to the view that the prison is an expensive way of making bad people worse.

A decade ago many followed Habermas (1976) and Offe (1984) into identifying a legitimation crisis at the heart of the Fordist KWS in parallel with its gathering economic crisis. Certainly there was no shortage of elements of such a crisis in the areas of criminal justice. As social polarisation increased, criminal justice agencies found themselves engaged in classic activities of generalised repression of the new marginalised in the inner cities. The latter achieved episodic cohesion in recourse to the streets, articulating demands for fairness and justice. Meanwhile new social movements demanded widening of the concepts of justice and appropriate procedures – such as revisions to legal notions of provocation and responsibility and the criminalisation of new forms of violence. These were joined by a growing critique of criminal justice in terms of its efficiency. The prison was joined by the police as institutions which 'fail to deliver' under conditions of continually rising crime and exploding prison populations.

Yet the dynamics of legitimation crisis are quite unclear. Habermas could speak of a growing demand for the 'discursive justification of values', yet how, precisely, this would lead to movements and pressure resulting in a social or political crisis in western capitalist states was never spelled out (McCarthy 1978; Ray 1993). The ambiguity was illustrated by the appeal of the theme of legitimation crisis to members of the New Right who observed 'a breakdown of traditional means of social control' (Crozier et al. 1975), and the need for a reassertion of authority by mobilising new bases of conservative support and the ending of the civic privatism of the middle classes. Fear of crime, the 'underclass', and criminogenic potential in any departure from traditional forms of socialisation was of course a key theme in such mobilisation. Meanwhile, attempts on the left to articulate a more precise concept of *hegemonic crisis* (Hall et al. 1978) tended both to read crisis symptoms too widely (for example with respect to increased class struggle in the early 1970s) and to misread strategies of consolidation (as with 'moral panic' about crime) as evidence of the exhaustion of hegemony. The real source of change in direction lay undoubtedly in changed economic conditions after 1970. In this context we can approach the issue of a transition to post-Fordism.

POST-FORDISM: A NEW FORM OF REGULATION OR DEEPER CRISIS?

The key question concerning the adequacy of the concept of post-Fordism is whether it describes the emergence of a new, stable, mode of development overcoming the limitations of Fordism or whether in fact it simply grasps, at an empirical level, the symptoms of deepening capitalist recession and confuses these with a new form of stability. This issue goes to the heart of the debate on the underconsumptionist tendencies associated with some varieties of regulation theory (Brenner and Glick 1991). If, for example, the expansion of mass consumption was what enabled stable post-war development (Aglietta 1979), then a new regime of 'flexible accumulation' (Harvey 1989a) involving flexible production systems catering for market diversity, and a return to smaller enterprises, might overcome the limitations of existing mass consumer markets. An alternative view would find the original cause of post-war expansion in the destruction of capital during the Second World War combined with a temporary post-war stability of the international monetary system. The expansion of consumption into new mass-produced commodities is seen as a consequence, rather than a cause, of profitable production. The current crisis is not a matter of the exhaustion of markets as such, but of over-accumulation of capital.[5] From this perspective what is central to the present transition is capital's determination to replace the KWS with a regime of low wages, impotent unions and highly flexible labour with a strong emphasis on women and ethnic minorities. Simultaneously much Fordist production is being 'decentralised' to low wage, politically authoritarian Third World areas. 'Post-Fordism' can be another name for the fact that in order to restore the conditions for profitable accumulation, capital must intensify its attack on the working class. It is only a new form of stability in that, if successful, the conditions for profitable accumulation will be eventually restored and the expansion of markets will result from the normal process of capital accumulation (Brenner and Glick 1991). From this perspective, diversification of production and consumption is entirely secondary. It is not the 'discovery' of new niche markets that replaces an exhausted Fordist mass consumption, but the restoration of profitability through the 'discovery' of a low wage, flexible, diversified working class. Much of the so-called post-modern diversity of lifestyles is a cynical inversion of this growing social polarisation.

So we are in transition to a condition whose contours we cannot yet fully specify. For this reason it is best to concentrate on the dynamics of transition itself rather than attempting the specification of an 'ideal' type of a stable post-Fordist mode of development. In the remainder of this chapter I shall therefore select a number of themes from the post-Fordist debate and attempt to assess their stabilising or destabilising effects in the area of crime and crime control.

THE GLOBAL CITY

A useful focus for many of the processes associated with post-Fordism is its impact on urban structure (Esser and Hirsch 1994). Issues such as the rediscovery of flexible low wage labour and the decentralisation of Fordist production to the Third World finds a focus in the literature on the 'global city'. Theorists such as Manuel Castells (1989) and Saskia Sassen (1991) see large cities like New York, Los Angeles and London moving towards a post-Fordist type of social structure characterised by the growth of highly polarised socio-economic relations.

The growth of high income employments in the financial sector are largely disconnected from the organic life of the city. In the classic capitalist city, even when part of an imperialist economy which dominated the world, the bankers and industrialists had some relationship with the urban working class. The function of the city was to allow capital and labour to combine and reproduce. In contrast, the global city is simply a convenient site for activities which could be located anywhere, since they concern not production but the increasingly computerised transfer of funds. Consequent upon this is the segregation of high income professionals who earn salaries determined by global rather than local market forces. Such professionals are cut off from local communities by segregated and guarded walkways; their presence generates little employment for locals except in the informal and consumption sectors and results in what Mike Davis called the 'militarisation of public space' (Davis 1990). The mirror image of the growth of footloose information-based sectors is the decline in Fordist manufacturing and its stable middle income communities. This is accompanied by the growth of an informal sector of low-wage flexible labour, especially in manufacturing enterprises that compete with Third World cheap labour, in newly privatised city services and in firms catering for the conspicuous consumption needs of the information and financial sectors. The growing pool of long-term urban unemployed increasingly inhabits the informal sector.

This scenario, which of course by no means represents all cities, is a backdrop against which to observe new trends in crime. Crime rates continue to rise, but what is specific to post-Fordism is changes in the organisation and functionality of various types of crime. We have noted that Fordism is contradictory. On the one hand, crime is assimilated to a general model of individualisation and marginalisation from normal social relations; the perfection of the juridical model. On the other hand, the 'widening and deepening' process rediscovers criminality in the normal processes of family life. The global city is the context for an intensification of this contradiction: a re-fusing of the normal processes of social and economic life with various forms of criminality.

Much of this concerns changing forms of organised crime, or the criminal economy, which takes on a new functionality in the 'flexible accumulation' of the informal sector. Under Fordism organised crime tends to follow a Mertonian dynamic as a route to social mobility essentially in parallel to legitimate structures. Under post-Fordism it becomes fused with them in more complex ways. As far as the informal sector is concerned, the method of organised crime (the willingness to use violence to achieve business goals) becomes especially appropriate as a form of 'resocialisation' of labour into new post-welfare state, post-trade union working conditions. 'Class consciousness no longer derives from the straight class relation between capital and labour, and moves onto a much more confused terrain of inter-familial conflicts and fights for power within a kinship or clan-like system of hierarchically ordered social relations' (Harvey 1989a: 153). The 'archaic' forms of organisation appropriate to the insecurities of the underworld, such as the role of ethnic and family loyalties (Reuter 1983), are precisely those of the new 'sweated labour' activities of the informal sector.

Organised crime is itself, of course, a form of economy, as in the drugs trade. The 'social crime' of early capitalism is turned on its head from the criminalisation of the working-class defence of traditional moral economy, and to the control of the latter by crime. The drugs economy, finding its labour force in the ranks of the permanently unemployed, brings together all the elements of the global city: that is, a major form of employment in the informal sector, linked, through a global division of labour and money laundering, to the financial sector. Thus Castells notes that

> booming criminal activities, particularly related to the drug traffic ... generate income and a kind of employment for some sectors of the ghetto population ... [but are] ... not limited to the underclass. In fact, the money laundering activities that are a substantial part of the drug economy lie behind the flourishing of many ephemeral busi- nesses, from restaurants to art galleries, that blossom and disappear in the space of a few months ... Ironically, these money laundering processes epitomise the oft praised flexibility of the new economy.
>
> (Castells 1989: 214)

Such crime becomes simultaneously more organised and more disorga- nised. Traditional professional 'project' crime – such as armed robbery – is becoming deskilled and relatively unplanned (Matthews 1995: 179) while, through the drugs trade, such 'disorganised organised crime' itself becomes globalised. Unlike traditional, neighbourhood or city-based orga- nised crime, drugs involve a global division of labour (in production or distribution, banking, etc.) and, particularly in cities concerned mainly with distribution, may become 'disorganised' and appear superficially as lacking any large-scale organisation (Dorn *et al.* 1991). Also, unlike traditional organised crime, there is less concern with status, with the achievement of legitimate social goals by illegitimate means (Massing 1992). The entrepre- neurs of global organised crime are increasingly shadowy figures shunning publicity or reputation. Partly a matter of the enhanced effectiveness of law enforcement agencies, this also reflects the growth of organised crime as not merely a route to capitalism but increasingly as one of its leading sectors.[6]

WORKFARE AND THE 'HOLLOWED OUT' STATE

The issue of the state brings us to the third theme. Post-Fordists such as Jessop (1994b) identify two processes at work. Firstly, the transition from the welfare to the 'workfare state' and, secondly, a process of 'hollowing out' of the state. The first is a fairly straightforward and familiar theme of the abandonment, under the impact of capital's need to reorganise the working class, of the relative autonomy of welfare policy from economic policy. The workfare state is aimed at guaranteeing labour flexibility, creating an attractive 'business environment' through vocational training and removal of restrictions on land use rather than guaranteeing universal- istic social rights and involves a shift to vocational training and innovation. This is not really a fundamental change in the relationship between state and economy in the sense that, during the Keynesian period, demand-led public contracts for welfare facilities – hospitals, schools – were seen as economic stabilisers maintaining predictable levels of effective demand. Now the state has to assist in the dismantlement of the gains of the previous period.

This has a number of implications for crime and its control. Obviously a dismantling of welfare 'citizenship' under conditions of income polarisation has criminogenic consequences through the removal of a cushion to relative deprivation. Attempts by vocational training schemes to secure a downward revision of expectations further reinforce criminogenic cynicism among the unemployed. But more fundamentally, there is a parallel between the transition from welfare to workfare and changes in the role of the state in the control of petty crime. If the growth of non-custodial and non-supervisory punishment (Bottoms 1983) exemplified some of the characteristics of the Fordist KWS period, such a tendency has been displaced by a *de facto* return to the prison, and to supervised non-custodial 'punishments in the community'. Bottoms's argument that the growth of non-supervised alternatives to custody presupposed that basic disciplinary functions were being exercised elsewhere, no longer holds. The growth of the permanently unemployed, the need to break down notions of social rights in favour of flexibility and 'responsibility', places new tasks on the agenda of social control. While the juridical relationship of criminal justice in many ways conflicted with the modes of operation of the welfare state – particularly around the notion of individual responsibility – in other ways the two were compatible. The social control and integration produced by Fordism and the KWS were foundations on which juridical responsibility could be imposed.

The transition to post-Fordism (that is, the dismantling of Fordism) involves a return in some respects to pre-Fordism, to the generalised surveillance and disciplining of the working class. Crime control thus becomes 'actuarial' (Feeley and Simon 1992, 1994), concerned with risk assessment, incapacitation and the management of delinquency. This takes a juridical – as opposed to a welfare – form, as it did in the early nineteenth century (Garland 1985). But the object is less that of preparing the new working class, through the experience of penal discipline, for the 'responsibility' required by labour for capital – factory discipline – and more that of introducing new flexibility, dismantling social rights and keeping the 'underclass' under control. The relationship between the workfare state and actuarial criminal justice continues to be that of reciprocity; the criminal justice system picks up those who are unwilling to bend to the new flexibilities of the workfare state. But since the workfare state increasingly sheds older welfare-guarantee functions, the criminal justice system increasingly also picks up those who simply cannot find work, rather than those actively refusing it. This reinforces the actuarial element in criminal justice (see below).

The 'hollowing out of the state' thesis involves the fragmentation of the old Keynesian planner welfare state, linked to a national economy and social citizenship, in two directions. Firstly, globalisation, or a loss of functions to global and supra-regional bodies, as economic processes can no longer be regulated at national level. This theme, which will not be pursued further here, has obvious implications for the development of international police agencies seeking to regulate multinational crime. Secondly, a process of localism, often combined with privatisation, in which regulatory functions are decentralised down from the national state to 'entrepreneurial' cities and regions which, at the economic level, compete for investment opportunities in new forms of partnership with local capital or other cities which cut across national boundaries. The 'hollowing out' process is made possible on the one hand by a collapse of Fordist corporatist, welfare and economic planning functions centred on the national state and on the other by 'flexible accumulation' and the establishment of new local state–private and inter-regional linkages that bypass the national territory. Privatisation and localism go hand in hand.

Such a process has a number of implications for crime and crime control. Local delivery of welfare state services is classically held to have weakened the basis for clientalism and organised crime by forcing client groups to articulate their claims in terms of universalistic categories of centrally administered need. Robert Merton saw the welfare state as a factor in the decline of American 'machine' politics: 'it was a basic structural change in the form of providing services, through the rationalised procedures of what some call "the welfare state," that largely spelled the decline of the political machine' (1957: 194). This is a one-sided view. Co-existence between powerful organised crime syndicates, big business and the planner state is now well understood (Ruggiero 1986). Nevertheless, a combination of localism and privatisation can be seen to offer new opportunities. Weakening of central supervision, and the subcontracting of services minimises accountability and may allow organised crime groups to repossess from the state some of their classic 'protection' functions.

At the level of crime control and criminal justice agencies, the actuarial tendency, precisely because it is concerned with generalised containment, can be privatised. There is a tendency to return to eighteenth-century local forms, as in the 'rebirth' of private policing (Johnson 1992). Private-based property protection, crime prevention and insurance schemes reinforce the polarisation of the city. They displace democratic or centralised bureaucratic forms of accountability – discourses of rights and justice – in favour of accountability to decentralised groups of customers. The last residues of a common welfare state citizenship fragment with the privatisation – alongside the militarisation – of public space. In a similar way criminal justice agencies begin to develop their own local criteria and strategies for managing disorder. Police forces function locally as semi-autonomous micro-criminal justice systems. This, *inter alia*, provokes a continual expansion of informal cautioning, in many cases resulting in a decline of reported crime rates reflected in traditional centrally recorded criminal statistics (Matthews 1995). Once established as a major employer, organised crime eventually becomes a major source of stabilisation and social control and reassumes some of its traditional functions of protection and dispute resolution.

However it would be wrong to interpret this process, as do some functionalist accounts of 'post-modernisation', as a withering away of the state, in which de-differentiation through new local public–private combinations is carried out to such an extent that the 'very notion of "the state" as a separate and autonomous institutional entity intimately linked with the notion of "politics" and "public sphere" and clearly separated from the domains of economy, societal community and culture, is increasingly problematic' (Crook *et al.* 1992: 104). Jessop, for example, is careful to distinguish 'hollowing out' from a process of demise, stressing that the maintenance of social cohesion 'still depends on the state's capacities to manage ... conflicts' (1994a: 274). The matter can be put in stronger terms: the national state – and to some extent the supranational state – appears increasingly in a 'Leninist' guise as 'marching bodies of armed men'; that is, the central core of force, the agency of last resort for the containment of resistance.

CONCLUSION

It might seem hazardous to draw conclusions from such a brief attempt to relate some of the themes from the debate around a transition to post-Fordism to issues of crime and crime control. The emphasis has been on seeing in 'post'-Fordism less the emergence of a new form of stability than a characterisation of the as-yet-to-be-resolved crisis conditions of late twentieth-century capitalism. However, the present phase of capitalist development may be a unique, slow and protracted crisis following the long post-war boom. Thus the need for capital is less to devise a sudden or 'episodic' strategy to restore profitable accumulation in traditional sectors than to develop new forms of economy and social control insulated from previous gains of the KWS. In this sense post-Fordism, as the concept of a social formation in 'slow crisis', may offer a useful direction of development.

NOTES

1   Echoed, in a different way, by the aristocracy and the very rich with their contempt for bourgeois universalistic notions of law and criminal responsibility and for the agencies of criminal justice – *vide* the impenetrable wall of silence thrown up to protect Lord Lucan who 'only' murdered a servant.
2   This is distinct from the argument that the whole concept of Fordism as a distinct stage of capitalist development is spurious (cf. Clarke 1990; Brenner and Glick 1991).
3   When one considers the continuous decline in crime from 1850 in 'traditional' working-class communities it might have seemed more appropriate to investigate these areas in terms of their successful social control of crime rather than their pathological features. This reveals the ideological nature of much sociological investigation.
4   The question of organised crime throws an interesting light on the dynamics of Fordism and anomie. The 'American' form of organised crime, as typified by Cosa Nostra, provided in many respects a classically 'Mertonian' solution in the form of surrogate routes to social mobility for social groups assimilated to the aspirations of Fordist mass consumption but excluded from its achievement (Bell 1961; Cloward and Ohlin 1960). In Britain, Fordism combined with a more consolidated KWS and high levels of employment kept syndicate crime localised in traditional communities even if some of its

members emulated the flamboyant characteristics of American mobsters (Hobbs 1988; Pearson 1985).
5 The issue goes to the heart of Marxist political economy and cannot be debated here. For a discussion see Mattick (1969).
6 This tendency can be seen writ large in the former USSR where the formation of a new business class is virtually indistinguishable from the growth of organised crime (Handelman 1994).

4

COOL TIMES FOR A CHANGING CITY

Rosemary Mellor

> Manchester may be cool, it may be fun, it may be action packed and
> spilling over with cultural innovation, but it is still a city in touch with
> its roots.
>
> (*Triangle*, April 1995)

The maintenance of the provincial city centres as symbolic cores to their
regions has been a consistent strand in British urban policy. In cities in
declining regions, as is Manchester, play and spectacle are increasingly the
crucial elements in reconstituting the city centre. In imprinting fresh style
on a city whose claim to fame was as 'Cottonopolis', there has been a policy
shift from a welfare agenda, in which the poor of the inner cities had a
modest priority, to a business/growth agenda in which the city centre itself
takes centre stage.

This account covers the emergence of a heritage industry in the 1980s,
the period of heady speculation about the role of Manchester in the new
Europe associated with the property boom of 1988–9, the accommodation
of urban Labour leadership to the expectations of partnership after 1987,
and also the emergent culture of urbanity extolling the merits of association in the city's public spaces. The reclamation of central space for a
lifestyle whose motifs are bars, boats and bistros (or, rephrased, youth and
success) has parallels in many other North American, West European and
UK cities (Harvey 1989a; Castells 1994).

THE CITY OF MANCHESTER

The city controlled a world market in cotton textiles for a century. It also
became the financial hub of the North of England, then one of the world's
wealthiest industrial regions. By the beginning of the twentieth century, it
was a wealthy commercial city fronting an industry and a region. In its
twilight, with the exaggeration proper to a local man, it was to be termed
'the last and greatest of the Hanseatic towns – a civilisation created by
traders' (Taylor 1976: 208).

The weaknesses in the regional economy were apparent long before the
recession of 1979–82. Low levels of investment, a ravaged post-industrial
environment, the image and reality of the cities and towns, as well as its

location peripheral to Europe, had been remarked upon in reports over the previous two decades (North West Regional Planning Council 1974; Rodgers 1980). But from 1978 to 1988 the North West Region experienced a net loss of 300,000 industrial jobs (32 per cent of the stock in 1979), and, as well, 70,000 in public services (Clark *et al.* 1992: 79–80). The stock of jobs in Greater Manchester alone had diminished by 23.5 per cent between 1965 and 1984 (GMRIPU 1985), but the mass redundancies continued throughout the 1980s. There were 500,000 redundancies (in layoffs affecting ten or more workers) in the period 1979–88 for a workforce that in 1988 totalled 1.2 million. Compulsory notifications ceased in that year.

For decades the city centre of Manchester had dominated commercial labour markets in the conurbation. There were 167,000 employed in its 1.5 square miles in 1961, approximately 14 per cent of the employment total of Greater Manchester. This had fallen to 98,000, 8.6 per cent, by 1977 (Manchester City Council Planning Department 1980b). There was then evident a massive erosion of the urban core economy. The basis of the decline was fivefold: the city had ceased to be the nerve centre for world trade in cotton textiles; its role as provincial business centre was diminishing; it was no longer efficient in servicing the region; its industries were closing; it was ceasing to be the town centre for the local population, which itself was much depleted by clearance.[1] Despite, or perhaps because of, a property boom before 1972, 20 per cent of commercial office space was vacant in 1977. The labour force was to retract further as printing presses, warehouses, and insurance companies decentralised in the next decade.

The demands of an ageing infrastructure, inefficient transport system, a dependent population, falling revenue, rising costs, and, as well, a pattern of spending inherent in regional status, are not peculiar to Manchester. They are burdens faced by the administrations of all core cities in Europe and North America. The political fragmentation of the Manchester conurbation may exacerbate the problems. The one comparative study concluded that in Manchester – with few affluent residents in the inner core, no effective public transport system, and 'strong' suburbanisation of office development – there were particular problems for the city centre (GMC 1985). Subsequent policies have been framed within this context of European disadvantage.

THE REGENERATION OF THE CITY CENTRE

Phase I: 1984–9

Regeneration strategies can be considered in two phases: before and after the collapse of the property boom in 1990. In the first phase, the major achievements were undoubtedly the establishment of the museums at Castlefield and the promotion of an urban heritage park; the reconstruction of Central Station, closed since 1969, as an exhibition centre and mass forum (G-Mex); the reopening of the two oldest theatres, investment in five (now twelve) large city centre hotels; and the tourist attraction at Granada Studios (which had 750,000 visitors in its opening year, 1988). All these were subsidised. An economy with the panache of a holiday camp, complementary to the business centre, was being promoted in the archaic shell of the old city centre.

In effect a heritage industry (Hewison 1987) was implanted in the city centre. The accreditation of the artefacts of the city's past with value was a total reversal of the previous policy of demolishing 'Cottonopolis'. Since 1980, archaeology (the reconstruction of the Roman fort), industrial history (the conversion of the world's oldest passenger station and its warehouses into a fine industrial museum), architecture (the renovation of the palatial mercantile headquarters of the textile firms into hotels), and the ambience of canal and riverside have all been promoted as conferring that aura of historic particularity on an otherwise inaccessible and uninviting environment. Local enthusiasts had been key figures in the early stages in demonstrating the palatability of 'heritage'; as decisive were the activities of local entrepreneurs. One particular investment – the conversion of the most splendid of the textile headquarters into a hotel by a local estate agent – showed its commercial potential.

The interests in regeneration of the city centre were many. There was central government, pledged to the social and political reclamation of the inner cities; the construction industry, deterred by the cost of greenfield sites and finding access to them slowed by planning controls; the financial institutions with substantial long-term investments in city-centre property; individuals and trusts adding to their property portfolios; established city businesses (including the banks) with freehold or long leasehold interests at stake. As well, there was the local authority, deprived of central government support,[2] facing diminished local revenue and influence. By 1989, there was a fledgling coalition of public agencies and private interests with an alternative vision of urban life and labour in a modernised city. As the agenda was set by the need to regenerate markets in property it inevitably marginalised those whose access to markets was restricted.

Manchester's assets were 'heritage' and space for recreation. Lefebvre commented presciently that 'leisure is becoming an industry of prime importance. We have conquered for leisure the sea, the mountains and even the deserts. There is now a process of reintegration of space at the heart of the cities' (1970: 265). His remarks have been partially confirmed twenty years later in this particular city. Manchester does not have a Pompidou Centre, but the strategies of the business-led growth coalition increasingly hinged on attracting leisure industries and tourism thereby securing an extra card in the bidding for business investment. The intriguing novelty was this symbiosis between business and leisure.

Manchester had been a city in which one did business, not one where there was licence to revel. That it was becoming a place of 'spectacle and play' was symptomatic of a profound urban revolution. Throughout the decade, despite the recession, opportunities for entertainment and eating, for real ale and clubbing, proliferated. And the developers and development agencies were increasingly using holiday motifs – bars, boats and bistros – augmented by theme parks and theatres. The economic development officer for the local authority suggested in 1988 that the city was to revert to 'how it had looked before the industrial revolution'. It was to be a backdrop to a new industry offering a ritualised experience of a city, complete with town crier!

The promotion of the arts, the heritage industry itself, the alternative lifestyles of artists, media professionals and the young, all presume new canons of cultured living in the cities. In Manchester, there was slow acceptance of the need to promote the arts both as an industry providing employment and as a stimulus to business or leisure investment (CLES 1989). It was then doubtful whether the promotion of the cultural industries would favour upper-income cultural aspirations. Perhaps the weakness of the Hallé Orchestra, once the city's declaration of worth to a national audience, symbolised the shift to a pluralistic urban culture. Presence at its concerts had had a ritualistic significance in the rhythms of the bourgeois community whose working and social life had focused on the old centre (Taylor 1976: 210). With the fading of that class as the old economy unravelled, the orchestra had to compete for audience and sponsorship in a market dominated by popular culture.

The last element in the regenerative strategies being explored was that of the '24-hour city'. The planning philosophy which had separated the public domain of work, commerce and industry from the private domain of home and leisure in a city of 'separate spheres' (MacKenzie and Rose 1983), since its articulation by the founders of the town-planning movement in the first decades of the century, was being challenged by a philosophy of urbanity. In the round-the-clock city a multiplicity of activities was to derive mutual benefit from proximity. The high costs of site recapture necessitated maximum yield from relatively low yield activities such as restaurants and flats. In effect, its instillation in property development is comparable to the introduction of three-shift working in the mills a generation previously. It is also a design strategy capitalising on the advantages of urban location in comparison with the suburban business park.

Throughout the decade there was a conspicuous reversal to privatism. Sociability in the cities was increasingly public, in the street, weather permitting. It has been argued that for minority and marginal groups in particular 'there is no identity without visibility, and the city spectacle encourages self-definition in its most theatrical forms' (E. Wilson 1991: 120), but milling in the crowd was becoming *the* social experience. Being seen in public is also an extension of the career. Work and leisure, whose separate spheres had been zealously pulled asunder by land-use planning, were to be reintegrated. Business and leisure, enjoyment and profit, day and night, are synthesised in this conception of the 'good' city.

In all this there was inconsistency and incongruency with everyday realities. First of all there was tension between the promotional rhetoric and the capacity to realise the setting for this urbane lifestyle. The city's infrastructure was old, and the revenue of the statutory agencies limited. The city population is poor and its needs manifold.[3] There was also a mythical element in the promotional campaigns: this urbane vision presents promenades as more important than motorways, bistros than conference catering, and public association in the crowd as more significant than private transactions. The designation of defunct tracts in the city centre as public arenas was to be the rationale for regeneration strategies which had to reincorporate a degraded environment into a modern city. Urbanity masks the development realities: expensive land, high costs of site recapture and marketing difficulties.

Phase II: 1989-94

At the end of the decade the central city, like others in the UK, experienced an extraordinary stake-out by property interests. Local place-entrepreneurs, construction firms, regional property companies and national developers, with the backing of banks, institutional funds and foreign investors, as well as local charitable trusts, were all staking a claim to the anticipated gains from the regeneration of what had become a most depressed property market. Speculation on the crest of the British property boom through 1988/9 resulted in gross exaggeration of values and prime office rents approaching those of Frankfurt.[4] There was every evidence of disconnection between what Lefebvre (1970) and Harvey (1977) had termed the 'primary and secondary circuits of capital' as the region's industrial economy showed little sign of recovery.[5] The expressed aim was the conversion of Manchester into a regional centre for North Britain within Europe.

The speculative dynamic of the property boom left little mark on the city centre. The main effect was on Salford Quays, where, as in London's Canary Wharf, much remained unlet (August 1994, 800,000 square feet; April 1995, 710,000 square feet). The recession (which led to losses of £9.1 million for the development corporation) terminated hopes of a speculatively led renaissance of the business centre. The two large schemes under construction in 1994/5 (adding a further 680,000 square feet and a 320-bed hotel) were linked to the two subsidised landmark developments – the Arena at Victoria Station and the Concert Hall complex alongside the Metrolink system. Nor have the leisure promotions been more successful: Granada's 'Media City' on the banks of the Irwell and a Dan Dare 'Space City' downstream, remain developers' dreams. Accordingly, the development corporation had to focus on residential conversion and tourism.

The sluggishness of property markets since 1989 is a more accurate reflection of the structural weaknesses in the regional economy than the previous euphoria. It is the only region in mainland UK to show consistent falls in GDP for twenty years; it also has the greatest rate of employment loss. The rate of decline has been aggravated by the termination of investment in nuclear energy and the defence cuts. Overseas contracts for the public utilities and the expansion in the many small 'high-tech' firms generate wealth, but this is insufficient to compensate for the loss of employment in the larger plants. Recorded full-time employment in both region and conurbation continues to decline and cuts in the finance sector aggravate job losses (GMLPU 1993, 1994, 1995). The ten local authorities that make up Greater Manchester constitute one of Europe's weakest urban economies with labour markets characterised by long-term unemployment and low pay. Undoubtedly there is a significant underground economy: expansion in the production of counterfeit goods complements the export of stolen cars, construction equipment, computers and antiques, as well as trade in drugs.

Nevertheless, in 1991 the city centre was still, in a qualitative assessment by professionals from other centres, rated as being the largest 'allround' business centre outside London (Wood 1991). Despite competition from Leeds and Birmingham, it retained the prestigious specialisms of stock-broking and overseas banking. In consequence, prime rents remained stable in the recession and institutional interest in investment in the office core may even exceed demand. At the heart of a poor region, within a local authority with the greatest concentration of poor people outside London, encircled by a wasteland of blighted commercial property, is a sought-after business district with its sustaining luxury services. This 'free-standing specialised service sector' (Sassen 1994: 66), embedded in the poverty belt, remains a crucial element in the prosperity of the outer rim of the region. It is one of the many nodes in the complex of professional businesses which service the national economy. As long as that can be sustained, there is restricted prosperity for both city and region. Its support, and that of corporate and institutional investment, has been the overriding aim of government since 1987. The nexus between state and the 'secondary circuit of capital' is national rather than local as in the US (Fainstein 1991).

Local partnership

The reassertion of business interests in urban policy by the Conservatives, along with the new competitiveness of regions and cities within Europe, has resulted in an unprecedented authority for the 'new managerial–technocratic–political élite' (Castells 1994: 26). In Manchester impatience with the local authority's inability to promote the city resulted in the rise of a self-designated 'Manchester mafia' of local influentials emerging from different factions of the regional business elite (Peck and Tickell 1995). Before 1990, comparison of the 'pro-growth coalitions' of the North American cities with the nascent partnerships between business organisations and local Labour parties was far-fetched. The structural parameters of British municipal politics – the dependence of local government on national mandate and resources, the detachment of local firms and their managers from the locality, and the strength of Labourism and its indifference if not hostility to local business interests – all pointed to the limits to the reconstitution of a 'business class' and its involvement in urban policy-making. There are limits to localism in Britain. All the trends in industrial and commercial organisation over the previous thirty years had furthered the integration of the national economy and polity. Localities have lost their bosses and their structural integrity as places with recognised elites.

The American model of local politics as being dominated by pro-growth alliances is a particular one. However, in the UK too, local businessmen have been co-opted to the 'quangocracy', urban policy has been levered from social welfare towards business growth, and local authorities have been propelled into promotion complementary to business interests. The corporatism implied by partnership between public and private sectors is now a reality. This is reflected in the considerable literature on local politics and research on local regeneration strategies (see Harding 1991). How long 'elite localism' would survive the removal of government patronage is another matter.

While seeking to protect commitments to welfare policies (notably pre-school provision and neighbourhood centres),[6] council leadership in Manchester has, since 1991, wholeheartedly advocated 'Euro' strategies. Endorsement of the Olympic Bid in 1993 (resulting in accusations of excessive promotional expenditure by local MPs) was the most blatant symptom of acceptance of the prestige model of urban regeneration. The sports facilities were conceived as the flagship developments which would re-present the city. Heightening the city's profile in the global marketplace, as 'an International City of outstanding commercial, cultural and creative potential' (Manchester City Council 1994) has become a criterion of successful local management. Of necessity the 'back-stage' neighbourhoods of the city have been relegated on the policy agenda in return for uncertain long-term benefits to that abstract value – the city's image. How much this is worth without the social investment to make the city a comfortable place to work, do business, live, and bring up children, is not openly debated.[7]

A concatenation of circumstances contributes to public acquiescence. First, the media and youthful public back the 'new' city. In particular, there was fervent support for the Olympic Bid, a populist cause. Secondly, there is no contest over occupancy or the symbolism of the terrain. The city centre is not a cherished European city but a run-down tract of redundant commercial space. The conversion of the derelict leftovers of the city's past into popular uses such as theme parks or nightclubs can be interpreted as social gain for mass culture. Thirdly, the local authority has balanced competing claims to expenditure from 'welfare' as well as 'growth' lobbies within its constrained budget. Fourth, there is the dislocation of inner Manchester. The institutional strengths and community ties of the former working-class city were broken by suburbanisation, clearance and redevelopment, and, finally, the death of the manufacturing economy. Colonial migrants to the inner city experienced all these ruptures to community organisation (Parry *et al.* 1987), repeated in the 1990s. Marginality in housing markets means vulnerability to exogenous development, transience and reliance on outsider advocates from the churches and local authorities. In a cosmopolitan poor city marginality has *not* 'become an increasingly strong presence through the new politics of culture and identity' (Sassen 1994: 124), nor is there any indication that it will become so.

The inner city neighbourhoods

Inextricably locked into the problem of the city centre is that of the inner city; that is, the region's poor living in districts which envelop its commercial core. The linkage is long-standing: as regions industrialised, the slums in and around their core business district housed the poorest of the poor, looking to the rough jobs in its services for employment. These notoriously unhealthy neighbourhoods – densely built, tightly occupied and heavily polluted – had therefore a symbiotic relationship with the regional centres which was broken by the withering away of the stubbornly traditional[8] central economy with its demand for poor workers. Its restructuring – from the handling of goods to that of people – disadvantages the uneducated, men, and people of colour. The so-called 'skill mismatch' – in reality a shortfall in acceptability – between inner-city labour force and central-city labour market is a recent phenomenon.

Unemployment levels in the inner city neighbourhoods are high,[9] as are welfare dependency rates. More than 60 per cent of households are reliant on housing benefit. The effect of urban renewal programmes has been to provide a superficially pleasant environment in some of these inner districts. The more recent housing is brick built, to conventional designs, landscaping can be luxuriant, school buildings are modern and shopping provision is improving, though there is a dearth of banks or other financial agencies. In environmental terms Manchester's inner city is not a terrible place in which to live. Forty years of municipal redevelopment have had effect. However, vandalism, arson and theft blight all community facilities, crime is intrusive, and poverty dictates the rhythms of everyday life.

Explanations of inner city poverty by reference to deindustrialisation, most recently by W.J. Wilson (1991, 1993), overlook the role of the city centre economy as the place for unskilled and casual labour. And, according to Sassen, the advanced service sector generates demand for the unskilled (1988, 1991, 1994). However, in Manchester the consensus is that those who live in stigmatised neighbourhoods do not have equal access to service work (post-code discrimination) and those who are categorised as black, irrespective of skill or qualifications, find barriers. The city centre workforce of Manchester, like that of Liverpool (Dennis 1988; Moore 1992a), but unlike that of London, is conspicuously white. City-centre employers may put a premium on acceptability much, or more than, suitability or skill (Jenkins 1986). The critical dimension is the slackness of the regional market in which 'employers can pick and choose, both in recruiting and promoting. They exaggerate the skill, education, and experience requirements of their jobs. They use diplomas, or color, or personal histories as convenient screening devices' (Tobin 1972). Black, and other inner city, residents will not benefit from central city regeneration because of the bar against their employment in service work.

Evidence of benefit of prestige developments to inner city populations is hard to ascertain. The conventional methods of evaluation have either looked at labour force recruitment to specific projects (Loftman and Nevin 1992), or the aggregate statistics for unemployment and welfare dependency in the locality (Department of Environment 1994). The first cannot take account of the effects of the development on other employment opportunities; the second overlooks the consequences of mobility in and out of adjoining districts. If the stock of poor households is continually replenished by others (Ward 1988) because inner cities have the regional reserve of undesired housing, no development strategy can affect the concentration of inner city poverty. The broader question of social benefit to the local population is avoided. What value will the 'leisure-domes' be to Manchester's children being brought up in households without a wage-earner (37.5 per cent in 1991) unless they can see that they have access to either the facilities or (the relatively few) jobs generated? Current 'spot' treatment of the fabric of the city accentuates the previous spatial and social discontinuities, jeopardising the security, and therefore economic viability, of the privileged spaces. Property crime is a considerable difficulty at Salford Quays and other developments outside the core.

Currently every stratagem open to the local leadership is being deployed to tie the city centre into a cosmopolitan circuit of work and play which will, at the same time, maximise its appeal to regional markets. The functional relationships of the inner city are very different. It constitutes a regional pool of low cost housing, a staging post for newcomers to the city, a place where poor people feel at home, and the site of informal industries such as drug-dealing and prostitution, as well as food-processing and clothing. The circumstances that brought this stigmatised space in proximity to the city centre have gone. While some of this space, notably Hulme, may be integrated into the 'Euro-city', the discontinuity between cosmopolitanism and poverty will remain.

The cool revolution

The opening photograph in the souvenir book of Manchester (Redhead 1993) shows open-air tables outside one of the twenty-five city centre café-bars listed in 1994. These, catering for a clientele ranging from the faded academic to the seriously 'cool', from the pin-striped to the 'cosmo-chic', (Greenhalgh 1994) have come to epitomise the 24-hour city which the growth alliance is pledged to promote. A revolution in style is being effected. Few could have envisaged adoption of the 'non-stop 24 hour city centre' (Central Manchester Development Corporation 1993b). Revelry in the public realm of the city centre has been tightly regulated for centuries. The people lived to a common rhythm of work and play regulated by religious and judicial systems, and common understandings of the time as well as the place for licentious pleasure. Underpinning the demand for reform in the 'closeted, prohibitive and therefore unwelcoming feel' (Stewart 1992) to British cities long remarked by foreigners (Schinkel 1993), are critical changes in attitude to city centres and in urban clientele.

The promotion of 'a new vision of the city which will also emphasise its nature as a means of communication, a place where people meet, talk and share experiences' (Mulgan 1989: 264) became a strategy of the Left which culminated in a model of a 'European' city with 'intense public life'. Architects and others disseminated the vision of cities 'where the commonest sounds are voices, footsteps and the buzz of the electric tram' (Rogers and Fisher 1992). Accordingly, in Manchester, Albert Square has been stone-setted in emulation of the central squares of Hamburg or Milan, and the streets pedestrianised fifteen years ago are being refurbished. The City Council sponsors public festivities – fun-days, carnivals, fiestas, and fireworks; there is an annual festival of the arts; the city was City of Drama 1994. There is much to see.[10] Increasingly, the local authority is a manager of spectacle, a more engaging role than that of mundane service delivery.

Civic spectacle complements other shifts in the social profile. Throughout the 1980s there was a sense of youth cultures bubbling under the surface of the conventional city. These culminated in 'Madchester' – the bubble of pop promotion that brought Manchester international repute from 1990–2 as the place to be. The mood was brilliantly evoked: 'Why Manchester? Where else could I go? There's nowhere in the world ... my God, I've got to get to Manchester ... so much to answer for. Day-trippers, sightseers, tourists, ravers, rovers, adventurers, scallys, op-kids, fugitives; all pouring into town' (Champion 1990: 12–13). Night-life is not without its problems: the lead club (Hacienda) had to close for part of 1991 because of gangland violence, and in 1994 ten clubs were closed down or stopped running black music nights because of protection rackets (Evans 1994).

The expansion of the university sector (to 52,000 students in 1994) has given demographic force to the image. Young money floods into the city-centre stores and clubs. In addition, the city has become known for its alternative cultures, and in the past three years has rapidly moved to the position of the gay centre for Northern England. By 1994 there was a promotable gay 'village', centred on the thirty-five listed enterprises in the city centre, with an annual festival drawing very large crowds. The entrepreneurs who colonised dead space in an accessible fringe to the downtown have nevertheless had to contend with restrictive policing.

The demographic profile of the inner core of the urban region is changing, and while the dimensions of class and race remain important, the other dimension of urban differentiation – lifestyle – is becoming more prominent (Shevky 1972). Increasingly the urban core is either an appropriate address at a given stage in the life-cycle, or the place to be different. In consequence there is a sharp social distinction emerging between city and suburbs which is not that of class or even race.

Analysis

The transformation of city centre Manchester into the 'cool' or 'vibrant' playground can be understood as part of a general process of reconquest of space in the urban cores (Zukin 1988). In the cycle of property investment the moment has come for reclamation of previously developed land and buildings: a rent-gap has opened between potential, or speculative, values and the values conferred by previous use. The role of the state agencies has been to facilitate a transition which will further the restructuring of the regional economy which led to the demise of the archaic city centre. The urban core economy is now dominated by two sectors – the knowledge industries and the professional and business service core – and it is the workforce of the former which is colonising the centre. In Manchester an urban bourgeoisie of merchants and local businessmen which once worked and relaxed[11] in the city centre has been replaced by a distinctive 'class fraction' which may work, relax and even live there (Wynne and O'Connor 1995). It is not therefore a process of gentrification so much as regentrification (one replicated in the older suburbs). The signal feature is the blatancy of the redefinition of urban policy to this end. The 'Manchester script' (Quilley 1995) has now been honed to perfection by the journalists and public relations consultants, and is articulated freely by politicians or other advocates of the 'cool' city experience.

The new cultural norms mark out the city centre as the setting for civilised appreciation of the city, its arts, and heritage. It is designated as the focus of the cultural industries on whose promotion, it is argued, city economies will increasingly depend (Bianchini 1989, 1991). Promoters can call on the ideas of a range of cultural entrepreneurs: the proclamation of café society and the delights of the urban promenade and the public square, the acclaim for the urban 'village', the linking of sustainability and central city living, the excavation of the texts of Baudelaire, Benjamin and/ or de Beauvoir. These are all symptoms of active cultural business. The revalorisation of deserted downtowns requires a redefinition of taste and of the symbols of cultural standing, if high-cost and – by suburban definition – ugly and inconvenient buildings in insecure settings, are to find a market.

However, very little investment directly services the professional/ business core to the core economy. Much of city centre entertainment and spectacle has middle mass appeal, and so many of the cultural industries, in particular the labyrinthine music industry with its 'postmodern hobos' (Terry 1995: 37), tell a different story – that of the clubs, old clothes-stalls and music stores. The urban cores are being colonised by the young and a-familial, poor and less poor, searching out abandoned and undesired abodes and the opportunities for enjoyment on their own terms.

None of the writers on gentrification take into account the effects of the second 'demographic revolution' in which longevity, affluence and state support for education and household independence result in a differ- entiation of opportunities in the life-course. City experience is becoming a statement of 'a-familiality' and urban living marks different stages in the life-cycle, typically those of youth and disruption to familial life. There is therefore evident a neat reversal to the Chicago School's proposition that city life leads to disorganisation and that, consequently, urbanism is denoted by the attrition of the family. In consequence the population of the inner core of British cities such as Manchester is a particular amalgam of opportunist lifestyle seekers and necessitarian survivors (Seeley 1966). It is this that gives central-city life its flavour of diversity and risk.

The majority of those who use the city centre do not live in the inner core. Many are drawn there by the 'mobilisation of the spectacle' identified by Harvey (1989a) as the novel feature of contemporary cities. While he overlooked the entrenched role of what Castells had termed the 'ludic nucleus' (Castells 1977: 225) in the urban cores, Harvey did highlight the capitalisation of 'spaces of representation ... constructed spaces for ritual'

(1990: 262) and the ensuing shift into fantastic architecture. In contrast to previous urban societies with the open spectacle of street, square or church, that in the contemporary city is being commodified. And, in addition, the spontaneity of play is being channelled into crowd spectacle. In urban design the mass promenade, 'one emblem of a society which clings to the public realm as an important realm of personal experience' (Sennett 1986: 218) becomes the centre of attraction. A theatrical building may substitute for history, custom or geography to draw the crowd.

In a declining city, such as Manchester, the generation of spectacle is also a product of relentless and demeaning competition. Cities, as investment outlets, are players in·a global marketplace which can only increase 'the capitalisation of the locality' (Urry 1982: 469). The growth alliances have a common goal – that of stretching potential resources in heritage and local customs to put 'their' place on the map. The corollary of globalisation is a drive for the bold statement, the search for the vital element, the one building that can be recognised subliminally, world-wide. The fun, the magical moments of time out in the city, cannot be shown in publicity or distilled in the submission for investment, and so the spectacular building is substituted as icon.

The work of 'making places in placeless times' (Robins 1991: 38) is demeaning because any memorable artefact or tourist-worthy quirk of tradition has to be hawked across the world. It is also demanding for it may have to overcome the dynamics of the place as it has become. The Olympic Bid campaign was unable to overcome the historically entrenched image of Manchester as dirt and pollution, poor living, work and rain, everything a sportive crowd wants to forget. Similarly the promoters of the city centre have to contend with media constructions of urban crime and pathology. The two districts of Manchester most likely to be identified by the national public are the notorious ones of Hulme (once the 'worst housing estate in Europe') and Moss Side ('Bronx of Britain') adjacent to city centre and university. And the local drug wars have given the city the tag of 'Gunchester', one difficult to dislodge when street crime and violence are rife.[12] If Manchester's city centre is to front the region as a place of success and pleasure, its own history as the core of a poor city will have to be overcome.

One incubus from the past is the social ecology of the city. Unlike continental cities the poverty belt envelops the city centre. These districts were notorious for their poverty ninety years ago (Hunter 1901: 116), and because of the circumstances of their rebuilding as slum clearance estates took on the additional stigma of 'inner city'. The regional centre is socially eclectic – extensively used by local poor as well as the young, and the regional majority. It is the shopping centre, marketplace, source of entertainment and relaxation for the inner-city populations. The Californian precedent of the 'fortress' city (Davis 1990) cannot be followed without redesigning the city's public spaces and the allocation of more resources to their policing. The privileged minority in Manchester have to navigate the city centre as they do the urban terrain – with trajectories of avoidance and disregard.

The poverty belt is as it is because poor people have always lived there (Mellor 1984). They did so, in large number, because of the demand for rough labour in the city centre as well as the availability of cheap housing. Now their presence is an impediment to the 'reintegration' of space at the heart of the city. The contrast between this still to be privileged space and the space of the poor is less acute than that of the American cities but it is also less defensible. British cities are relatively permeable and current policy is to retain that characteristic (Manchester City Council 1995). And while the business core can be protected, the urban playground, by definition public space, cannot.

However, the ultimate limit to the 'city of the future' – vibrant, cosmopolitan, entertaining and happening – will be the regional economy. If this is further depleted then it will become ever harder for the professional business core to retain its critical mass as the commercial centre into which insurance funds and others invest. The second limitation will be the counter-magnet of the suburbs: the city centre will become increasingly irrelevant to the economic and social life of the region except as 'a kind of liminal zone where some of the rules and restrictions of routine life are relaxed' (Lash and Urry 1994: 235). The third limitation will be that of the poverty belt. To the stigma of association has to be added the risks of work and play in the 'cool' city.

NOTES

1   The population of the local authority district fell from 710,000 in 1951 to 420,000 in 1991; that of the innermost six wards by 75 per cent; some 79,000 dwellings were cleared between 1956 and 1980, only 39,000 being replaced in the city (Manchester City Council Planning Department 1980a).

2   Cuts in the rate support grant and allocation for housing investment from 1979–89 had deprived the City Council of £1,500 million (at 1989 prices) (City Executive's Office, July 1989).

3   The borough, Manchester City, had a higher proportion of welfare-dependent households than any other local authority district in Britain in 1994. In October 1994 an estimated 42.3 per cent were receiving housing benefit.

4   *Financial Times*, 17 November 1989, *The Economist*, 21 October 1989 and *Daily Telegraph*, 19 December 1989. Prime rents had trebled between 1981 and the end of 1989, increasing by 90 per cent in 1988/9 to reach £14.50 per square foot.

5   In 1988 it was 'forecast to fare the worst of all regions, suffering the biggest fall in employment ... output growth barely half the national average and a growing exodus of the population' (Cambridge Econometrics Economic Research Centre 1988). See also *The Economist*, 1 April 1989, in which the North West was ranked eighth out of eleven UK regions for growth.

6   The Manchester Labour Party has been more cautious than those of Birmingham and Sheffield. The former's spending of £380 million on the International Convention Centre and the National Indoor Arena, as well as refurbishment of the city centre, 1986–92, is argued to have been a contributory element in the underfunding of the city's education and housing budgets (Loftman and Nevin 1992).

7   The letters page of the local newspaper is the only forum. The irony of bidding for the Olympic Games whilst unable to maintain park tennis courts was remarked on in 1992/3. Quite small sums of money can make a great difference to local life: a £25,000 grant to the Manchester Schools FA, or a similar sum for a playground, close to the £9 million velodrome in East Manchester, where 'residents are extremely angry to see the only facility for children in the area under threat at a time when millions of pounds are being

poured into the area in the name of regeneration and the Olympic bid' (*MEN*, 19 March 1993).

8   A procession of horse-drawn lorries and wagons traversed the city centre from Salford Station to the warehouse district to the south of the business centre twice a day because the cotton merchants kept to the practice of inspecting yarn and cloth at each stage of the process of manufacture at the city centre warehouses (*Official Guide to Manchester City 1950*, and oral evidence).

9   Registered unemployment peaked at 20.3 per cent for the local authority area in January 1993. The rate in October 1994 was 17.3 per cent, twice the national average. Male unemployment rates were more than 29 per cent in ten wards (all but one in the inner city). Six were areas of Afro-Caribbean and South Asian concentration; four out of five wards with the highest levels of women registering were areas of non-white concentration (*Unemployment and Welfare Benefits Bulletin*, no. 13, 1994, Manchester City Planning Department; 1991 census).

10   The Tourist Board reported that the city was sixth in the UK tourism league with 330,000 overseas visitors in 1993 (and also 1994), an increase of 47 per cent 1984–92 (*Manchester Evening News*, 14 July 1994, 11 July 1995).

11   The day of the independent textile merchant had a definite rhythm: office in the morning, coffee, dominoes or backgammon, lunch through the middle of the day in one of the large coffee houses, back to the office before returning home to the suburbs in the evening (oral evidence).

12   In one neighbourhood alone there have been an estimated 1,000 street attacks in a year. Pickpockets work the crowds in the city centre, bag snatches are common, bus passengers are the target for violent thefts; the car parks require extra protection. Attraction of the leisure pound has to be tempered by caution (as in the cryptic advice to cruise along a particular section of one canal only in the *mornings* (Central Manchester Development Corporation 1993b; emphasis added). The risk is that of banditry by young men.

Part II

MANAGING AND MEASURING
CITY LIFE

5

BEYOND 'CULTURE CITY'

Glasgow as a 'dual city'

Gerry Mooney and Mike Danson

INTRODUCTION

One of the main arguments emerging in urban studies in recent years is that social and economic changes, together with government policies, have led to the creation of various marginalised groups, or further excluded sections of the population long considered disadvantaged, primarily located in declining urban areas. Within the contemporary city social and economic polarisation has been accompanied by a corresponding reorganisation of the urban spatial structure, so that emerging 'post-industrial' cities contain within them groups who have 'lost-out' through economic transformation (Wilson 1987). This in turn has prompted claims of a 'dual city'. Castells has argued that the dual city image has long been a classic theme of urban sociology (Castells 1989: 224). However, of late the dual city metaphor has become a popular means in academic and media circles of describing urban spatial change and the growing divide between rich and poor, or affluent and 'socially excluded'.

In many American studies in particular, the dual city is interpreted primarily in terms of an impoverished inner city contrasting with affluent middle-class districts located, though not exclusively, in suburban areas. 'Elite enclaves' are thus contrasted with areas housing 'marginalised' social groups (Winchester and White 1988). The prevailing image is one which portrays the inner city as home to the poor or the new 'underclass', an area where 'urban problems' are contained. Sharkansky has argued that one of the dominant characteristics of modern American society is the development of cities with 'two sides':

> Their attractive side includes productive manufacturing, innovative service industries, striking architecture, and experimental programs on the frontiers of social policy. Their unattractive side features slum housing, grinding poverty, widespread crime and attendant social programs that seem unable to cope with people's needs and occasional disorder that threatens the political fabric.
>
> (Sharkansky 1975: 71)

While these dualist models are more developed in American studies, it is becoming a convenient tool for describing the contemporary urban landscape and for urban analysis in a European context. Here we wish to consider the applicability and usefulness of the dual city notion in the context of the 'regeneration' of Glasgow in recent years. We focus on Glasgow as it has been widely regarded as *the* model of urban renewal in Britain, having successfully navigated the path from a declining industrial to a reinvigorated post-industrial city. Further, in the context of Glasgow, ideas of a dual city take a different form from those depicted in the vast number of studies: while a distinction is still drawn between the 'affluent city' and the 'deprived city', for the most part the 'deprived city' is defined as the large post-war housing estates located on the perimeter, which have been largely bypassed by Glasgow's 'regeneration'. This is not to argue that spatial divisions are a new feature of cities such as Glasgow. As in many other British cities, historically spatial divisions existed between different parts. In Glasgow such divisions were accentuated in the post-war period by the rapid development of large 'peripheral estates' and in many accounts of Glasgow's regeneration it is these estates which represent, to borrow Sharkansky's phrase, the 'unattractive side' of modern Glasgow (for example, Keating 1988, 1989; Pacione 1986, 1990, 1993).

In seeking to explore the dual city notion we begin by considering its use in previous studies. We turn then to focus on Glasgow and examine the particular ways in which the dual city idea has been used there, drawing on academic studies, media coverage of Glasgow's regeneration and local authority programmes for the 'deprived segments'. We conclude by questioning the usefulness of the dual city notion, examining the spatial patterns of poverty and disadvantage which characterise the city in the mid-1990s.

THE DUAL CITY IDEA

The dual city notion is by no means novel but has tended to re-emerge in different historical contexts in attempts to grasp the complexity of urban social and spatial patterns. However, several developments are responsible for its renewed popularity. The uneven impact on urban areas of global and national processes of economic change are widely regarded as increasing the economic and social marginalisation of particular social groups and the abandonment of much of the urban (industrial) landscape. In several American studies (Mollenkopf and Castells 1991; Savitch 1988; Sassen 1991) this process has been interpreted in the framework of a post-industrial transition. Mollenkopf and Castells, for example, claim that New York City has undergone a post-industrial transformation in recent years. While some groups have clearly benefited from the expansion of well-paying service jobs, they also highlight the negative aspects of this post-industrial shift in terms of the growth of poor quality employment.

Sassen has further emphasised the impact of processes of work informal-isation on the social structure of 'global cities' such as New York (Sassen 1991). Occupational polarisation is accompanied by growing segregation on the basis of ethnic background whereby the less skilled and others unable to compete in the new labour market are concentrated in the less desirable areas and poorer housing.

The growth of poverty over the past two decades has become a major characteristic of urban areas. Augur (1993) has argued that in the United States there is an increasing 'urbanisation of poverty', the product of a combination of economic decline and government policies which have drastically reduced the scope and level of services for disadvantaged groups in American cities. This point is also taken up by Kantor who interprets the development of dual cities as a consequence of political failure to respond to those processes which generate urban inequalities (Kantor 1993).

The dual city idea has gradually entered debates about urban polarisation in Europe. The notion has been explored in investigations of poverty in Amsterdam (Van Kempen 1994) and in Hamburg (Dangschat 1994) with both studies questioning its adequacy as an analytic tool and highlighting its vagueness.

In Britain it is the residents of run-down inner-city districts and large local authority housing estates who are regarded as socially excluded. MacGregor argues that these areas have become central, not only to much of the contemporary discussion of social and spatial polarisation but also to the very language of urban poverty itself.

> Urban poverty, the underclass, the inner-city and the outer estate –
> these terms become associated with drugs, prostitution, a walk on the
> wild side, living on the edge – stepping over the boundaries of
> normality and correctness.
>
> (MacGregor 1994: 67)

For Robson, these processes of polarisation suggest that the future for many of Britain's major cities is bleak:

> The gloomy prospect that cities face is one of living with the ghetto,
> of the physical containment of the urban underclass, who might form
> 10 per cent of the national population but perhaps one-third of that
> of the big cities. Unwanted, allowed to develop a subculture which sets
> them apart from mainstream society, such an underclass must form a
> recurring threat to the achievement of economic affluence for the
> majority. One increasingly plausible response may be that of contain-
> ment. And where better to contain than in the run-down housing
> estates on the fringe of large city centres, or in the girdle of deprived
> populations lying outside the central city.
>
> (Robson 1989: 22–3)

The key organising concept which serves to link debates about urban poverty and polarisation is the 'underclass'. It is unusual for sociological concepts to enter into popular discourse, but the notion of an underclass is clearly an exception. In both academic studies and literary works alike, not to mention in a wide body of journalistic writing, versions of the underclass thesis have been used to give expression to a wide range of popular fears, and moral panics over contemporary social 'problems'.

The resulting image is one which portrays an increasingly divided city: a relatively affluent and increasingly suburbanised white (and growing black) middle class on the one hand and a poor black underclass, economically and socially isolated in inner city ghettos. Cities are thus becoming more economically polarised and spatially segregated with a widening divide between those who have benefited from the new job opportunities in well paying sectors, and those who are forced to rely upon casualised employ-ment. Interwoven with this are inequalities deriving from divisions of race and gender. The divide is generally portrayed as between the rich and poor, between those who have been able to participate in the consumer booms of recent years and a growing population who are both welfare-dependent and socially excluded.

The dominant view is one which claims that economic transformation and social change are producing an increasingly isolated mass of poor people, cut-off from and largely bypassed by centres and processes of economic growth. The outcome is the creation of two cities in a shared spatial context: one for the rich and one for the poor; a city doing 'well' and one doing 'poorly', and a dramatically widening gulf between the two.

THE REPRESENTATION OF GLASGOW AS A DUAL CITY

The apparent success story of Glasgow's attempts in recent years to restructure its economic base and reverse decades of economic decline has placed it increasingly in the academic and media spotlight. Glasgow was *the* place to visit to explore successful place-marketing; cultural-led urban regeneration programmes and public–private agency partnership at its most successful.

However, the spotlight did not fall only on the 'Miles Better Campaign', the National Garden Festival in 1988 or the European Year of Culture in 1990. The national British media, some sections of the international press, policy-makers and several academics, while praising policies applied in Glasgow, were also increasingly drawing attention to the 'problems' of those areas neglected by the image-makers and bypassed by urban regeneration. For many it was the 'problems' of the peripheral housing estates which required particular attention.

Glasgow's 'outer' (or 'peripheral') estates were a product of slum clearance programmes and the need to tackle severe housing shortages in the 1930s, 1940s and 1950s. Starting with Pollok in the mid-1930s, for the next twenty-five years a series of large public-sector estates were con-structed. The biggest estates, at Castlemilk, Drumchapel, Easterhouse and Pollok, were the main recipients of the slum clearance population who were rehoused within the city. At their peak in the late 1960s and early 1970s, the four large estates accommodated around 200,000 people, almost exclu-sively in social housing. One outcome of these housing and renewal programmes was the creation of a new layer of spatial segregation, superimposed on those patterns of residential divisions laid down in previous periods.

From being the solution to Glasgow's housing problems in the immedi-ate post-war period, by the late 1960s the peripheral estates were figuring on the table of deprivation indicators. While in the early 1970s this was largely confined to areas of declining industrial activity and districts with private-rented housing along the Clyde, by 1981 the four large peripheral estates had become significant locales of 'multiple deprivation'. This was reflected in the large number of estates identified as *Areas of Priority Treatment* by Strathclyde Regional Council at this time. During the 1970s the spatial distribution of urban deprivation in Glasgow had significantly changed, partly as a consequence of urban renewal and slum clearance programmes in the inner city, which led to dramatic falls in inner-city populations (Pacione 1993). Glasgow's outer estates were built at a time of relative economic growth and increased state housing provision. But by the late 1960s and 1970s, its economic base had dramatically declined, reflecting the long-term de-industrialisation of the economy. Lee highlights the ways in which the changing (and declining) economic fortunes of Britain's older industrial cities impact on outer estates. His comments about Liverpool's overspill estates apply directly to Glasgow:

> The residents of its hurriedly constructed and under-serviced outer estates, like Kirkby, Speke, and Halewood, were decanted from the inner-city as part of the Fordist processes of urban restructuring during the long boom. They now live lives in which many are deprived both of a livelihood in the capitalist economy and of support from a welfare economy devastated by the effects of the urban fiscal crisis.
>
> (Lee 1989: 69)

For Pacione, results of the 1991 census confirmed arguments that the 'urban crisis' was becoming particularly acute in such estates (Pacione 1993). In contrast to other parts of Britain where the inner city remained the key '*deviant*' area, home to the urban underclass (MacGregor and Pimlott 1990), in Scotland it was the peripheral estates dotted around the main cities which had become the '*problem spaces*' (although to some extent outer estates in English cities were beginning to figure in accounts of urban deprivation). By the mid- to late 1980s, when Glasgow's regeneration was well under way, opponents of the regeneration strategy and media commentators alike did not have far to look to highlight the other side of culture city.

How was the dual city/two city idea expressed in the Glasgow context? From the late 1980s it is possible to identify this notion in both national and local newspapers, on national and Scottish-based television, in several academic accounts of Glasgow's regeneration and in studies of rising poverty levels on Clydeside. Of late it has begun to emerge, albeit implicitly in some instances, in economic strategy reports produced by public agencies in Strathclyde (for example Glasgow City Council 1991; Glasgow Regeneration Alliance 1993). In 1992 Glasgow's new image was shaken by the publicity given by the media to a gangland murder trial which lasted for several months. The two city idea was grasped by sections of the media keen to explain the co-existence of 'Merchant City', a renewal area adjacent to the city centre which is seen as representing the 'new Glasgow', along with gang 'warfare' and rising crime. This also characterised some newspaper accounts of violence in the city in August 1995. But in the main the dual city idea has been grasped by those eager to account for increasing levels of poverty at a time of economic change and substantial private sector investment in the city.

It was Keating in *The City That Refused To Die* (1988) who was among the first to popularise and apply the notion in a Glasgow context. Previously Keating and Boyle (1986) had explored Glasgow's 'dual economy': a situation whereby large-scale city centre renewal and inward investment was in marked contrast to the underfunded peripheral estates. While the populations of these estates were largely characterised by poor health, unemployment, low skills and a life of poverty, there had been little opposition to the growing social and spatial divide within Glasgow. The reason Boyle later provided was stark:

> Glasgow's poor are simply no longer part of the city. In economic, political, or social terms, their alienation from the city is now almost complete. Years of isolation bred hopelessness; the response of the very poorest has been to withdraw into a personal world of survival, far removed from city centre renewal, waterfront housing, and new shopping centres.
>
> (Boyle 1990: 129)

This theme had also been taken up by Keating. He saw Glasgow as a prime example of an economically 'stagnating city', with few growth sectors. Urban restructuring and renewal programmes, while improving Glasgow's image, had heightened social and geographical inequalities, increasing the isolation of the populations of the outer estates.

> [The] result is a 'dual city', with few dynamic sectors and a consider-able revival of downtown amenities ... but, overall, with a stagnant economy, considerable social distress, and a growing housing problem.
>
> (Keating 1989: 516)

Large public sector housing programmes in the post-war period had created a spatially divided city, wherein outlying estates would be largely cut-off from inward investment in the city centre. As opposed to the entrepreneurial dynamism of the core, the peripheral estates could be seen as a 'welfare city', where the majority of the residents survived either on welfare benefits or on poor quality, low paid employment. But this 'dualism' would be further exacerbated by policies which saw these estates in isolation from the wider Glasgow and Strathclyde economies.

The idea that the peripheral estates represented a 'welfare city' was also expressed by Pacione in his study of the changing pattern of poverty in Glasgow. Pacione saw the outlying estates as typically 'cashless societies', characterised by high levels of welfare-dependency (Pacione 1990: 308). The conditions prevalent in this city stood in marked contrast to those which characterised Glasgow's *other city*.

While Keating, Boyle and Pacione sought to avoid a 'blame the victim' type of argument, and argued that the 'problems' of the peripheral estates had to be seen in relation to the overall economy of Glasgow, their uncritical use of some of the concepts and terms characteristic of much of the underclass debate allows for different interpretations of their arguments. Despite the call for regeneration programmes to be extended to include the peripheral estates, the language of dual city or two cities allows the problems in the peripheral estates to be seen as residual, particularly by the policy-makers. The print and television media were quick to pick-up on some of the emotive language following from the dual city argument and the wider debate emerging in Britain about the underclass and social polarisation. A number of articles appeared in both the Glasgow-based press and national press which applied the dual city idea with renewed vigour. The following extracts are indicative of many of the press reports which appeared around this time:

> But hidden behind the logoed smiles of the Glasgow's Miles Better campaign is another Glasgow, a city in deep economic crisis, and a city haunted by the reality of growing poverty ... Glasgow in 1988 is a tale of two cities and two competing economies.
>
> (*Sunday Times*, 7 August 1988)

> So much of the new Glasgow remains irrelevant to so many. On the surface the city is going great guns but for a substantial slice of the population the city which is miles better is a mirage. They can see it from their peripheral estates where they are sentenced by Glasgow's new social imbalance to live under economic house arrest. They can look on but they cannot touch. For them the Glasgow which is miles better is miles away.
>
> (*Glasgow Herald*, 5 December 1988)

> Easterhouse, with Castlemilk, Drumchapel and Pollok, the other 'peripheral estates' which ring the city, is cut-off from Glasgow's much-mooted renaissance, its residents trapped in a spiral of poverty and economic decline. Boom time in the centre has thrown poverty on the margins into stark relief. In Glasgow, the last decade's deepening divide between rich and poor is probably at its sharpest.
>
> (*Independent*, 24 April 1989)

> When urban poverty is concentrated at a city's heart it cannot easily escape notice by those who have avoided it directly. Exported to the literal margins of conurbations it can be easily unnoticed ... All around the periphery of Glasgow, and other Scottish cities it might be added, are large districts with daunting problems of social and economic deprivation.
>
> (*Glasgow Herald*, 5 January 1990)

> Glasgow, for all the strides made in the 80s, is still teetering on the brink. In real terms it remains one of Britain's more impoverished cities. And unless the momentum for change and renewal is maintained, there is a danger it will slip back down the ladder. Or merely perpetuate its existence as a tale of two cities, with a confident up-beat

centre – and away from the bright lights, a hinterland of unemployment, run-down housing schemes, and chronically under developed
urban 'black holes'.

(*Glasgow Evening Times*, 3 July 1991)

Again the predominant themes which tended to emerge from these
newspaper reports were ones which focused on welfare 'dependency',
'cashless economies', 'deserts of despair', 'hopelessness' and the growing
concentrations of single-parent families. Numerous other articles provided human interest stories of the 'hell' of living in Glasgow's outer
estates. Indeed the *Sunday Times*, when devoting space to Charles
Murray's arguments about an emerging British underclass, highlighted
Easterhouse in particular as an example of a council estate 'consistent
with reports from inner-city Washington and New York' (*Sunday Times*,
26 November 1989: 30).

One of the main ideas to emerge from these reports, and in a number
of television programmes broadcast during 1990, was the growing marginalisation of the outer estate populations, cut-off from processes of economic regeneration. Thus the peripheral estates were not only peripheral
in geographical terms, but were peripheralised economically, socially and
politically. The picture which dominated tended to stereotype the peripheral estates as uniformly run-down and deprived. The two Glasgows – the
'old' (here depicted by the not-so-old peripheral estates) and the 'new' (as
represented by Merchant City, tourist attractions and new shopping
centres) – were starkly counterposed.

While thus far these ideas have not been wholly accepted by the policy-
makers who drive Glasgow's regeneration programme, there is some
evidence that the two city notion has begun to influence a number of public
and private sector agencies which are operating in the city. In 1991 Glasgow
City Council's Planning Department warned of the long-term consequences
of ignoring the outer estates, which could undermine the regeneration of the
entire city (Glasgow City Council 1991: 10). This perspective has emerged
explicitly in arguments made by the Glasgow Regeneration Alliance (GRA)
(G. Mooney 1994). This Alliance, which comprises four public sector
agencies, was launched with the promise of a £1.5 billion investment package
for 'disadvantaged areas', including the peripheral estates. Continuing
population decline had left Glasgow with an 'unbalanced social structure',
increasingly marginalised in deprived areas. For the GRA, Glasgow's long-
term economic revitalisation was dependent upon utilising the resources of
such areas. Further, the threat to Glasgow's new image which such areas
posed, particularly to the growing tourist trade, was also highlighted as a
major cause for concern. The four large peripheral estates offered considerable land development opportunities together with abundant labour sup-
plies. Easterhouse and Pollok were adjacent to the existing and planned
motorway network and thus were 'strategic gateways' to the city offering
economic development opportunities.

Despite claims that the GRA was committed to 'unlocking the full
potential' of disadvantaged areas throughout Glasgow, it is not difficult to

identify the attractiveness of the peripheral estates in terms of their land development potential. In other words it was not the space occupied by the peripheral estates which was redundant, but sizeable chunks of their populations.

Population decline in the outer estates during the 1980s and early 1990s had led to proposals that at least one estate should be completely demolished, with the population being rehoused in the 20,000 empty council houses spread across Glasgow. While such proposals were not fully developed, the thinking that lay behind them illustrates the extent to which over the past 10–15 years the outer estates have come to be regarded as *the* key urban problem in Glasgow. Claims that they have become in some sense 'surplus' to requirements have not been hard to find, particularly in press coverage. By the early 1990s the idea that the peripheral estates had become 'outcast Glasgow' or Glasgow's 'second city' had been clearly established.

What emerges from this discussion is the language of much of the underclass debate. While references to the underclass in the Glasgow context have been few in number thus far, ideas of dependency, exclusion, marginalisation, hopelessness and despair have dominated the accounts of the emerging socio-spatial divide in the city. The portrayal of the peripheral estates in particular as uniformly depressed and welfare-dependent has been widely reported. Such views tend to regard these areas as residual problems. But how adequate are such claims and how far is the problem of poverty a problem of – or confined to – peripheral estates?

THE GEOGRAPHY OF POVERTY IN STRATHCLYDE

Glasgow is the major city within the Strathclyde Region of central Scotland. In Strathclyde Region the long-established 'Social Strategy' is based upon a spatial social policy implemented through the concept of 'Areas of Priority Treatment' (APT). These are defined using a number of indicators which have been identified as being closely correlated with poverty. Other social indicators tend to confirm the results delivered by these statistics and recent analyses testify to the validity of using these proxies (Strathclyde Regional Council 1994).

Analysis of the 1991 Census of Population suggests that the extent of relative poverty and deprivation appears to have become more widespread in the decade 1981–91, requiring a broadening in the coverage of APTs. The notion of priority treatment has been reduced, though, by this depression in the living standards of many in the working class across the metropolitan area of Glasgow, the Glasgow conurbation and the wider Strathclyde Region. However, in its strategic role the Council has continued to promote the concept of APTs on the grounds of the persistence of concentrations of poverty; in Glasgow and Paisley especially, multiple deprivation has become even more focused on specific areas in the last decade (Strathclyde Regional Council 1994). Nevertheless, the Region highlights a more dispersed and varied deprivation in the rest of Strathclyde, with many of the poorest living outside the worst areas of poverty. In other words, poverty has become deeper and more widespread throughout Strathclyde, questioning the idea of a spatially concentrated and well-defined underclass.

Although the Regional Councils in Scotland have been abolished under local government reorganisation in 1996, the reappraisal of the area-based approach to social strategy is of importance to more than the authority itself, as many other agencies have adopted this method of focusing on the deprived, enumerated by communities and households. Given the rigour, the well-established acceptance of the methodology, and the availability of the analysis, the Strathclyde Region approach to measuring the extent and distribution of poverty and multiple deprivation has been adopted here also. If an underclass or dual city does exist, then unique concentrations of multiple deprivation would be expected and so the APT definitions hold promise in the pursuit and identification of an excluded people.

The 1980s witnessed a major restructuring in the Clydeside economy, with 44 per cent of manufacturing and 5 per cent of service jobs disappearing from the city over the decade. Unemployment, however, is not highly correlated with the other principal indicators of poverty, such as lone parents, elderly or disabled. As the poor earn their poverty, suffer from debilitating illnesses, struggle to raise a family single handedly, or carry these burdens into old age, so they may be concentrated with similar people, but not exclusively or comprehensively with all such groups.

As in previous Censuses, the figures for 1981 and 1991 show that while the city has continued to suffer from relative multiple deprivation, the old industrial districts on the periphery of the conurbation have also deteriorated since 1981. The populations of Glasgow, Renfrew and Inverclyde are over-represented compared with the share expected from a simple count of their residents. In total, 12 per cent (280,000) of the Regional population live in the areas of severe deprivation designated as Priority 1 or 'Major Social Strategy Initiative Areas'. All of the Glasgow APTs are included in the priority areas of the government quangos and public/private sector partnerships in Clydeside, including Scottish Homes and the Glasgow Regeneration Alliance. In none was unemployment below 27 per cent, lone parents headed up between 35 per cent and 52 per cent of households, while the lives of 13–21 per cent of the non-elderly population were limited by long-term illnesses.

Few of the Priority 2 or 'Smaller Social Strategy Urban Initiative Areas and Priority Rural Areas' have instances of the very worst Enumeration Districts (EDs), the smallest local units of the Census, but any degree of concentration of poverty is to be found in Glasgow city. The Priority 3 areas are either 'Urban Programme Eligible Areas' or 'Other Deprived Rural Areas'. As the local authority document notes, however, some elements of deprivation in the latter are not addressed by the Census (for example, access).

The Census has confirmed the city's position as the centre for poverty and deprivation in the region. On a range of indicators (unemployment, lone parents, overcrowding and vacancy rates), Glasgow appears as the worst district in Strathclyde, non-elderly illness being the exception.

Glasgow has 50 per cent of EDs in the worst 10 per cent in Scotland and 87 per cent of the worst 5 per cent in Strathclyde. In dynamic terms, comparing the City with its wider Region suggests that couples tend to move out to the suburbs when they are newly married or otherwise ready to start a family, a standard pattern of mobility.

Unemployment is appreciably higher in the city. Although 'race' is a poor indicator of deprivation in Scotland, the relatively low numbers of ethnic minorities in Strathclyde are concentrated in the city (21,500). While a higher proportion of the elderly have a limiting long-term illness, the differential is greater for younger age groups. A much higher proportion of households have no car, again a common large-city phenomenon.

Other non-census indicators show that age-specific death and morbidity rates are higher in Glasgow than elsewhere in the region, UK and indeed Europe. Wage and income data suggest a higher dependence on the benefit system and basic pensions, with a greater proportion of jobs in low paying sectors. The proportion of the relevant population receiving free school meals, income support, housing benefit or clothing grants are all highest in Glasgow in a list of Districts in the Region.

Together these data suggest that Glasgow has suffered and continues to suffer from the aftermath of decline and stagnation. Moreover, the large expansion in the new service sectors of the 1980s (banking, insurance and finance, personal services and public and private administration), all promoted as key elements of the post-industrial city and as compensation for the haemorrhaging of skilled manufacturing employment, has over-whelmingly benefited commuters outside the city. Nearly half of all jobs are now taken by residents of the dormitory suburbs, of satellite towns, and of other regions within daily travelling distance. 'Trickle-down' processes of regeneration are difficult to discern in this evidence. Yet mobility out of the city and the widespread levels of multiple deprivation throughout Strath-clyde suggest that Glasgow is not simply home to a new regional underclass, made redundant by the restructuring of the last quarter century. To determine how concentrated the poverty is within Glasgow, it is necessary to look at the peripheral estates and renewal areas of the city.

Between 1981 and 1991, population loss was especially severe in the peripheral estates (PEs) (30.4 per cent) and the renewal areas (RAs) in general (20.5 per cent) compared with under 4 per cent in the rest of Glasgow, suggesting a relative move from the poorest areas into the wider city. This in itself undermines the notion that a permanently excluded underclass exists with limited mobility to the rest of the community, or that poverty is concentrated in certain areas, or is dominant in those areas, or therefore in those areas alone.

As to the composition of the respective areas, the proportion of all households with children is highest in the PEs (39 per cent), lower in the RAs as a whole (30 per cent) and only 22 per cent in the rest of the city. The proportion of lone parents has increased across the city. There is a significant concentration of lone parents in poorer areas, with 70 per cent of all lone parents in the city living in RAs, half in the PEs alone.

Another group subject to poverty and deprivation are the single elderly, yet these are under-represented in the poorest areas: 12 per cent in PEs, but with similar proportions in the RAs (17 per cent) and in the wider city (18 per cent). This demonstrates that the deprived communities are themselves of different histories and structures. Older industrial districts are deprived because of the redundancy of their populations' skills and networks in the 1970s, with induced and institutionalised immobility concentrating poverty locally. The new concentrations of single parents in some parts of some peripheral estates, for instance, are created no less by economic, housing and family interactions, but give rise to different areas of multiple deprivation.

Critically, therefore, the areas where the poor live cannot be explained simply in one dimension; by extension, there is not a class defined by different criteria from the rest of the working class, rather they are a heterogeneous set of the population that is often concentrated in particular parts of the city, region and nation. Many of their number can be found beyond the 'areas for priority treatment'; that is, the areas defined as having the worst problems of poverty and deprivation.

CONCLUSION

The conclusion which is drawn from the analysis of poverty and deprivation in contemporary Glasgow presented here is not one which lends support to the dual city model. In this respect our conclusions follow those made by other critics of the two city notion. This is not to deny however, that there is an uneven distribution of poverty in the city or that poverty is concentrated in certain areas. What is being contested is the usefulness of the dual city argument for our understanding of such distributions and the processes which contribute to it. While there is an important distinction to be drawn between simplistic uses of the dual city notion, exemplified by press reports, and more sophisticated sociological accounts (for example Mollenkopf and Castells 1991), they tend to suffer from similar problems.

The language of the two city/dual city argument is one which is seriously flawed by definitional and conceptual difficulties. Despite the continuing use of concepts such as polarisation, underclass, exclusion and marginalisation, we are little clearer about the underlying factors which are viewed as contributing to such processes. In this respect the dual city perspective and its implicit arguments about growing socio-spatial polarisation are plagued by ambiguity and vagueness (Fainstein et al. 1992; Hamnett 1994; Marcuse 1989; Van Kempen 1994; Woodward 1995).

In discussions of the emerging 'tale of two cities' in Glasgow, the attention which the peripheral estates received does not relate directly to the levels and proportions of poverty to be found there. In part this is a consequence of reluctance to define adequately the areas or social groups concerned. Further *within* peripheral estates there is a marked differentiation between the various component parts in terms of unemployment, poverty and deprivation. This is almost completely neglected in the dominant picture of these estates which has emerged in recent years which stereotypes the estates as homogeneous enclaves of 'despair' or 'hope-lessness'.

It is also evident from the analysis of the spatial distribution of poverty in Strathclyde that the situation *throughout* Glasgow is deteriorating relative to the rest of the Region. Only in two other Strathclyde Districts – Renfrew and Inverclyde – is there an increase in the concentration of poverty. This raises a major problem with the dual city concept – that of scale (Van Kempen 1994: 996). Suburban areas have continued to prosper, largely at the expense of other parts of the region. Such a pattern may then justify the fears of politicians that there will be a continuing population exodus from Glasgow as a whole with an increasingly welfare-dependent population and an even more 'unbalanced social structure'.

That the dual city model fails to capture the complexity of social and spatial divisions within the urban setting is apparent in many of the studies mentioned here. Mollenkopf and Castells, for instance, question the continuing use of the term for implying a simple dichotomy between rich and poor areas (Mollenkopf and Castells 1991: 405). Despite this, Castells in particular has continued to utilise the notion. The dual city, he claims, is the fundamental urban dualism of our time:

> It opposes the cosmopolitanism of the elite, living on a daily connection to the whole world ... to the tribalism of local communities, retrenched in their spaces that they try to control as their last stand against the macro-forces that shape their lives out of their reach. The fundamental dividing line in our cities is the inclusion of the cosmopolitans in the making of the new history while excluding the locals from the control of the global city to which ultimately their neighbourhoods belong.
>
> (Castells 1994: 30)

But the continuing use of the dual city idea obscures more than it illuminates our understanding of the dynamics which underlie the divide referred to by Castells. What are the links between growth and decline and poverty and affluence in urban areas? Much of Glasgow's economic regeneration has been founded upon the growth of relatively low paid and temporary employment, increasing the proportion of the population who have only a tentative hold on the labour market.

Despite the arguments that the peripheral estates are essential to the long-term economic future of the city, at present the dominant representation is one which sees such areas as residual problems. In this respect the dual city notion gives rise to a 'poor versus the rest' type of argument which serves to obscure the fundamental relations of power and profit in the modern city (Marcuse 1989: 707). Following from this, Beauregard is right to highlight the politics of the dual city representation:

> All dualities are political statements. They convey a hierarchical positioning that reinforces prevailing relations of power and privilege and they do so in a historically contingent and rhetorically embedded way.
>
> (Beauregard 1993: 227)

The peripheral estates have become symbolic of the '*dark side*' of contemporary Glasgow: the '*city of despair*' in contrast to the '*city of hope and splendour*' (Van Kempen 1994). But such symbolic representations tell us little about the realities of an economically depressed city. In this respect, then, it is not only the idea of a 'city of despair' which is problematic. With its declining position on the European periphery, and rising levels of poverty and deprivation, can we speak of Glasgow as a 'city of hope and splendour' either?

6

'RACE', HOUSING AND THE CITY

Peter Ratcliffe

INTRODUCTION

The analysis which follows stems from a growing concern at the apparent inability of the literature, both beyond the discipline and within it, to provide a convincing theorisation of the structural position of Britain's minority populations within the housing market. Given that large-scale post-war migration from Africa, the Caribbean and the Indian sub-continent began in the 1950s, and that significant numbers of black citizens had settled in Britain many decades earlier (Fryer 1984; Hiro 1991; May and Cohen 1974), this is somewhat surprising. Within the obvious confines of such a brief chapter, I shall endeavour to sketch out the basis for a re-evaluation of existing debates, and demonstrate how newly available empirical data can provide insights into the value (or otherwise) of various substantive theoretical positions.

'RACE', ETHNICITY AND HOUSING INEQUALITIES: THE KEY DEBATES

If we are to analyse inequalities in housing, we need to be clear about (a) the bases of these inequalities, and (b) the groups of people or households who are to form the focal point for comparison. As to the first of these, there are a number of dimensions; principally, tenure, dwelling type, location, structural condition, amenities and overcrowding levels. Although apparently unproblematic, variations in definition and modes of data collection almost inevitably create problems for a comparative analysis, as is demonstrated below. It is, however, the identification of comparator groups which raises the key sociological questions.

Although there is much confusion in the literature as to the appropriateness of various 'race'/ethnic group categorisations (not to mention underlying theoretical debates concerning the ontological status of 'race' – Bulmer 1986a; Mason 1995) there is little disagreement about the *existence* of major inequalities in the housing market. Thus, the 'Black-Caribbean' population is characterised as traditionally exhibiting a much lower level of owner-occupation than the general population (and other minority groups, with the notable exception of the 'Bangladeshis'), and a correspondingly higher dependence on the social housing sector. For a variety of reasons, the least favoured property types and locations have tended to be a consistent feature of these lettings (Henderson and Karn 1987; Phillips

1986; Simpson 1981). Despite this, Black-Caribbeans have scored quite highly on basic amenities largely on the grounds that, irrespective of structural condition, public sector housing will almost inevitably have such things as a fixed bath, running hot water and an inside WC.

The 'South Asian' groups, once again with the exception of the Bangladeshis, have been characterised as having far higher rates of owner-occupation than the general population, and a correspondingly low (if gradually increasing) presence in the social housing sector. Rather than painting a positive picture of achievement, most commentators point to the fact that many of these dwellings are amongst the very worst of the housing stock, and are often either in a serious state of disrepair, or are actually unfit for human habitation (Karn *et al.* 1985). The clear exceptions are twofold. On the one hand, there is the growing (predominantly 'Indian') middle class who tend to own rather better quality property (though still usually in close proximity to the inner urban areas). On the other are the Bangladeshis who, as a relatively recently arrived migrant group, and a predominantly poor one at that, have tended to become concentrated in poor quality local authority property, such as in Tower Hamlets in East London (Phillips 1986). Although segregation levels have in general been much higher for all South Asian groups, as compared (say) with the Black-Caribbeans, the Bangladeshi levels have been exceptionally high (Peach 1996); high both with respect to the majority White population and to other minority groups (except at times the other predominantly Muslim group, i.e. the Pakistanis).

Explanations of these differentials, in the UK at least, have invariably talked in one form or another about either the *constraints* faced by migrant groups, or the *choices* they have made in providing a roof over their heads (Rex and Moore 1967; Dayha 1974; Ballard and Ballard 1977; Karn 1977/8; Ratcliffe 1986; Smith 1991). The more convincing contributions to the debate have attempted to balance the two sides of the equation, accepting the force of the argument that migrants of all groups had both individual and collective aims (and political strategies), whilst clearly living and working in a society which was (and is) endemically racist. Dissatisfaction with the apparent sterility of much of the choice-constraints-based literature has, however, led some to look for more sophisticated forms of analysis. Sarre *et al.* (1989) suggest that a development of Giddens's structuration theory might provide a way forward. This ostensibly permits a dynamic, dialectical analysis, highlighting the interplay between material conditions, institutional forms and structural forces (though it could be argued that ultimately it simply produces a more elaborate version of previous, well-rehearsed arguments).

The key sociological questions appear to be largely evaded, however. In claiming, for example, that 'ethnicity explains' housing market location via the notion of choice, we need to ask what is meant by 'ethnicity' and in what sense this 'explains' observed patterns. It seems at best implausible that 'ethnicity' as a conflation of cultural and religious traditions, and/or a sense of 'group identity and belonging' (say), would influence attitudes towards housing tenure. However, first-hand experience of the workings of a housing market in a migrant's country of origin, may. But, then, the underlying social relations of production and exchange arguably have little directly to do with 'ethnicity'. And to isolate and prioritise 'ethnicity' as an explanatory factor seems to beg the question as to the relative significance of factors such as class, gender, age/position in life-cycle, household size/ structure, and so on. As to 'explanation', we are able to provide little more in practice than a collective characterisation which then serves as a representation of the summation of individual actions.

On the constraints side of the equation, we have a negation of 'ethnicity' as a mode of explanation, and its replacement by individual or collective acts of discrimination, 'institutionalised racism', and/or the 'racialisation' of the housing market. These accounts portray the migrant essentially as victim of external forces, and deny, or at least downplay, the efficacy of agency on the part of the individual/household. In its 'purest' form, therefore, this constitutes a highly deterministic mode of explanation, and lacks the capacity to account for the widespread variations in housing position of households with differing (*and even the same*) ethnic heritage(s). To suggest, as some commentators have, that 'different racisms' are at work, does not seem to present a fruitful line of enquiry (though it is undoubtedly the case, for example, that *discrimination* can take different forms and have uneven effects). In practice, the constraints are seen to be of greater or lesser significance in the light of an individual's gender, class position, and so on. Also, in practice, even those who adhere to the 'choice' agenda, acknowledge the existence of discriminatory mechanisms, some (e.g. Ballard and Ballard 1977) even admitting that these factors are logically prior to the individual choices of minority households.

The present chapter seeks to add to the theoretical literature, but not through an extension of existing, ultimately arid, conceptual debates. Employing (necessarily brief) summaries of detailed analyses of 1991 Census data (to be published in full elsewhere – Ratcliffe forthcoming), it aims to demonstrate that large-scale secondary data on factors such as tenure, dwelling type, amenities and levels of overcrowding can be used to interrogate existing theoretical debates. Having said this, there are natu- rally many features of the housing scene which are *not* covered by the Census, and there are certain problems with the Census data itself.

SECONDARY DATA ANALYSIS AND HOUSING DIFFERENTIALS

Perhaps the key issue is the interpretation of 'ethnic group' deployed by the Census; the fixed categories (excluding the 'Other' boxes) being 'White', 'Black-Caribbean', 'Black-African', 'Indian', 'Pakistani', 'Bangladeshi', and 'Chinese'. This 'identity conflation' confuses phenotype, geography, and perhaps nationality; but in terms of the underlying aims of the Office of Population Censuses and Surveys (OPCS)[1], and the Departments of State sponsoring the Census, it 'works' in that it enables the data to be reduced ultimately to four categories, namely 'White', 'Black', '(South) Asian' and 'Chinese and others'. A whole series of ethical and political questions are raised by the question itself (and indeed about the uses to which the data may be put), and by the way the question was answered (in particular whether it can ultimately be regarded as measuring self-identity – as it is claimed), but these are beyond the scope of the present chapter. For present purposes the question is whether the data can safely be used for our analysis of housing differentials. The answer is 'yes, but with extreme care'.

The first point to make is that whatever the categories *do* measure, it is *not* 'ethnicity', at least in any meaningful sociological sense. 'White' includes, for example, 'Greek Cypriots', 'Turkish Cypriots' and the 'Irish'. 'Indians' of East African origin may find themselves in either the 'Indian' or the 'Other-Asian' category, depending on how they describe their 'ethnic group' – a point which is critical for an analysis of the housing situation given the radically different experiences of Indian migrants and the 'twice migrants' (Bhachu 1985). In addition, all the 'Asian' categories conflate the various religious communities. (These problems are compounded by the need for data imputation in the light of a significant degree of underenumeration/undercount, particularly serious amongst urban minorities.)

On the positive side, the introduction of the 'ethnic' question in 1991 coincided with the production, again for the first time, of what Americans call 'public use' samples. Fears of a potential loss of anonymity and confidentiality resulted in the repeated rejection of the idea prior to 1991. The resulting samples, known as SARs (Samples of Anonymised Records) take two forms: a 2 per cent sample of individual records and a 1 per cent sample of households (which may be used either as a sample of households or as a sample of individuals who lived in these selected households). Their availability means that for the first time, social scientists can follow their own agenda in data analysis terms, rather than being limited to that dictated by the OPCS or, alternatively, going through the expensive (and often time consuming) procedure of commissioning special tabulations.

As pointed out earlier, however, the Census still lacks data on some of the key housing indicators, most notably in the area of housing quality. This is understandable given the potential measurement problems, but it nevertheless weakens any analysis based solely on census data. Despite the addition in the 1991 exercise of central heating, current amenity measures lack discriminatory power. The potential addition of a new revised deprivation index in relation to small area data will give a useful surrogate measure of environmental context, but will clearly fail to distinguish between (say) two ostensibly similar houses in the same area which are very different in terms of structural condition and state of repair. And even if this index were to be added to the SAR data files, there would be an analytical problem due to the large spatial units which have been introduced to ensure anonymity and confidentiality.

The English House Condition Survey (EHCS) has routinely collected data on repair costs and on such matters as resources – that is, household income (again a factor excluded from the Census) – but little attention is given in the published reports to the question of ethnicity. We do know from the 1986 EHCS, however, that 9 per cent of households with heads born in the New Commonwealth and Pakistan (NCWP) were living in dwellings designated as 'unfit', and a further 22 per cent were in property deemed to be 'in poor repair'. The corresponding figures for those of UK origin were 4 and 13 per cent respectively. Although slightly ambiguous and confused by changes in key definitions, data from the 1991 EHCS suggests, as will be shown later, that the position has not improved markedly.

As research has consistently demonstrated a link between poor housing and ill health (Audit Commission 1991; Commission for Racial Equality 1994; S. Smith 1989), housing quality is of prime importance. We cannot assess from the Census the relative likelihood of householders (a) having the resources (and the inclination) to rectify defects, and/or (b) having access to renovation grant aid. Research reported in Ratcliffe (1992) and Commission for Racial Equality (1994) suggests, however, that minorities are probably less likely than 'Whites' to have either sort of funding. Furthermore, and despite strongly worded exhortations from the Commission for Racial Equality (1984) for local authorities to adopt rigorous and active ethnic monitoring, by 1992 a clear majority of authorities (74 per cent) still lacked such procedures in the area of service delivery (Commission for Racial Equality 1994).

Although the Census did (for the first time) attempt to enumerate the 'roofless', it did so very patchily; and in any case failed to cast light on the more general question of homelessness. As to whether minority groups are more prone to homelessness than others, we have to rely on a handful of local studies. A recent survey of London Boroughs showed, for example, that 'black households are up to 4 times as likely to become homeless as white households' and that '40 per cent of London's homeless acceptances are either "African", "Caribbean", "Asian" or "Black UK"' (Friedman and Pawson 1989: 54).

Although difficult to quantify, and clearly beyond the scope of the Census, racial harassment is a key element of the housing picture. The available evidence suggests that such harassment is on the increase, both in the UK and on mainland Europe (Skellington 1992). The success in 1993 of a British National Party candidate in a local council election in east London, widely interpreted as having resulted from his playing the 'race card' in relation to the council's housing allocation policy, amply demonstrated the level of 'racial' antipathy. As Phillips (1986) showed, allocations policy is a key element of the harassment matrix. In Tower Hamlets it effectively increased the level of segregation of the Bengali community and at the same time lowered their standard of housing by placing them in hard-to-let blocks of flats. Rather than confronting 'racial' harassment by tackling the perpetrators, the authority took the easy option and moved the *victims*.

THEORISING ETHNIC DIFFERENTIALS IN HOUSING POSITION

In what follows the central aim is to enhance our understanding of the housing position of Britain's minority ethnic groups, and in particular to assess, on the one hand, the relative importance of 'ethnicity' and 'racial exclusion/marginalisation', and on the other, questions of class, gender, life-cycle/-stage, and household type/size/structure. As one might imagine these issues are rather simpler to state than to actualise. In the final analysis it will become clear that the empirical data can only take us so far: further research will be needed to test out a number of possibly conflicting explanatory schema.

For reasons of space, the analysis focuses largely on the core issues of tenure, dwelling type and location. Starting with housing tenure, the first point to make is that there were major differentials between the various 'ethnic groups' covered by the 1991 Census. Owner-occupation in Britain was highest amongst those of Indian origin (82 per cent), followed by Pakistani households (77 per cent), Whites (67 per cent) and the Chinese (62 per cent). Outright ownership levels were highest amongst the White population, as one would expect given the typical length of residence, but almost one in five Pakistani households, around one in six Indian households and one in seven of the Chinese also belonged to this group. Given the general decline in the public sector during the 1980s and the consequent rise in owner-occupation and the private rental and housing association sectors, it is hardly surprising that the overall level of council/ new town rentals was down to 21 per cent (approaching 10 per cent less than ten years earlier). The 'true' figure may in fact have been even smaller given the suggestion that some respondents whose council properties had been transferred to a private landlord appear to have recorded their original tenure position (Dorling 1993). Despite this dramatic fall, renting from a local authority remained very common amongst all three 'Black' groups – 36 per cent for the Black-Caribbeans, 41 per cent for the Black-Africans and 35 per cent for the 'Black-Other' group. The only South Asian group with a similar figure were the Bangladeshis, at 37 per cent.

This raises a number of issues: first, that of explaining the high level of outright ownership amongst Indian and Pakistani migrants. The key lies essentially in the type of property purchased, as intimated earlier. Discriminatory mechanisms in the housing market meant that renting property was often difficult, and pooling of capital to purchase property (whether a conditioned 'choice' or an imperative) was a feasible strategy even in the early days of settlement, given the availability of relatively cheap, but poor quality, housing in inner urban areas (Karn 1977/8; Ratcliffe 1981).

Secondly, there is the question of housing market transformation. Owner-occupation in Britain increased from around 59 per cent to over 66 per cent during the period 1981–91, largely as a result of government policy. Amongst minorities, however, the changes were rather different. The combination of a high base figure in the early 1980s and few council tenancies meant that the picture for Indian and Pakistani households was bound to be somewhat different. As Ratcliffe (1994) shows, data from the 1982 PSI survey (reported in Brown 1984) and the Labour Force Surveys of 1984 to 1990 give a consistent figure for the Indian group of 77 per cent, and a corresponding figure for Pakistani households of 80 per cent (1982) falling to 76 per cent by the end of the decade. Allowing for sampling error, it is possible to conclude that tenure levels probably remained virtually static over the decade. Not so for the Bangladeshis: from around 30 per cent at the beginning of the 1980s, their figure had risen to over 44 per cent by 1991. The Chinese exhibited a similarly dramatic rise from approximately 50 per cent to 62 per cent. Without change matrices it is difficult to assess the precise character of tenure shifts, but in the former case council tenancies have dropped quite sharply (by a similar amount to the gain in ownership levels in fact) suggesting for some a change of tenure *in situ* (via Right-to-Buy). In the case of the Chinese, both the private rental and council sectors contributed to the observed shift.

Tenure patterns for the various Black groups appear to have remained largely static, except for some evidence of an upward shift in owner-occupation amongst those of Caribbean origin (around 40 to 48 per cent). Of the East African Asians little can be said, on the basis of the Census at least, as they are submerged within the 'Indian' and 'Other-Asian' categories. The best estimate, from Ratcliffe (1994) and Jones (1993) would put the 1991 figure at around 80 per cent, this representing around the same level of upward shift as in the general population.

In sum, with a few notable exceptions, we appear to be witnessing a significant narrowing of ethnic differentials in tenure patterns. It was always a theoretically dubious argument to suggest that ethnicity (however conceptualised) could 'explain' the different tenure patterns of the various minority groups. Peach and Byron (1993), for example, using data from the General Household Survey (GHS), argued that class explained about 39 per cent of the tenure pattern of the Caribbean population and adding gender to the analysis increased the explanatory effect to 50 per cent, family structure also emerging as a powerful explanatory factor.

Performing a parallel exercise using Census data is fraught with difficulties, from conceptual problems with the notion of 'head of household' to high levels of 'missing data' on variables such as 'socio-economic group' and 'social class' (in the event of an individual having had no paid employment during the previous ten years). Constraints on space also limit the level of analysis. However, looking separately at tenure patterns, controlling for 'household type' and sex of 'household head' reveals some pointers to the underlying determinants of tenure position.

Amongst male-headed households in the SAR, the Black-Caribbean ownership rate was 58 per cent compared with 73 per cent for White households. Making the same comparison for female-headed households, the figures were 37 and 52 per cent respectively. For male-headed households who were local authority tenants, the Black-Caribbean rate was 28 per cent compared with a White figure of 16 per cent. The figures for female-headed households were 46 and 32 per cent respectively. Even amongst those South Asian groups with extremely high ownership rates overall, the public sector features significantly when the household is female-headed. Thus a quarter of Indian and three out of ten Pakistani households in this group rented local authority property.

It does appear, then, that the gender issue is of some importance here. The nature of a female-headed household (taking as read the general definitional problem) varies of course in terms of such factors as age and marital status, and the distributions of these variables will differ markedly between the 'indigenous' White population and the various minority groups. This raises more general questions about the salience of household structure.

Ratcliffe (forthcoming) shows that ownership rates for Black-Caribbean and White married couple households were uniformly high at over 70 per cent. This appears to negate the simplistic ethnic stereotype (supported at least implicitly by some of the academic literature) which suggests that Caribbean households are pre-disposed to rent rather than to buy property. (It also lends further support to the findings of recent research by Peach and Byron, which showed, amongst other things, that households of Caribbean origin displayed at the very least an equal propensity to Whites to participate in Right-to-Buy schemes.) In the case of lone parents with dependent children, tenure distributions were once again similar: 60 per cent of Whites as against 52 per cent of Black-Caribbeans owned their homes and 32 and 39 per cent respectively rented in the public sector.

It is clear that, for those of Caribbean origin at least, household type accounts for much of the variation in tenure structure. Regional differentials in settlement patterns clearly play their part, as do such factors as the timing of migration flows and the wealth and class composition of migration cohorts (both, of course, beyond the scope of the Census). Thus, the relatively recent arrival in the UK of the major part of the Bangladeshi population, combined with low levels of personal capital and their settlement in large numbers in London, probably contributed greatly to their initial dependence on public housing, and to the fact that, despite the marked shift towards owner-occupation during the 1980s, their figure was still well below that of (say) the other South Asian groups. High concentrations in the metropolis also go a long way towards explaining the tenure distribution of those of African origin.

We have suggested that, in addition to household structure and geographical location, a key factor influencing tenure position is social class. In the general population there has traditionally been a fairly strong positive correlation between class and propensity to buy. Among some minority groups (notably those of Indian and Pakistani origin), however, the relationship has been weaker or even negative, with ownership levels being at their highest amongst the semi-skilled and unskilled working class (Brown 1984: 100; Jones 1993: 144). This has been explained in terms of a variety of market constraints, the availability of cheap property in inner areas and the desire to maintain cultural and religious ties by buying into these spatially well-defined locations. With the advent of the SARs we are now in a position to explore some of the (empirically accessible) components of these hypotheses, and also take the argument one stage further. For example, assuming that first-generation migrants *did* have as part of their agenda the desire, for ostensibly 'cultural' reasons, to maintain areal homogeneity, would this also apply to the UK-born? Would they perhaps move more closely to 'local' norms both spatially (i.e. by becoming less segregated, especially from the White population of similar social class background), and in terms of tenure outcomes?

Changes in spatial patterns and segregation levels over the last decade and, in particular, developments in respect of the UK-born of migrant origin, are the subject of current ESRC-funded research by the present author and David Owen from Warwick University's Centre for Research in Ethnic Relations. As to the question of comparative tenure patterns for households with UK-born as against non-UK-born heads, the SARs provide useful data in all cases except for the Bangladeshis and Chinese where the sample sizes are too small to provide stable estimates. Whereas UK-born Whites exhibited an owner-occupation level of 67 per cent, the figure for Black-Caribbeans was 34 per cent, for Indians 61 per cent and for Pakistanis 66 per cent. Parallel figures for the non-UK-born groups were as follows: Whites 62 per cent, Black-Caribbeans 55 per cent, Indians 83 per cent, and Pakistanis 81 per cent.

Households with UK-born heads of Indian and Pakistani origin were much more likely (than Whites) to be found in private rented accommodation; 24 and 17 per cent respectively as against 7 per cent for the Whites. In the public sector, however, the opposite was true. Whites were more than twice as likely to be renting from the local authority as either of these groups. For the UK-born South Asians, then, tenure patterns were markedly different from those of the first generation. For the latter, renting of any kind is quite rare. Black-Caribbeans, irrespective of the birthplace of household head, were much more likely (than the Indians or Pakistanis) to rent in the public sector; 34 per cent for the non-UK group and 41 per cent for the UK-born; and a similar point could be made in the case of the other Black groups identified by the Census.

A completely convincing explanation of these differences is rather difficult without additional data. Some points are clear, however. The larger number of female-headed households among the Caribbeans and the concentration of the other Black groups in London can be linked to the relatively high levels of public sector renting. The younger age structure of the UK-born cohorts, combined with relatively high unemployment levels and a distinctive pattern of household structures, may have led to a greater propensity to rent in the public sector. The lack of a 'tradition' of local authority tenancies amongst the Indian and Pakistani groups, combined with the declining availability of such properties and the lower than average prevalence of female-headed (or lone parent) households, may contribute to the under-representation of the UK-born in this sector of the housing market.

It remains to be seen whether renting privately (possibly from family/kin in some cases) continues to be an important source of housing for the new generation of South Asians: for many it may simply represent a transitional state (on the way to owner-occupation). (It was certainly more common amongst the current UK-born Indian cohort aged under-25 than it was amongst the 25–34-year-olds – taking over from owner-occupation as the most common tenure.) We may be about to witness a levelling out of ownership levels overall (as between Indians, Pakistanis and Whites), with the gradual fall from the 80 per cent plus figures seen amongst the first generation, accompanied possibly by a rise in the average quality of minority owned property (due to delayed purchase).

The relationship between class (seen in occupational status terms) and tenure still appeared to hold as far as the first generation were concerned. The household SARs revealed interesting differences for those with UK-born heads, however. Amongst Caribbean households with UK-born heads in professional or intermediate occupations, the level of ownership was 61 per cent. Rates then fell consistently moving down the occupational scale. Cell frequencies were too small to come to firm conclusions about the various South Asian groups, but ownership levels appeared to fluctuate around the 50 to 65 per cent level. More research is needed here.

Turning to property type, the academic literature has a great deal to say about ethnic differentials and the reasons for them. The Black population in general (using the Census definition of 'Black') is seen as being much more likely to be accommodated in flats than either Whites or South Asians (with the exception of the Bangladeshis). This is argued to be due to their significant presence in local authority stock, and a particular sector of it, due to discriminatory allocation policies based on class, 'race' and gender (Henderson and Karn 1987; Phillips 1986), or in the case of Africans (and also Bangladeshis) due to their concentration in London. Households of Indian and Pakistani origin are characterised as heavily concentrated in inner city terraced housing (for reasons discussed earlier). Of the two groups, the former, because of their higher proportion of white-collar workers, are seen as being the more likely to acquire semi-detached or detached housing (Jones 1993).

The 1991 Census data essentially confirms the empirical propositions underlying these remarks (Ratcliffe 1996). Thus, whereas around half of GB households lived in semi-detached or detached property, only 17 per cent of Black-Caribbeans, 11 per cent of Black-Africans and 13 per cent of Bangladeshis did so. The minority with the highest figure was that of Indian origin (with just under 40 per cent). Terraced housing was indeed by far the most common form of dwelling for Indian and Pakistani households, with over three out of five of the latter and more than 40 per cent of the former accommodated in this way. The Black groups in general were not only much more likely to be living in flatted accommodation but were also much more likely to be found in converted dwellings, and in those which were not self-contained. Taken together, the last two categories of dwelling accounted for almost one in five African households and around one in eight of the Black-Caribbeans (and incidentally one in ten of the Chinese, who were also heavily dependent on flatted accommodation, much of it linked to their principal economic niche, i.e. flats over shops, restaurants and take-away outlets).

The determinants of these distributions are complex, ranging from historical factors concerned with the housing markets in initial settlement areas to the behaviour over time of exchange professionals in both public and private sectors, and the social class background and structure of individual households. One thing is clear from even a cursory reading of the literature: within tenures one would expect minorities to be living in very different property types. The relevant SAR table confirmed this, and, incidentally, provided further support to the arguments in the literature questioning the fairness of many local authority allocation systems (Simpson 1981; Phillips 1986; Henderson and Karn 1987; Habeebullah and Slater 1990).

ETHNIC DIFFERENTIALS IN HOUSING QUALITY

Whatever the evidence on the narrowing of tenure differentials amongst certain class groups and household types, this is not to argue either that housing market discrimination is a thing of the past (for there is ample evidence from CRE investigations and elsewhere that it is not) or that the property acquired by minorities is of a similar standard (within tenure categories) to that of Whites.

The 1986 EHCS, as noted earlier, presented clear evidence of global differentials between minorities as a whole and the White population. In the 1991 EHCS rather more detail on ethnicity was given, with minorities being divided into three groups: 'Black', 'Asian' and 'Other'. A simple measure of dwelling condition was used: this divided the total stock into 'worst', 'best' and 'rest', where the 'worst dwellings are the 10 per cent with the highest repair cost, the cut-off being £26 per square metre' and 'the best dwellings are the 30 per cent of homes with no or minimal repair costs, the threshold being £1.45/sqm' (Department of the Environment 1993: 74). For owner-occupiers (where sample sizes were sufficiently large), ethnic differentials mirrored those observed five years earlier. The percentages of both 'Black' and 'Asian' samples in the worst housing (which comprised 7 per cent of the total stock) were more than double that for Whites.

Overcrowding levels are clearly a key element of housing standards (Ratcliffe 1981, 1994; Jones 1993). If anything the problem worsened during the 1980s, such that by the 1991 Census the (admittedly rather crude) indicator of over one person per room produced a Black-Caribbean figure of 5 per cent, and Pakistani and Bangladeshi figures of 30 and 47 per cent respectively. Almost one in five of the latter group were found to be living at a density of over 1.5 persons per room. The EHCS told a similar story.

Turning to amenities, the Census confirmed the earlier remark that few households, of whatever ethnic origin, lacked exclusive access to a bath/shower and/or inside WC. Those lacking central heating varied widely, however, with well over a third of Pakistani households but around one in five of most other groups in this category. Taken together, these provide certain circumstantial evidence of 'relative disadvantage', but even then the key issues are whether (a) people can *afford to use* the central heating, and (b) the 'amenities' are of an acceptable standard.

A detailed analysis of the household SAR shows that, as far as overcrowding is concerned, class background and whether or not the household head was UK-born, are key predictors. (Overcrowding levels were markedly lower for households headed by the much younger UK-born cohort.) As far as central heating was concerned the 'social class gradient' reappeared, with the UK-born faring slightly *worse* on average.

Although of much interest, it should be added that none of this data gives an unambiguous picture of differentials in housing quality, or quality of life. Overcrowding levels ignore such vital points as room size and layout. The form of heating in a particular dwelling may be a matter of choice, and central heating may correlate with flat living. But along with the other material discussed earlier, especially that from the EHCS, the data adds weight to the general picture of ethnic inequalities.

SUMMARY AND CONCLUSIONS

To summarise the key points: first, although there remain major disparities in the tenure patterns of Britain's majority and minority communities, these do not unambiguously reflect inherent ethnic differences in the propensity to enter a particular tenure category. Factors such as household type/structure, class background and life-cycle/generational status account for many of the observed differences.

Secondly, there remain major housing quality differentials, both between majority and minority and between the various minority groups. To the extent that these are not 'explained' by class/economic factors, they provide continuing evidence of a process of 'racial'/ethnic exclusion/marginalisation. 'Red-lining', residence requirements, housekeeping standards, and the blatant refusal to sell or rent property to 'Blacks' may belong to an earlier era, but, as recent CRE investigations amply demonstrate, discriminatory practices have by no means disappeared.

In terms of the future *policy agenda*, the latter issues, combined with homelessness and harassment, are the key issues. There is, however, little evidence of political will; the will, first, to deal with the housing crisis as a whole, as evidenced by the general shortage of properties, the shrinkage of the social housing sector (despite the raised profile of Housing Associations) and the failure of urban renewal/regeneration policies and, second, the will to address housing inequalities based on 'race', ethnicity and gender (not to mention disability and sexual orientation).

As to the *sociological agenda*, there is an urgent need to theorise the sociological dimensions of economic, social and demographic change. To initiate this project, the current chapter has explored what the SARs can tell us about changes in the housing position of Britain's minority populations, and in particular the 'new' generations of UK-born. Despite the obvious problems created both by small sample sizes and by significant differences in age structure between these groups and the first-generation migrants, a few tentative conclusions can be reached.

We may be witnessing a shift towards the equalisation of tenure patterns between young White households and minority households with UK-born heads; at least if we control for social class and household structure. Levels of overcrowding appear to be significantly lower amongst the second generation. Furthermore, the use of more diverse sources of housing (than first-generation migrants) may lead on average to higher standards of housing than those in evidence hitherto.

Against this positive scenario, however, it is worth stressing in conclusion the limited (and reducing) options in the housing market for such groups as single males and the young unemployed (of whom a disproportionate number are of minority origin). Furthermore, the lack of political will to intervene decisively in the housing market is mirrored by a similar lack in the area of anti-discrimination legislation. The current Race Relations Act has remained on the Statute Book for twenty years, and is generally regarded as woefully inadequate. At the same time, its policing body (the CRE) lacks the funds and the political status to influence the behaviour of the key actors in the housing scene.

NOTE

1   The Office of Population Censuses and Surveys organised the 1991 Census. Subsequently, in April 1996, it was merged with the Central Statistical Office to form the Office for National Statistics.

7

VIOLENCE, SPACE AND GENDER

The social and spatial parameters of violence against women and men

Jayne Mooney

BACKGROUND

The North London Domestic Violence Survey – a general population survey – involved interviews with 1,000 people (571 women and 429 men) in the north London borough of Islington.[1] The first report (Mooney 1993) examined women's experiences of violence from husbands and boyfriends. This chapter widens the study out to explore the social and spatial parameters of violence against both women *and men* from known and unknown persons. It delineates the overall level of violence, the social characteristics of victims and perpetrators and its location, in terms of public and private space. This enables the testing of various hypotheses derived from the theoretical literature about the nature of violence in contemporary society.

Respondents were asked by an interviewer whether anyone, including close friends or members of their family, had threatened them or used any form of physical violence against them in their home or in a public place in the last twelve months. A sample of all violent incidents was then obtained by asking about the last incident that had occurred; this facilitated the collecting of more detailed information regarding the specific nature of the violence, its impact and the relationship of the victim to the perpetrator. Since more women than men were interviewed the data were weighted.

THE FOCUSING OF VIOLENCE AS PRESENTED IN THE LITERATURE

In the literature various positions can be identified on the focusing of violence. The main points made by the new administrative criminologists, left realists, the family violence theorists and radical feminists are outlined below.

New administrative criminologists

New administrative criminology – which developed around the work of researchers associated with the Home Office's Research and Planning Unit

– has tended to downplay the problem of crime. The findings of the various sweeps of the national British Crime Survey conducted by the Home Office have shown the risk of violent victimisation to be low and less common than non-violent property offences which are themselves presented as infrequent occurrences (Hough and Mayhew 1983, 1985; Mayhew *et al.* 1989, 1993). The 'average' person, it was suggested in the report of the 1982 survey, can expect 'a robbery once every five centuries, an assault resulting in injury (even if slight) once every century, the family car to be stolen or taken by joyriders once every 60 years, a burglary in the home once every 40 years ... and a very low rate for rape and other sexual offences' (Hough and Mayhew 1983: 15, 21). And one of the conclusions of the 1984 survey was that:

> Offences involving violence are very heavily outweighed by offences involving theft and damage to property. Some undercounting of non-stranger violence in the survey is likely, but present figures show wounding, robbery, sexual offences and common assaults to comprise only 17 per cent of all BCS offences (Excluding common assaults, the figure was 5 per cent).
>
> (Hough and Mayhew 1985: 16)

With respect to the focusing of violence the 'typical' victim is presented in the British Crime Surveys not as someone who is 'defenceless' or elderly but as a man, aged under 30 years, single, widowed or divorced, who spends several evenings out a week, drinks heavily and has assaulted others. Victims and offenders are, therefore, most likely to resemble each other and in a significant number of cases will be known to each other (Hough and Mayhew 1983; Gottfredson 1984). For example, in the 1988 survey, victims knew their assailants in about half of the cases (Mayhew *et al.* 1989). Whilst it is acknowledged that the surveys undercount domestic violence and sexual offences, the risk of violence for women is generally presented by the new administrative criminologists as slight. Moreover, in line with the apparent maleness of the phenomenon and lifestyle characteristics of the victims, violence is seen as a feature of public space, occurring mostly in pubs, clubs and other places of entertainment. According to Gottfredson, 'those who stay in and around the home have lower likelihoods (of personal victimisation) than those working outside the home' (1984: 18).

Left realists

On the overall focus of the level of violence, left realists have been critical of the incidence figures produced by the national crime surveys. They consider crime to be extremely geographically and socially focused in certain areas and amongst particular groups of people. Poor areas of the city are seen to be more likely to be victimised than rich areas (Kinsey *et al.* 1986). Thus, it is argued that to add crime rates for a suburban area to that of an inner city area – as the British Crime Surveys have done – produces 'blancmange figures of little use to anyone' (Young 1992: 50). Surveys of local areas conducted by left realists have, therefore, yielded much higher incidence figures of interpersonal violence for women and the elderly, as well as for men. Indeed the first Islington Crime Survey uncovered higher assault rates for women than men: in the year of study there were 213 incidents for women, 152 for men per 1,000 households (Jones *et al.* 1986).

The spectrum of violence experienced by women, particularly young women, is seen by left realists to be much wider than that for men, ranging from harassment to more serious assault. Violence against men is more likely to be experienced at the more serious end of the spectrum. Indeed, women encounter harassment on a level that is unknown to most men, as Young has pointed out:

> The equivalent of sexual harassment for men would be if every time they walked out of doors they were met with catcalls asking if they would like a fight. And the spectrum which women experience is all the more troublesome in that each of the minor incivilities could escalate to more serious violence. Sexual harassment could be a prelude to attempted rape; domestic verbal quarrels could trigger off domestic violence ...
>
> (Young 1992: 50)

On the invisibility of violence, it has been stressed by left realists that much violence against women is, in fact, concealed. It does not appear in agency statistics and is less likely to be picked up using the conventional survey method. This is believed to be particularly true for domestic violence and sexual offences (Young 1988, 1992; Crawford *et al.* 1990).

Finally, from a left realist perspective, people are seen as having a differential vulnerability to crime and, therefore, to talk of a general risk, the experiences of the 'average' person, assumes that everyone is equal in their capacity to resist the impact of such experiences. For left realists there is no such thing as an equal victim. People are more or less vulnerable, depending on their place in society; those who are poor with little political power will suffer the most from crime (Lea and Young 1984; Kinsey *et al.* 1986; Young 1992). The relatively powerless situation of women – economically, socially and physically – is seen to make them more unequal victims than men (Young 1988).

The family violence approach

The work of Straus and others in the United States is solely concerned with emphasising the problem of violence in the family. In the introduction to *Family Violence*, Richard Gelles writes:

> Twenty years ago, when people were concerned about violence they feared violence in the streets at the hands of a stranger. Today we are aware of the extent, impact and consequences of private violence.
>
> (Gelles 1987: 13)

Violence between husbands and wives is seen as part of a pattern of violence occurring amongst all familial members. The family violence approach is an attempt to look at the whole picture of family violence. As

Gelles and Cornell have remarked, 'while it is important to understand the nature and causes of ... wife abuse, concentrating on just one form of violence or abuse may obscure the entire picture and hinder a complete understanding of the causes and consequences of abuse' (1985: 11).

The family violence researchers have conducted two national surveys in the United States, in 1975 and 1985 respectively, which have not only uncovered high levels of domestic violence but, in terms of focusing, have resulted in the highly controversial finding that men are as much at risk of violence from their wives, as women are from their husbands (Straus 1980; Straus and Gelles 1988). This is seen to contrast to women's behaviour outside of the family where it is said they are much less likely to use violence (Straus and Gelles 1988). Thus, on the basis of the 1975 survey, Steinmetz (1977–8) concluded that there was a 'battered husband syndrome' which had not previously been acknowledged, and Straus commented:

> violence between husband and wife is far from a one way street. The old cartoons of the wife chasing the husband with a rolling pin or throwing pots and pans are closer to reality than most (and especially those with feminist sympathies) realize.
>
> (Straus 1977–8: 488)

This has had serious policy implications in the United States. It has been used against battered women in court cases, cited by men's rights groups lobbying for custody and child support, and to argue against funding for refuges (Pagelow 1984; Dobash and Dobash 1992; Brush 1993).

Radical feminists

Radical feminist research has centred on violence against women. The studies conducted by radical feminists in this country, like those of left realists, have highlighted the myriad forms of violence experienced by women and been used to challenge the figures produced by the British Crime Surveys conducted by the Home Office. In the *Violence Against Women – Women Speak Out Survey* carried out in the London Borough of Wandsworth by feminist researchers, 44 per cent of women, for example, reported being the target of a violent attack within the past year. This, together with other findings uncovered by the research, was said by its co-ordinator, Radford, to, 'cast real doubt on the figures cited in the British Crime Survey which reported a very low rate of offences against women' (1987: 35).

On the focusing of violence, feminists have emphasised the gender dimensions of violence against women; that is, it is made clear that violence is largely perpetrated *by men on women*. Whilst there has recently been an acknowledgement of women's violence against other women, particularly in the context of lesbian relationships (Lobel 1986; Kelly 1991; Mann 1993), female on male violence is presented as rare and when it does occur is seen as mainly in self-defence (Dobash and Dobash 1979; Breines and Gordon 1983; Kurz 1993). The impact of violence against women in terms of psychological trauma, avoidance behaviours, injuries experienced and the difficulties inherent in their structural positions is, in addition, stressed by feminists.

With respect to the relationship to the perpetrator and locality of the violence, women are generally seen to be more likely to be assaulted by men who are known to them in their homes than by strangers in a public space:

> By far, most violence and threat arises from those who are familial and familiar. Rather than the street constituting the greatest threat to personal security, violence often happens in places such as the home or worksite.
>
> (Stanko 1992: 3)

This position has led radical feminists to be critical of official crime prevention literature which tends to be fixated on the problem of 'stranger-danger' (ibid.). Violence from known men, however, is seen as less likely to be reported to an interviewer due to its intrinsically personal nature (Hanmer and Saunders 1984; Radford and Laffy 1984). Indeed when Hanmer and Saunders (1984) found that 78 per cent of violence against women was by *unknown* men and more than half of violent incidents occurred in public space, they questioned the validity of their own results. They noted that when women were asked about violence they had witnessed in the neighbourhood, 69 per cent was between people known to each other with a higher proportion occurring in the home. And when the pilot for the Wandsworth survey, mentioned above, failed to uncover any violence on women by their husbands, brothers and boyfriends, Radford and Laffy commented, 'our conclusion is not that this has not occurred, as that contradicts what we know of domestic violence from Women's Aid but rather ours was not the right type of survey to explore such very personal and possibly continuing experiences' (1984: 113). On the location of the violence in terms of public and private space, Hanmer and Saunders further make the point that incidents in public space may not necessarily be from strangers:

> Arguments and assaults between acquaintances, friends or married couples may begin and/or end outside the home or in any public location . . . specific violent events are not sealed off into private versus public domains.
>
> (Hanmer and Saunders 1984: 45)

FINDINGS

The various theoretical positions on the focus of violence suggest a series of propositions, which are addressed by research data from the North London Domestic Violence Survey. The figures in the tables refer to threats of, or actual, physical violence.

OVERALL LEVEL OF VIOLENCE

1   *The risk of violent victimisation is low in comparison to property crimes (new administrative criminology).*

The results already presented in *The Hidden Figure: Domestic Violence in North London* show violence against women from their husbands and boyfriends to be a relatively common occurrence. This chapter reveals this to be true *for violence overall.* As Table 7.1 demonstrates, nearly 20 per cent of the total sample – comprising both men and women – had experienced a threat or some form of physical violence against them in the last 12 months, with equal proportions having occurred in the home or in a public place. Three women and three men, in addition, had incidents against them in both the private *and* public spheres. This study has, therefore, refuted the finding of the British Crime Surveys conducted by the Home Office which show the risk of violent victimisation to be low in comparison to property offences. It is likely that the use of highly trained, sensitive interviewers together with the general emphasis placed on violence in the survey has encouraged the reporting not only of domestic but of non-domestic violence.

Table 7.1 Overall level of violence by location, per cent of total sample
(N = 1,142, weighted data), survey conducted in 1992

Location	Number	%
Home	111	9.7
Public place	109	9.5
Both places*	214	18.7

*'Both places' does not equal the sum of Home and Public because some people were victimised in both spheres

GENDER AND AGE RELATION OF OVERALL VIOLENCE

2   *Men are the predominant victims of violence (new administrative criminology).*
3   *Men are the predominant perpetrators of violence (new administrative criminology, left realism, radical feminism).*

Tables 7.2 and 7.3 show the women and men in this survey to have fairly

Table 7.2 Overall focus of violence by gender, per cent of total sample
(N = 1,142, weighted data), survey conducted in 1992

Victim	Home		Public		Both places	
	No.	%	No.	%	No.	%
Women	67	11.7	39	6.8	103	18.0
Men	44	7.7	70	12.3	111	19.4
All people	111	9.7	109	9.5	214	18.7

Table 7.3 Overall focus of violence by gender and locality, per cent of those experiencing (N = 214), survey conducted in 1992

Victim	Home		Public		Both places*	
	No.	%	No.	%	No.	%
Women	67	60.4	39	35.8	103	48.1
Men	44	39.6	70	64.2	111	51.9
All people	111	100	109	100	214	100

*'Both places' does not equal the sum of Home and Public because some people were victimised in both spheres

equal risks of violence against them. The supposition of the new administrative criminologists that it is men who are the predominant victims of violence is obviously based on an underestimation of violence in the home.

Respondents were asked further details about the last incident of violence that they had experienced. With respect to the perpetrator of the violence, the general assumption of radical feminist work, where it is made particularly explicit, and that of new administrative criminology and left realism, is that the perpetrator is most likely to be a man. The findings for the last incident, presented in Table 7.4, confirm this proposition: in 85 per cent of cases the assailant was found to be a man.

Table 7.4 Perpetrators of violence by gender and locality, per cent of those experiencing (N = 206)

Perpetrator	Home (%)	Public (%)	Both places (%)
Male	85.2	84.7	85.0
Female	14.8	15.3	15.0

4   *Young men are the predominant victims of violence (new administrative criminology).*
5   *Young women are more at risk of violence than older women (left realism).*

The findings detailed in Tables 7.2 and 7.3 have refuted the new administrative criminologist's position with respect to the usual gender of the victim. However, as Table 7.5 demonstrates, when men are looked at as a category *by themselves*, it is younger men – those aged 16 to 24 years – who are most likely to be victimised both in the home and in a public place. Further, it is of interest to note that, within this age group, 90 per cent of those who had experienced violence in a public place from an unknown man estimated his age to be under 25 years. New administrative criminology is, therefore, correct when the focus is specifically on young men's

Table 7.5 Violence against men by age and locality, per cent of total sample
(N = 571)

Age	Home (%)	Public (%)
16–24	19	27
25–34	6	11
35–44	5	13
45+	4	9

experiences: violence on young men is largely perpetrated by other young men.

Table 7.6 displays the age profile for women. In the home the risk for women decreases significantly after the age of 45 years which must, at least in part, relate to the increased number in this age group who live alone through being divorced, separated or widowed and whose children have left home. In public space women of all ages had similar levels of victimisation against them.

Table 7.6 Violence against women by age and locality, per cent of total sample
(N = 571)

Age	Home (%)	Public (%)
16–24	13	7
25–34	15	8
35–44	17	7
45+	7	9

LOCALITY OF VIOLENCE

6   *Most violence occurs in public space (new administrative criminology).*
7   *Most violence occurs in pubs, clubs and other places of entertainment (new administrative criminology).*

As was seen in Table 7.1, this survey found violence to be equally distributed between the private and public spheres. Again the position held by the new administrative criminologists is based on an underestimation of violence against women, a large proportion of which is domestic. When focusing specifically on violence in public places (Table 7.7), the most common location for both women and men was found to be the street. Thus neither of the above propositions is supported.

Table 7.7 Location of violence in public space by gender, per cent of those experiencing (N = 109)

Location	Women (%)	Men (%)	All people (%)
Street	44	47	46
Pub/restaurant	13	11	12
Shop	8	10	9
Housing estate	21	16	17
Work	3	0	1
Other	11	16	15
Total	100	100	100

THE GENDERED DISTRIBUTION OF THE LOCALITY OF VIOLENCE

8 *Most violence against men occurs in public space (new administrative criminology).*
9 *Most violence against women occurs in the private sphere (new administrative criminology, left realism, radical feminism).*
10 *Men are the predominant perpetrators of violence in public space (all perspectives).*
11 *Men are the predominant perpetrators of violence in the private sphere (new administrative criminology, left realism, radical feminism).*

This study confirms that most violence against women is private, most violence against men is public. However, as is apparent from Tables 7.2 and 7.3, in neither instance is the focus overwhelming. Table 7.3 shows 36 per cent of violence against women was in a public place, while 40 per cent of violence against men occurred in the home. Furthermore, it is interesting to note that the ratio of violence against women in the home compared to the public sphere is nearly equal to the ratio of violence against men in the public sphere compared to the home. Propositions 10 and 11 are additionally confirmed; as demonstrated in Table 7.4, men are the predominant perpetrators of violence in the domestic sphere and to an identical level (85 per cent) in public.

INTER- AND INTRA-GENDER DISTRIBUTION OF VIOLENCE

12 *Most male violence is against men (new administrative criminology).*
13 *Most female violence is against men (family violence researchers).*

Table 7.8 shows that male violence is directed more against women than men although not by a great extent. Twice as much female violence is, however, against men than women albeit on a much smaller scale. The first proposition is, therefore, refuted; the second is substantiated.

Table 7.8 Inter- and intra-gender distribution of violence (N = 206)

Relationship	Home (%)	Public (%)	Both places (%)
Male to male	26	56	40
Male to female	59	29	45
Female to male	13	7	10
Female to female	2	8	5
Total	100	100	100

INTER- AND INTRA-GENDER DISTRIBUTION OF VIOLENCE BY LOCALITY

14 *Most male violence in public space is against men (new administrative criminology).*
15 *Most male violence against women is in the private sphere (radical feminism).*
16 *Most female violence against men is in the private sphere (family violence researchers).*

It is apparent from the results presented in Table 7.8 that most male violence in the public sphere is against men, although the ratio of 1.9:1 male to female victims is not perhaps as high as might have been thought. The new administrative criminologists position is, therefore, supported. Indeed it is of interest to mention that there is a degree of symmetry here, with male violence in the private sphere being 2.3:1 female to male victims, almost the mirror image of the public sphere. The amount of male violence against males in the private sphere is likewise not insignificant. But, overall, twice as much male violence against women occurs in the private compared to the public sphere. The radical feminist position is thus substantiated. Female violence – *which is much less common* – does not have such a symmetry between the two spheres. An equal proportion of female violence in the public sphere is against men and women. In the private sphere, however, female violence is directed at men (6.5:1), thus the last position is validated.

OVERALL SEVERITY OF VIOLENCE

17 *Most violence is minor (new administrative criminology).*

Respondents encountered a wide range of violent behaviours against them, most commonly being punched and slapped. A weapon was involved in 15 per cent of cases, and 34 per cent resulted in some form of injury. Nearly a third of those experiencing a threat of, or any form of, violence had experienced more than one incident. On the impact of the violence, a significant number sought medical treatment and experienced various emotional and psychological effects after the last incident. In the light of these findings, violence cannot therefore be considered to be minor.

SEVERITY OF VIOLENCE BY GENDER

18 *Violence against men is likely to be more severe (new administrative criminology, left realism).*
19 *Violence has a greater impact on women (left realism, radical feminism).*

Overall women and men were found to experience a similar range of violence against them and similar injuries. However, in the home women were 56 per cent more likely to experience more than one incident than men. With regards to impact, whilst men's experiences were not insignificant, violence was found generally to have a greater effect on women. For example, 4 per cent of women had stayed overnight in hospital – which underscores the seriousness of the injuries inflicted – in comparison to no men, and 49 per cent reported feeling depressed or losing self-confidence in comparison to 25 per cent of men. The degree of impact experienced by women is, of course, hardly surprising given the inter-gendered nature of violence against women. Thus, the results fail to support the first proposition but substantiate the second.

SEVERITY OF VIOLENCE BY LOCALITY

20 *Violence is more severe in public space (new administrative criminology).*
21 *Violence is more severe against men in public space (new administrative criminology).*
22 *Violence is more severe against women in the private sphere (radical feminism).*

With respect to the range of violent behaviours used, the survey found little difference between the home and public space. In the home, however, the risk of injury was greater (36 per cent) and respondents were 71 per cent more likely to experience more than one incident. In public space there was a higher risk of the incident *involving* a weapon. The impact of violence was significantly greater in the home. When looking at the psychological effects of violence in particular, this is hardly surprising given that the home is where one is supposed to feel safe and secure ('a haven in a heartless world'). Violence in the home is, in addition, more likely to be carried out by a known person and, as indicated by the incidence data, may be part of an ongoing experience. Finally there was little difference in the nature of the violence experienced by men and women, either overall or in public and private space.

THE RELATIONSHIP BETWEEN VICTIMS AND PERPETRATORS

23 *Most violence is committed by someone who is known to the victim (new administrative criminology, radical feminism).*
24 *Violence against women in public space is more likely to be from an unknown man (conventional wisdom).*
25 *Violence against women in public space is likely to be from a known man (radical feminism).*

The new administrative criminologists and radical feminists have suggested that the surveys they have conducted undercount non-stranger violence due to the methods used. The assumption generally made in their writing is that violence from known people is much greater than that revealed. The findings presented here in Table 7.9 support the notion that violence is usually perpetrated by a known person. This is not to say, however, that violence from a stranger is insignificant, Tables 7.10 and 7.11 show that it accounts for 20 per cent of violence against women and 32 per cent

Table 7.9 Overall violence by relationship and gender, per cent of those experiencing (N = 214)

Perpetrator	Women (%)	Men (%)	All people (%)
Unknown male	15	32	24
Unknown female	5	0	3
Current partner	23	7	15
Ex-partner	10	6	8
Other male family member	7	9	8
Other female family member	2	1	2
Male friend	11	9	10
Female friend	0	1	1
Male acquaintance	22	23	23
Female acquaintance	2	3	3
Not specified	2	7	4
Total	99	98	101

Table 7.10 Violence against women: relationship to the perpetrator by locality, per cent of those experiencing (N = 103)

Perpetrator	Home (%)	Public (%)	Both places (%)
Unknown male	0	38	15
Unknown female	0	12	5
Current partner	34	5	23
Ex-partner	13	7	10
Other male family member	12	0	7
Other female family member	3	0	2
Male friend	18	0	11
Female friend	0	0	0
Male acquaintance	18	29	22
Female acquaintance	0	5	2
Not specified	2	4	2
Total	100	100	99

Table 7.11 Violence against men: relationship to the perpetrator by locality, per cent of those experiencing (N = 111)

Perpetrator	Home (%)	Public (%)	Both places (%)
Unknown male	2	51	32
Unknown female	0	0	0
Current partner	15	1	7
Ex-partner	9	4	6
Other male family member	24	0	9
Other female family member	3	0	1
Male friend	20	1	9
Female friend	0	1	1
Male acquaintance	17	27	23
Female acquaintance	2	4	3
Not specified	7	9	7
Total	99	98	98

of violence against men. The figure uncovered for women is even more notable given the extraordinary avoidance behaviours adopted by women to avoid such victimisation (see, for example, Painter 1988; Painter *et al.* 1990). It is clearly important in highlighting the reality of domestic violence that women's experience of violence from unknown men is not forgotten.

Table 7.10 shows women were found to be at greatest risk in the home from first their current partner (34 per cent), secondly a male friend (18 per cent) or male acquaintance (18 per cent), and thirdly an ex-partner (13 per cent). In public, the assailant was most likely to be an unknown male (38 per cent), a male acquaintance (29 per cent) or an unknown female (12 per cent). For men, the perpetrator in the home was most likely to be another male family member (24 per cent), secondly a male friend (20 per cent), thirdly a male acquaintance (17 per cent), and fourthly a current partner (15 per cent). The 'other male family member' most usually cited by men was a brother. In public, men were most likely to be victimised by an unknown male (51 per cent) and secondly by a male acquaintance (27 per cent).

If we analyse non-stranger and stranger violence in public we find that both women and men have about a 50 per cent chance of the attacker being a stranger. For men this stranger is invariably male and for women there is a three to one chance of the assailant being male. These findings refute the notion that violence against women in public space is more likely to be from an unknown man – he is just as likely to be known as unknown. And, of course, it refutes the opposite assertion often occurring in the radical feminist literature.

VIOLENCE BETWEEN HUSBANDS AND WIVES/BOYFRIENDS AND GIRLFRIENDS

26 *Most violence in the private sphere is between husbands and wives/boyfriends and girlfriends (all perspectives).*

Table 7.12 indicates that most violence in the home was found to be perpetrated by a current partner. However, it is important to point out that violence in the home from non-family members is not insubstantial, particularly by a male friend (19 per cent) or male acquaintance (18 per cent).

Table 7.12 Overall violence in the home by relationship, per cent of those experiencing (N = 111)

Perpetrator	All people (%)
Unknown male	1
Unknown female	0
Current partner	25
Ex-partner	12
Other male family member	17
Other female family member	3
Male friend	19
Female friend	0
Male acquaintance	18
Female acquaintance	1
Not specified	4
Total	100

27 *Men are as likely to experience violence from wives/girlfriends as women are from husbands/boyfriends (family violence researchers).*

28 *Women are more likely to experience violence from their husbands/boyfriends than men from their wives/girlfriends (radical feminism).*

29 *Women use violence against their husbands/boyfriends in self-defence and are more likely to be injured and experience a greater degree of impact (radical feminism).*

The findings detailed in Tables 7.10 and 7.11 suggest the risk to women from their current partners was over three times greater than that for men. Moreover, methods used at this stage of the project probably underestimate domestic violence against women; that is face-to-face interviews as opposed to self-complete questionnaires (see J. Mooney 1993, 1994, 1996). Thus this data clearly contradicts the findings of Straus and others and undermines Steinmetz's notion of the 'battered husband syndrome'. Therefore proposition 27 is dismissed and proposition 28 confirmed.

This survey also shows that women were more likely to endure a wide range of violent behaviours, be injured and have a weapon used against them by their partners or ex-partners than was the case for men. In fact no man was found to have had a weapon used against him by a partner. Women were also more likely to experience multiple incidents and the impact on them was, not surprisingly, worse. Qualitative work shows further that women who experience violence from their partners often use violence in self-defence. Thus, as occurred above, the radical feminist position on this form of violence is found to be valid. Furthermore, as left realists in particular have stressed in their work, there is no such thing as an equal victim; people have a differential vulnerability to crime. Thus violence on women, because of their structural position, is likely to be worse and have a greater effect than that against men.

SUMMARY OF FINDINGS AND CONCLUSION

Summary of findings

This chapter set out to explore the social and spatial parameters of violence. Its main findings are as follows.

- Violence is a relatively common occurrence.
- Women and men have fairly equal risks of violence against them.
- Men are the predominant perpetrators of violence.
- Violence is equally distributed between the public and private spheres.
- Most violence against men occurs in public, most violence against women occurs in private, but in neither instance is the focus overwhelming.
- Men are the predominant perpetrators of violence in both the private and public spheres.
- Most male violence in the public sphere is against men, most male violence in the private sphere is against women, although male violence against women in the public sphere and male violence against men in the private sphere is not insignificant.
- Violence is serious; respondents experienced a wide range of violent behaviours against them, injuries and the impact was correspondingly severe.
- Women and men experienced a similar range of violent behaviours against them, use of weapons and injuries. Violence had a greater impact on women.
- There was little difference between the home and public space with respect to the range of violent behaviours. In the home the risk of injury was slightly greater and the impact was worse.
- Most violence is committed by someone who is known to the victim, although violence from a stranger is not insignificant in public space. Violence from strangers entering the home is negligible.
- Women were most at risk from their current partners, followed by male acquaintances and then unknown men.
- Men were most at risk from unknown men, followed by male acquaintances and then male friends.

- The perpetrator of violence in a public space is equally likely to be a non-stranger as a stranger whether the victim is a woman or man.
- Violence from partners or ex-partners in public space was relatively infrequent.
- Women are at much greater risk of violence from partners or ex-partners. Violence against men from partners or ex-partners was relatively uncommon. Women are more likely to use violence against their partners or ex-partners in self-defence, are more likely to be injured, have a weapon used against them and experience a greater degree of impact.

Conclusion

These findings with regards to the distribution of violence cut across the predictions of the major theories, invalidating many whilst supplying answers where there has previously only been conjecture. In particular they contradict the widespread notion that violence is a relatively infrequent occurrence which focuses on men in public space and is perpetrated by strangers. On the contrary, violence is a common event and not the 'poor cousin' to property offences in the criminological agenda; it focuses equally on men and women and occurs in equal proportions in the public and private spheres and is frequently committed by non-strangers.

Patterns of victimisation have been found to be distinctly gendered. For a man the public sphere is twice as likely to be the arena of risk in comparison to the home; for a woman the pattern is exactly the opposite. For a man, strangers are the greatest risk, followed by acquaintances and then partners: the risk decreases with intimacy. For a woman the reverse is true; partners are by far the greatest perpetrators of violence, followed by acquaintances and then strangers. However, for men and women the one constant factor is that it is *men* who pose the greatest threat. Thus, this survey to a large extent has validated the radical feminist arguments, although, in highlighting the problem of domestic violence for women, we must not underestimate the danger they face in public space from male acquaintances and strangers; this has also proved to be not insignificant.

NOTE

1   The number of households in the survey area was 2,410; one household in two was targeted for the sample (i.e. 1,205). At each household an alternative male/female respondent, aged 16 years or over, was identified for interview. To ensure a random selection within the household a Kish grid was used (Kish 1965). The response rate was 83 per cent; that is, 1,000 individuals were interviewed.

8

CHALLENGING PERCEPTIONS

'Community' and neighbourliness on a difficult-to-let estate

Janet Foster

Public housing estates are rarely seen as environments where 'community' and neighbourliness flourish. Indeed they are more often characterised by rapid tenant turnover, adverse physical design with high levels of crime and low levels of tenant satisfaction. The few studies of housing estates demonstrate that these generalisations conceal a considerable diversity in residents' experiences (see Parker 1983 and Reynolds 1986 as examples), but a mixture of nostalgia about communities past (see White 1986; Pearson 1983) and the failures of public housing (see Coleman 1985; Power 1989) have led to continuing assumptions about the patterns of social relationships in these settings.

This chapter, as the title suggests, seeks to challenge some of these popular stereotypes. It describes tenants' experiences of community and neighbourliness on a difficult-to-let estate in London which emerged from ethnographic research for a Home Office funded evaluation of the Priority Estates Project (PEP) and its impact on crime and community (see Foster and Hope 1993). The study involved eighteen months' overt participant observation on the estate and seventy interviews with residents, housing staff, police officers and other 'professionals' associated with it (see Foster and Hope 1993 for detailed discussion of methodology).[1]

The account begins with a brief history of Riverside (a pseudonym), tenants' recollections of the estate when it opened, the intense neighbouring which occurred at the outset and how the estate rapidly went into decline. This description forms the framework for subsequent discussion of residents' perceptions of community and neighbourliness on the estate at the time of the fieldwork and the networks which existed there.

RIVERSIDE

Riverside, in the heart of London's East End, was a multicultural estate assumed to have many of the problems associated with post-war council housing. Opened in the early 1970s it comprised two concrete medium rise blocks of flats and maisonettes and was based on Le Corbusier's designs (see Eisenham 1972). 'There's no comparison between the estate today and as it was then' a tenant remarked:

In them days we used to have architectural students from all over the world coming to look at Riverside because it was one of the original concepts of the 'streets in the sky'. If them same architects came back now, I wonder what they'd think.

Many tenants, irrespective of whether they liked living on the estate or not, often referred to it as a 'prison'. 'Let's be honest,' one said, 'Riverside always does look like a prison, the design of it.' But this did not prevent many tenants moving there at the outset: 'It was lovely,' one recalled, 'although there was lots of concrete, the estate was nice, it was very clean and the flats were lovely' (Foster 1995: 567). When the first occupants moved in the fact that the estate was new produced a feeling of pride and investment and as there were no established networks people easily developed contacts:

Everybody seemed to be all in together and all trying to be sort of nice and stay nice and friendly . . . In those days people used to take more pride outside their door. They used to take pride in the whole outer part . . . The place at that stage was a show place so everybody wanted to keep it oh so nice. (See Foster 1995: 567.)

'Believe it or not it was quite nice then,' another said, 'all sort of friendly . . . I moved here just before Christmas and I remember like on the new year night I opened the door and I couldn't believe it everyone was dancing up the landing you know and inviting you in each other's houses.' 'We had a great lot of neighbours' another tenant recollected:

They made yer feel welcome. It was like you used to have in the houses if anybody was ill everybody used to rally round . . . We had a neighbourliness which doesn't exist now, not really.

As in the established working-class neighbourhoods where women played a pivotal role (Young and Willmott 1957; White 1986; Whipp 1990), neighbouring was most frequent and intense among female tenants: 'In the early years a lot of the women didn't go to work', an original tenant explained. 'So we'd all sit outside . . . gossiping and chatting.' Children were also an important link because as the same tenant remarked: 'It was yer children who was yer interest, we were all neighbourly because our children were the common factor . . . children can be great ice breakers between neighbours.'

The initial and intense neighbouring which occurred at the outset soon faded (a common occurrence, see Abrams 1980) and within a short period of time Riverside went into decline in an all too familiar manner (see Power 1989; Bottoms et al. 1989). 'A number of factors' contributed to Riverside's problems, an estate officer explained:

One is the sheer physical appearance of the estate, it's forbidding, it's ugly . . . Two, lettings policies . . . Whereas in 1971 you had all the original residents and quite a few of those are still around as the[y] . . . filtered out . . . people have been dumped here literally – it's one offer, take it or leave it and that doesn't exactly help to foster pride.

Riverside hasn't been popular with people, it's always been the last resort.

Those tenants who had lived on the estate since it opened argued that the process of decline began as the original tenants 'died, moved out to better theirselves, or got transfers to bigger places'. They were replaced by 'different' people, often students and couples without children who did not have housing priority (Foster and Hope 1993: 29). Some of these had been offered more than one property and therefore still had a degree of choice but were not seen to have the same commitment. Consequently they were frequently blamed for the estate's difficulties:

> The type of people that they're moving in the flats now, they're calling them 'hard to let' which I don't think they are – they're very nice flats, but they're just moving in single people who don't go and wipe their balconies down or their window sills or put their rubbish out. It is ... the ones that are by themselves or new couples who are doing the damage, because we've still got a lot of people from when I first moved in and we never used to have the rubbish like we do now, and the lifts so dirty and the balconies dirty ... That's the type of people they're moving in here now.

One tenant suggested that two distinct groups of people resided on Riverside: 'There's people who see being here as a stop gap to going somewhere better' (many of whom had been on the transfer list since the day they arrived and were reflected in the significant numbers – 55 per cent – of tenants who reported in a Home Office survey that they would like to move – see Foster and Hope 1993: 23); 'and there's people I suppose like us, [who] like our flat, not particularly mad about the state of the lifts, the graffiti and the fact that it isn't kept clean, but basically like the flat.'

As the tenant profile of the estate became more diverse, neighbourliness assumed a different character. Those with established networks were often reluctant to extend them, and consequently new tenants moving onto the estate found it harder to establish links. A woman who moved in just six years after the estate was opened said: 'we never saw anybody and I lived here five years before I spoke to the ... next door neighbour ... You'd ... see people but they just never spoke' (see Foster 1995: 567). Common residence then was not enough to create friendly relations especially in circumstances where, as on Riverside, the estate came to house an increasingly heterogeneous population who perceived themselves to have little in common.

Given Riverside's poor status, it is unsurprising that approximately a quarter of the estate's population were Asian (7 per cent), Chinese/ Vietnamese (9 per cent) and Afro-Caribbean (10 per cent) (Foster and Hope 1993: 44–5), as it is generally acknowledged that these groups are structurally disadvantaged (see Henderson and Karn 1987) and receive the worst housing allocations (Commission for Racial Equality 1988; Ratcliffe 1992). The most recent ethnic minority settlement was the most controversial, involving the allocation of flats to previously homeless families, the majority of whom were Bengali (see Forman 1989; Docklands Forum

1993). The policy was problematic on a number of fronts, but most importantly because it effectively eliminated any tenant choice. Families were forced to accept the single housing offer made to them and to settle in areas of East London which had previously been predominantly white.

> He was offered this flat ... It was his only offer. He didn't have any alternative but to move in here. He did complain ... cos it's too far out, concerned about his kids ... [and told the council] 'I don't think it's a suitable flat'. [The reply was] 'well you've gotta take it cos there isn't any other alternative ... He was a bit angry but because he didn't have an alternative he took this flat.
>
> (Bengali resident, Riverside, speaking through an interpreter)

Not surprisingly, the Bengalis, coerced into moving to an area which was commonly perceived as hostile, were frequently fearful, and the first Bengali families moved to Riverside even before the homeless families policy was implemented, experienced harassment, including in one case 'trouble with people putting fires ... through their letter boxes'.

The rapidly expanding number of Asian households (which by the end of the research formed 17 per cent of the population – see Foster and Hope 1993: 45) led to specifically racialised comments among many white tenants about the 'different' people moving to Riverside who were not perceived to maintain the same 'standards' and 'values' as original tenants. This was aptly demonstrated by a resident who immediately interpreted a question about changes on the estate in racial terms: 'Oh it has changed. It's changed a lot. Well the people they've put in. They was ever such nice people they were when we came here. I know these coloured people aren't the same.' Ethnic minority households became a convenient scapegoat as this white tenant remarked: '[When] we first moved on the estate we had very few coloured or Bangladeshi people or Vietnamese people and there's a lot more of them moved in and I feel that most people are talking about them ... there is a lot of hostility.' She continued:

> People generally in the East End [of London] are very racist. They don't like foreigners at all, they don't want them here ... they feel that they're the cause of all the problems.
>
> (Foster and Hope 1993: 29)

At face value the description above does not suggest that Riverside tenants, whatever their ethnic origin, were either likely to feel positive about the estate or to develop patterns of neighbourliness in this context. However, during the course of the research it became evident that tenants' perceptions of the estate and the patterns of interaction there challenged many of the stereotypes conventionally associated with life on such estates.

PERCEPTIONS OF NEIGHBOURLINESS AND 'COMMUNITY' ON RIVERSIDE

Few Riverside residents perceived themselves to be part of a 'community', a term which conjured up the kinds of images invoked by this tenant:

'People popping in and out of doors, that happened in me mum's day, when you had rows of houses and the family lived in the road ... people left their keys on a string and doors were never locked – it don't happen now.' Some pointed to the abuse of public areas on the estate as indicative of the absence of community:

> People have ... a total lack of concern for other people by peeing in the lifts or letting their dogs ... foul the landings and not putting rubbish out. To me things like that are [signs] that people just don't care where they live and don't care who their neighbours are because if they did you wouldn't do it.

Yet, despite these feelings, the same residents also felt Riverside did have elements of neighbourliness and 'community' as the tenant quoted above continued: 'I think generally that people ... look out for each other and a lot of people are very friendly ... I feel this is quite a community.' 'It just seems that most people know one another on the estate, if not to talk to, to nod to ... there's not a lot of bad feeling ... there's not a lot of animosity' (Foster and Hope 1993: 31). This view was not limited to white households as the comments of this Bengali man speaking through an interpreter demonstrated: 'He thinks it's [Riverside] good ... because he lives in a friendly environment [and] local people are all right.'

More than 50 per cent of respondents in the estate survey 'talk[ed] to or were friendly with two or more neighbours', were 'friends with two or more households on the estate', and over 60 per cent had 'neighbours who kept watch on their property when they were out' (Foster and Hope 1993: 31).

Ironically those who had lived on the estate longest seemed least likely to feel that Riverside was friendly. This was because they compared their current experiences with the period of intense neighbouring when they first moved in. For example, one original tenant said: 'I think it's very sad that the neighbourliness and friendliness has gone.' Yet she also felt: 'There's still a community but not like it was.' These contradictions lie at the heart of the difficulties of trying to define and understand 'community', which as Crow and Allen (1994: 183) point out 'has many meanings; it involves different sets of experience for different groups of people, and indeed for the same people at different times in their lives'.

Rather than focusing on those problems here, I want to discuss the patterns of social interaction which existed among different groups of residents on Riverside, beginning with the established tenants. Despite considerable tenant turnover established residents retained a significant number of contacts on the estate, especially on their own landing. A female tenant, for example, who had lived on the fifth floor of block one since 1972 knew half of the forty-one households along the landing. The core of her network was centred on ten original tenant households.

Despite the number of tenants involved and the importance of this network for providing support, where tenants 'look[ed] out for each other', the established participants perceived themselves to be a beleaguered minority and felt threatened by the arrival of new tenants with whom they felt unable to identify (although in some cases they did establish contacts with them). Original tenants therefore perceived the estate to be increasingly occupied by 'strangers':

> There's so many strange faces we don't know who lives there and who shares a flat with somebody. But we did know before who was here and who wasn't and eventually got to know their relations if they come up to visit. 'Oh that's so-and-so's son's wife ... that's so-and-so's young son ... all that sort of thing. You had that certain familiarity.
>
> (Foster 1995: 575)

The networks of more recently arrived tenants tended to have a more diverse base and promoted different perceptions of community and neighbourliness. On the eighth floor of block two, for example, an active network with the same degree of contact as the original tenant in block one (where half the balcony was known to the tenant) was perceived very differently. Here tenants saw the estate as 'friendly' and familiar rather than a place occupied by 'strangers'. The eighth-floor network was comprised of residents of different ages, sexual orientation, class and lifestyles. The central figure (Carol) in the network had lived on Riverside for eleven years but did not know any other tenants for several years after moving to the estate. 'When I had [the baby]', she said, 'I thought enough's enough. When new people move in I'm going to introduce myself and that's what I do.' Five years after her initial overtures, the network was thriving:

> This balcony has got what the old fashioned streets used to be like ... We have got a couple up here that just don't speak ... but I would say that half this balcony know each other and at one time or another have popped in and had tea and coffee. It's really nice up here ... My door and my phone's for ever going. Last week I got called the den mother for the eighth floor because if anything goes wrong they always knock on me ... A lot of people along here I have their keys ... for them ... or when they're on holiday I go in and feed ... cats ... [or] pick ... up ... mail and mak[e] sure there's no leaflets in the door.

I asked Jill and her partner Pete who lived on the same landing how long it took to meet their neighbours:

> Quite soon actually ... we were sort of knocking and bashing around ... the neighbours Terry and Madge next door, they sort of came out and were sort of looking. We said 'We're moving in.' They said: 'That's fine, it's just that we heard knocking and wondered what was going on.' So we met them and ... I asked her then would she ... have the keys for us because the day we were moving in I'd arranged for the electricity and gas to be put on.

When Jill came home the electricity had not been connected: 'I saw a light on in Carol's and just took a chance really', Jill said. 'She was really sweet – gave us a candle or two. They were the first neighbours really that we sort of met. We realised that they were very nice and very helpful indeed.'

A gay man on the same landing said he had initiated contact with his neighbours:

> My attitude in situations like this is to say hello first and I in fact did. Because I'd met Barry (another gay man on the estate) Barry introduced me to somebody else and it just went on from there and when I met Carol ... we became good friends. It's vital for me to have contact like that.

When I asked how many people he knew on the balcony he said:

> to stand and talk to about nine flats ... but there are different degrees of cognisance that I actually know them by. There's Carol, she's the major contact on the balcony itself. Barry has left now but he was on the fifth floor ... Jill and Pete is next ... then Jo, then again my opposite neighbour since they've moved in I've got quite close to them. I mean I knocked on their door when I ran out of sugar and they knocked on my door when they didn't have any change for the meter or whatever. Errol, the black guy next door ... he's a really nice fellow ... and his girlfriend ... then Georgina at the end.

Neighbourliness seemed to be facilitated by the landing itself (as was intended in the 'streets in the sky' design) because it provided the opportunity for people to meet and talk to one another and made interaction between those who might not otherwise have established contacts easier, as Carol explained:

> I used to chat to [Georgina's] fella ... If he was out [on the balcony] he'd have a walk down and have a cigarette and a chat and then one afternoon he said 'Could my girlfriend come down and have a chat with you?' ... We really became good friends ... It's like when Justin and Scott moved in, we probably would never have spoken to them; they'd have probably have [to have] spoken first. It was only that we'd had the gas cut and they come along [the balcony] with an electric cooker and me and Jo was in such a good mood we was having a laugh and joke and that and I said 'Fancy going out and buying an electric cooker, the gas is coming on tommorra!' And they started laughing and chatting ... They'd only been there a couple of weeks ... and Scott said 'Could you have the keys for me?'

Unlike the established residents who found heterogeneity difficult to deal with, diversity was not a problem in itself for more recent tenants, as a small fifth-floor network in block one comprised of students, young families and elderly tenants, and the eighth-floor block two networks, demonstrated. Tenants however were not oblivious to the differences. The 'den mother', for example, saw herself as 'ordinary' but acted as an important support to a diverse range of tenants. 'We're getting some very weird people moving into these flats', she said:

> For instance Justin right. The other week he goes to this pub ... He walked into the gents toilet and there was a girl in there rolling a joint

so he borrowed £20 off her and give her the keys to his flat. Now I mean is that weird? ... He was ringing me up every half hour, 'Is my door still shut? Have you seen anyone go in? Can you get John [her husband] to go in and check? ... I'll ring you back in half an hour.'

Despite Carol's belief that the balcony operated like 'the old fashioned streets', and that she knew many of the tenants along her balcony, she did not perceive her neighbourly relations as constituting community: 'I would say ... in general, that it's not a community ... People know each other but, as I say, we are quite rare up here because we do all get on with each other so well and pop in and out of each other's places.'

PRESSURE ON NEIGHBOURLINESS

Although neighbourliness appeared to be common, it existed under considerable pressure because of mistaken impressions of the estate and continuing difficulties in finding common ground. No matter how successful the networks, an underlying suspicion about the potential for hostile encounters persisted among most residents and made them reticent about establishing contacts. For example the young men, Justin and Scott, that Carol met on the balcony invited her in for a cup of tea the day they moved in. Carol's immediate thought was: 'I didn't know who they are. They could have been murderers for all I knew. I'm not that gullible just to walk in.' (See Foster 1995: 569.) While Jill, when she asked her neighbours to hold her keys said: 'Bit of a risky thing because you don't know, but they seemed like nice and very ordinary and we didn't have that much stuff.' Interactions then were overlaid with the expectation of trouble.

The perceived differences between tenants also led to assumptions about the way they would respond, particularly in neighbour disputes. Tenants often anticipated hostility and were consequently on their guard, which not unnaturally influenced their willingness to get involved. Neighbour disputes sometimes went unresolved for long periods because residents were fearful of intervening. For example, a female tenant was driven to distraction by the music being played by a tenant on the landing below and finally decided to confront him. He apologised and said he 'didn't know' he was causing a disturbance, 'no-one's said anything to me'. His two immediate neighbours whose lives were equally disrupted by the noise said to her: 'How did you knock on his door? He'll pull a knife on you ... That music's driving us up the wall.'

CULTURAL DIVERSITY AND ITS CONSEQUENCES

The indigenous white community think oh they're [the Bengalis] dirty, they're rubbish ... Those people if they could have had a choice they would not have chosen to come to such an estate, they would probably have gone to better places but because there is no choice ... they're making the best to be there and make a peaceful life.

(Bengali support worker, Riverside)

The preceding discussion outlined the patterns of interaction among groups of largely, though not exclusively, white tenants on two landings in the Riverside blocks. This section focuses on the burgeoning networks of Bengali tenants on the estate and the strength that was derived from these alongside the support provided by the PEP initiative (see Foster and Hope 1993). By the end of the research the Bengalis, initially the most vulnerable, perceived themselves to be 'empowered' while their white counterparts, especially original tenants, perceived themselves to be a defeated and outnumbered minority (see Foster and Hope 1993: 42–4).

It is well recognised that ethnicity can provide an important basis for networks and the Bengalis had a number of factors in common: ethnicity, religion, country of origin, and in many cases the same area within Bangladesh. Although these commonalities were important, differences did exist between Bengali tenants who were more educated and relatively financially secure and those families who had little education or income. These differences, however, were less important than the desire to improve the lives of all Bengali households on the estate and to create an environment which would be relatively safe and supportive.

One young Bengali man with whom I made contact was a member of one of the first families to move to Riverside. Before the research began he knew all fifteen Bengali households on the estate but knew only one of the residents on his landing (the fifth floor of block two). Three years later, with the burgeoning Bengali population (which increased by 10 per cent in three years, see Foster and Hope 1993: 45) and his active involvement in the tenants' association and the Bengali Association which welcomed new families to the estate, his network included forty-five households – almost a fifth of households on Riverside – but he still knew only four households on his landing. While the networks of white tenants tended to be based on individual balconies and there was very limited interaction between landings let alone blocks, the Bengali networks provided strength and support across the estate.

The network included both Bengali and white households because of his involvement with the tenants' association: 'We had white neighbours but I'd never actually spoken to them', he explained. 'Through [the] TA we got to know them and they got to know us quite well. Better relations as a result. Better neighbours' (Foster and Hope 1993: 41). His experiences on Riverside led him to suggest that the estate was 'the best estate to live on at the moment in the whole of ... Tower Hamlets, in terms of race relations'. A perception which was very important given the negative experiences of Bengali families moved onto the Isle of Dogs just a short distance away (see Foster 1992, 1996, forthcoming). 'Riverside hasn't had that bad name as other [estates],' the Bengali support worker explained, 'where everyone wants to move out, very unprotected, alone, defenceless ... Bengalis are not coming [to Riverside] with a great fear now.'

Many Bengali residents, despite their initial trepidation, felt positive about the estate. For example this man said: 'I like the Bengali Society and our community, everything's all right you know.' This growing confidence and security was reinforced by the fact that most new tenants housed on the estate were Bengali: 'Within the last three or four years a large concentrated number have come to settle down in Riverside. And new ones coming every day'; this increased familiarity and reduced fear, as the comments of this Bengali resident demonstrated: 'If you go out [of] any flat you see Asian faces everywhere ... whereas three years ago you didn't see any ... so they feel a lot safer' (Foster 1995: 576).

Despite the many positive comments about Riverside a small minority of Bengalis were dissatisfied because its high rise design was unsuitable, especially for children, and the estate's location some distance from the mosque and other facilities in Whitechapel created difficulties. Language barriers also led to isolation: 'I don't know the language, it's isolating', one of the men said through an interpreter. 'He knows the ... white faces and black faces living here but he doesn't know them personally because of the language problem he's got.' This was even more acute for Bengali women.

White tenants rarely mentioned the Bengali households who were known to them when they described their networks, although they did include Afro-Caribbean residents and sometimes the Vietnamese or Chinese (though these contacts tended to be relatively superficial). This was because many white tenants felt threatened by the burgeoning Bengali population and perceived insurmountable barriers in establishing contacts with them. 'Different cultures are not friendly', a tenant said. 'They've got their way of life and we've got ours.' Another said:

> They outnumber us in here now ... I love my flat ... they're nice flats, I wouldn't like to move [but] ... if they give me the opportunity to move out of here I would go. ... I feel I'm being pushed out ... by who's sort of coming in ... they're just driving other people out.
>
> (Foster and Hope 1993: 43)

Such negative responses were not unique to Riverside (see Cornwell 1984; Holme 1985). Although white tenants may have perceived themselves to be in the minority they still formed the largest group on the estate. However, in three years their relative position had changed from 73 per cent of the population to 58 per cent (see Foster and Hope 1993: 45).

When white tenants were highly sensitised to the Bengali population on Riverside, and underlying distrust and hostility was openly expressed towards them, why did the Bengalis feel positive about the estate? Part of the explanation lay in their networks because as the Bengali support worker observed:

> among their own group there's a welcoming, ... so they ... settle down and feel quite comfortable. [They are] confident that some-body [is] at hand, that their children will not be alone, there will be other children at school and if they have a problem there is someone to help.
>
> (Foster and Hope 1993: 41)

These feelings of relative security may also have been due to the response of white tenants too. 'We are tolerant of each other I suppose in our backhanded sort of way', one explained. 'We do [think] they're here to stay, that's it, end of story, so live and let live. Our resentment we keep more or less to ourselves, hence we became apathetic' (Foster and Hope 1993: 44).

CONCLUSION

This short chapter has outlined the patterns of interaction among residents on a London housing estate where, despite adverse physical design and a changing tenant profile, networks had been established. In the case of the original Riverside residents, despite their dwindling numbers, a support network survived but was perceived to be increasingly threatened. By contrast, Bengali households, despite their initial vulnerability, formed a successful community of 'interest' (Willmott 1986) across the estate where common factors such as ethnicity and residence combined with fears about their safety and the intense stage of neighbouring to encourage the development of links.

Although common factors were key elements in both the established and Bengali networks, diversity was not a problem in itself, especially where networks were facilitated by design or the energies and enthusiasm of key individuals. The differing types and composition of networks on Riverside aptly demonstrate that different forms of neighbourliness can occur in the same setting simultaneously among different groups of people. These networks played an important role in an environment where Asian, white, black and Chinese/Vietnamese households alike lived with an underlying suspicion about their neighbours and expressed concerns about their safety (see Foster 1995).

The very existence of these networks suggests that popular perceptions of council housing – and the very poorest and most difficult-to-let estates in particular – as alienating environments in which there is little tenant interaction and support, are too simplistic. Instead of condemning such places as 'dreadful enclosures' (Damer 1974) we should look more closely at the patterns of interaction between tenants in these contexts. We need to understand more about how they are characterised, in what ways they influence tenants' perceptions of the estates on which they live, and how different individuals and groups, who have had little or no choice in their housing allocation, manage to co-exist.

NOTE

1 Survey research (before the PEP initiative began and three years later) was also conducted for the Home Office (see Foster and Hope 1993) and the data are included here where appropriate, but it is important to note these figures refer to the *whole* experimental site in London and not simply to that part of the estate discussed here.

Part III

NEW FORMS OF REGULATION: PARTNERSHIP AND EMPOWERMENT

HEGEMONY AND REGIME IN URBAN GOVERNANCE

Towards a theory of the locally networked state

Chris Collinge and Stephen Hall

INTRODUCTION

The recent proliferation of inter-agency 'networks' and 'partnerships' at the local level in Britain has now reached a point where these are seen as a primary vehicle for urban policy development and implementation. This process has been associated with increased fragmentation of the local state through the internalisation of the market and the transfer of responsibilities to centrally appointed quangos. It has also been associated with the commodification of urban policy through the establishment of a market in regeneration funding. In each case these changes have conditioned a phase of experimentation, with new institutional roles and relationships arising in and around urban governance.

The newly emerging pattern of urban governance has recently been theorised in terms of the transition from Fordist to post-Fordist modes of regulation or state forms (e.g. Tickell and Peck 1992). But, whilst historical changes have been described in regulationist terms, much less attention has been given within this school of thought to identifying the causal links through which gross transformations of society are supposed to have occurred (see Goodwin *et al.* 1993). The appearance during the 1980s of promising strands of theory from within American political science, and from within Gramscian state theory, does however suggest certain alternative formulations which may allow the processes involved in macroscopic change to be specified more clearly. Regime theory, for example, has emerged from within the pluralist tradition as a model for the analysis of urban politics and local state restructuring, focusing upon the crystallisation of interests in urban coalitions with particular emphasis on powerful representatives of private capital (e.g. Stone 1993). Progress has also been made from within the Marxist tradition in the development of neo-Gramscian theory of hegemony, to the point where (despite the national focus of much writing, and despite its association with the regulation approach) it is possible to investigate the spatial diversification of hegemonic projects and accumulation strategies, and to analyse the co-ordination of locally specific power blocs (Jessop 1983b; Cox and Mair 1988; Peck 1995).

This chapter reviews the development of regime theory and the theory of hegemony, compares and contrasts these approaches, and identifies their implications for the analysis of the state and society at the local level. It then examines these theories by reference to the elaboration in recent years of urban policy networks and partnerships as part of the restructuring of the local state, politics and civil society. This is investigated through a case study of regeneration policies in Birmingham since the early 1980s.

THEORIES OF HEGEMONY AND REGIME

The theory of hegemony derives from the humanistic reading of Marx and Engels undertaken by Gramsci during the 1920s and 1930s. It also derives from the anti-humanist, structuralist appropriation of this analysis in the writings of Althusser and Poulantzas, and subsequent reactions to this structuralism. Regime theory has been developed from within the liberal pluralist tradition of political science, in opposition to neo-classical economic models of local government, to provide a method for the analysis of political processes in US cities.

Neo-Gramscian theories of hegemony

During the 1980s neo-Marxist state theory was reformulated by Hirsch, Jessop and others in order to relate it to more substantive concerns, and to draw upon emerging regulation theory (e.g. Hirsch 1983). The regulation approach takes up the Gramscian notion of a hegemonic apparatus, which combines political and civil power in the process of social regulation, and places this within a theoretical framework reminiscent of Althusserian structuralism. The state is viewed as the central core of a constellation of social institutions and relationships (the 'mode of regulation') that orchestrates arrangements between production and consumption within a given 'regime of accumulation' to ensure their mutual compatibility (De Vroey 1984).

In a broadly regulationist context, Jessop develops an account of the formal properties of the state, together with the substantive character of 'hegemonic projects' and 'accumulation strategies', which is intended to resist the extremes of structuralism and instrumentalism. The state gives form to social power but also constrains this through, for instance, the differential representation of social interests. There are three formal features of the state that are decisive in mediating the rule of capital: forms of representation, forms of intervention, and the form of the state as an ensemble of institutions (Jessop 1983a: 154). Jessop distinguishes three different forms of political representation (clientelism, corporatism and parliamentarism), each of which links the state to the interests of capital and helps to 'manage' anti-capitalist interests, but each of which contains its own drawbacks. The effectiveness of these different forms of representation in reproducing the circuit of capital (the value form) and the institutional integrity of the state is, according to Jessop, not given by capital but is a contingent matter that depends, for instance, upon the substantive articulation of hegemonic projects and accumulation strategies.

Jessop defines hegemony as the 'interpellation and organisation of different "class relevant" (but not necessarily class conscious) forces under the political, intellectual and moral leadership of a particular class (or class fraction) or, more precisely, its political, intellectual, and moral spokesmen' (Jessop 1983b: 100). He argues that successful leadership requires the development of a hegemonic project which asserts a general interest behind activities that advance the long-term requirements of the hegemonic class or fraction, and opposition to activities which might confound these interests (Jessop 1983a: 155). For example, Jessop et al. (1984) argue that Thatcherism succeeded in replacing the old 'one nation' Tory hegemonic project by a 'two nations' project of divide and rule between the productive market core and the less productive periphery. A hegemonic project involves the granting of concessions to non-hegemonic classes and fractions, and differs from an accumulation strategy in that it is directly concerned with wider social or political themes 'such as military expansion, moral regeneration, social reform, or political stability' (Jessop 1983a: 155). Jessop views hegemony as provisional and allows for the possibility that it may fall into crisis or encounter opposition in particular places at particular times. An accumulation strategy is described as an economic 'growth model' together with the means of its achievement (Jessop 1983a: 149). Accumulation strategies may be articulated by business leaders, or by other agents including politicians, academics or bureaucrats (Jessop 1983a: 160). Just as the substantive reality of the value form in each context is contingent upon (for instance) the particular accumulation strategy that is adopted, so the substantive reality of the state form depends in part upon the hegemonic project that is pursued (Jessop 1983b: 107–8).

The preceding theorisation takes the nation-state as its focus but in recent years efforts have been made to extend and adapt this analysis to subnational power structures and state apparatuses. Following Harvey's concept of 'structured regional coherence' (Harvey 1985), Cox and Mair have analysed urban politics in the USA in terms of 'local dependence'. Capital and the local state cannot escape dependence upon local resources, customers or taxpayers, and so they must confront it through mutually beneficial accumulation strategies which, typically, take corporatist forms (Cox and Mair 1988: 309). A pro-development coalition will, for instance, seek to co-opt class interests behind a hegemonic project supportive of its objectives. This project may assert that class-based resistance will discourage investment and employment in the locality and that sacrifices are required if this area is to compete effectively with others. Cox and Mair thus argue that the hegemonic project, by appealing to community loyalty, displaces local class conflict into a competitive rivalry between localities (Cox and Mair 1988: 318–21).

From the late 1980s there have been various attempts to develop a regulationist account of the local state and 'local spaces of regulation' (Tickell and Peck 1992: 209; Goodwin et al. 1993). Goodwin et al., for instance, argue that following the post-war settlement the local state assumed a central role in organising production and reproduction, and establishing new forms of consumption via the welfare state. Since the 1970s, however, the class alliances underpinning local Fordism have been broken down, and the state nationally and locally is being restructured as part of the preparation for a new mode of regulation. Most local authorities have adopted a 'new realism' involving compliance with the central government agenda, but in some areas there is positive emphasis upon 'a two-nation model based on private provision for the affluent worker, with only a minimal "social security state" for those excluded from this' (Goodwin *et al.* 1993: 81).

Peck has also developed a structural, 'institutionally embedded' analysis of business elites. He points to a contradiction in Thatcherism between the ideological centrality of business leadership in urban redevelopment, and the practical dependence of this leadership upon (central) state sponsorship and a centrally established framework of local institutions. Local business leadership is not to be understood as a spontaneous expression of the interests of local capital, but as a force that is constituted and sponsored through action by the nation-state in the creation of a non-elected tier of local government: ' "business interests" are currently being mobilised, given their form and presented with their function by the state' (Peck 1995: 17). For old style macroeconomic tripartism, Thatcherism has substituted a bipartite corporatism based on 'partnership' between government and individual 'maverick' or disorganised capitals at the local level. An important element of political discourse in late Thatcherism was that of 'localism', and through institutional changes business leaders have been encouraged to see themselves as speaking for their city as a whole, creating a situation in which the interests of business are hegemonic (Peck 1995: 30).

Neo-pluralist regime theory

Regime theory developed as part of a broader response within US political science to economistic analyses of urban development, the most important being Paul Peterson's seminal *City Limits* (1981). Peterson acknowledges that conflicts over policy do occur but argues that they are theoretically unimportant; it is the economic system as a whole that constrains the choice of policy-makers. The most important function of city government is to preserve the economic vitality of its territory and thus its fiscal base. Peterson regards cities as unified entities, competing with each other to secure economic investment. This basic competitive dynamic precludes the possibility that city governments might pursue redistributive, social welfare strategies.

Clarence Stone (1984: 289) argues that Peterson is correct to suggest that economic development enjoys popular support, but he underestimates the extent to which the actual process of economic restructuring is subject to conflict. Sanders and Stone (1987: 528) suggest that the debate is based on a dichotomy between those who regard cities as unitary entities and those who regard cities as complex entities through which political and economic competition is mediated. Regime theorists fall into the latter category. They reject economic determinism and argue that politics matters because different cities have responded differently to economic change (Swanstrom 1988: 107). Policy grows out of the characteristics of the governing coalition, so politics produces policy (Sanders and Stone 1987: 538).

Regime theory is concerned essentially with local power structures, although some more recent formulations have stressed the importance of economic restructuring and inter-governmental fiscal support. Regime theory agrees with pluralism that, given the highly fragmented nature of modern society, it is unlikely that any one group could monopolise power but argues that the threat of monism is so negligible that it is uninteresting (Stone 1993: 8). Consequently, regime theory adopts a social production model of power in contrast to conventional pluralism's social control model. The social production model addresses the power of local elites to achieve certain policy outcomes rather than to exercise control over the public, and regime theory, therefore, emphasises 'power to' rather than 'power over'. Stoker and Mossberger argue that conventional pluralism addresses the well-known question 'who governs?', whereas regime theory is also concerned with *the capacity to govern* (1994: 197).

Traditional pluralism assumes that political authority is adequate for the state to achieve its objectives and economic factors are largely absent from its analyses. Regime theory, on the other hand, adopts the familiar neo-pluralist dictum that there exists a fundamental division of labour in liberal democracies between state and market (Lindblom 1982; Elkin 1985: 11). In this context, the state must co-opt non-governmental actors (Elkin 1985: 12), and public policy choice is constrained fundamentally by the need to build and rebuild governing regimes. A regime is the set of agreements (or perhaps substantive policy dispositions) by which the division of labour between political and economic institutions is managed (Stone 1993: 2) or, as Swanstrom (1988: 110) puts it, how a compromise is reached between economic and political logic.

Non-governmental resources are of course skewed strongly towards capital, not least in the massive discretionary powers of corporations to invest and disinvest in particular localities (Stone 1984: 294). Government cannot command economic performance, it can only induce it (Elkin 1985: 13), and the private sector, therefore, occupies a particularly advantageous position in urban regimes. This is reinforced in the United States by a number of factors, including the instrumental control of city government by business interests and the lack of equalising federal grants to local government (Harding 1994: 359). However, regime theorists are not (generally) as pessimistic as Lindblom (1982) regarding the constraints imposed on public policy by the market (Logan and Swanstrom 1990: 6).

Regime theory is, therefore, as DiGaetano and Klemanski (1993: 368) put it, an amalgam of urban political economy and the community-power paradigms. It is American in origin but ethnocentricity is not necessarily a problem. Harding (1994: 366), for instance, suggests that the fundamental division of labour between state and market in liberal democracies makes the variations in institutional structure between nations of secondary importance. Nevertheless, the activities of urban regimes differ spatially and temporally and the approach, therefore, lends itself to the construction of ideal types to facilitate empirical analysis. For a number of regime typologies see Stone (1993: 18–22), Elkin (1985: 15–24) and Swanstrom (1988: 108).

Comparisons and empirical implications

Neo-Gramscian theory and regime theory clearly demonstrate a degree of convergence, and the similarities between these are substantially greater than those that attended previous generations of Marxists and pluralists. They include the following:

1   A rejection of economism as it appears in their respective traditions. Both perspectives therefore agree that 'politics matters'.
2   Both theories resist 'instrumentalism' by recognising the impossibility of monistic control and emphasising the participation of a plurality of interests within the political process, forming a ruling coalition or hegemonic bloc.
3   Both theories stress the necessity of building and rebuilding political alliances to achieve and sustain the capacity to govern. Both recognise the importance of ideology in forming and cohering these alliances.
4   Despite their resistance to economism, both approaches acknowledge the impact of economic interests (particularly the requirements of capital) upon political processes.

Beyond these similarities, however, there are some fundamental differences between the two perspectives which stem in part from the traditions in which they are embedded:

1   Although regime theory postulates the separation but interdependence of politics and economics, this is taken as given and is not theorised to any depth. Neo-Marxism views the separation of 'politics' and 'economics' as problematic and subject to renegotiation according to the development of class conflict.
2   Neo-Marxism acknowledges a plurality of 'groups' and 'categories' within or around the state but it suggests these are underpinned by class relations and the interpellation or displacement of class interests and identities. Regime theory has a more pluralistic concept of community interest and pressure groups.
3   Neo-Marxism deals with the articulation of 'projects' and 'strategies' in the co-ordination of 'categories', 'groups' and 'class fractions' into hegemonic blocs. Regime theory deals with interest groups and parties, and their composition into coalitions which have a stable policy orientation referred to as a 'regime'.
4   Neo-Marxism generally is less committed than regime theory to the

empirical investigation of hegemony (of hegemonic projects, accumulation strategies and the building of hegemonic blocs) and in particular
to the examination of case studies in urban politics.

5   Neo-Marxism regards the form of the state as an important determi-
nant of its relationship to class interests and its ability to serve these
interests. Regime theory tends to take these two formal features as
given and to examine the dynamics of coalition formation against this
background.

6   Neo-Marxism postulates a structural relationship of the state both to
class struggle and to the development of capital, with different degrees
of relative autonomy or contingent causation for the state. In regime
theory the causal emphasis is placed upon the political composition of
the ruling coalition and the importance of system or structural
variables is, therefore, down-played.

There is, then, an underlying difference between neo-Marxist theories of
hegemony, with their formal analysis of the state and its relationship to the
structures of capital and class in which empirical investigation is neglected,
and regime theory with its more open-ended investigation of political
process in which there is greater empirical emphasis, but in which the form
of the state apparatus and its structural relationship to economic interests
are neglected.

URBAN GOVERNANCE IN BIRMINGHAM

The next step is to investigate these rival theoretical perspectives through
a brief case study of the governance of regeneration activities in Birmingham. As Britain's second largest city, with a population of approximately
one million people, Birmingham is the centre of the West Midlands region.
The city has suffered disproportionately from industrial decline since the
1970s, losing more than half its manufacturing jobs during the decade and,
by 1980, unemployment exceeded 20 per cent (Wright 1994: 1). In the
space of two decades Birmingham has declined from a thriving prosperous
city to one of the most deprived in Europe (Martin and Pearce 1992: 500).

The West Midlands County Council moved politically to the left from the
late 1970s and responded to the economic crisis with a range of inter-
ventionist initiatives targeted at indigenous industry. However, the right-
ward shift in national politics brought conflict between (especially)
metropolitan counties and the Thatcher government, which intensified to
the point where in 1986 the upper-tier councils in the English conurbations
were abolished. Birmingham City Council's response to the economic crisis
contrasted with that of West Midlands County Council and local authorities
in other major cities. Under the leadership of Sir Richard Knowles, the City
pursued a strategy linked explicitly to civic 'boosterism' and place-
marketing. This strategy has been extensively documented, critically
(Loftman and Nevin 1992) and less critically (Carley 1991; Martin and
Pearce 1992). However, the government's programme of disciplining,
fragmenting and de-democratising urban governance was proceeding, and

by the late 1980s there was a proliferation of local development agencies.

Davies (1993), for instance, identifies no fewer than fifty-three local 'executive bodies' (including Heartlands Development Corporation and Castle Vale Housing Action Trust) in Birmingham. This is a conservative estimate, however, as it excludes joint bodies created after the abolition of the County Council and, crucially, a number of key economic players (the Chamber of Commerce, the Training and Enterprise Council). Moreover, several territorial levels of the state in and beyond the UK are active locally. The European Commission, for instance, is involved through its Structural Fund policies, from which Birmingham has benefited more than most British cities (Martin and Pearce 1992: 500). Central government's presence takes the form of a number of locally specific direct measures (e.g. a City Action Team, a Task Force), and it operates several grant regimes from which Birmingham has benefited (Regional Assistance, City Challenge, Single Regeneration Budget). On the other hand, the city has suffered from the Conservative government's fiscal austerity regime. The Government Office for the West Midlands is responsible and *centrally* accountable for the management of the regional European Operational Programme, and the Single Regeneration Budget. Finally, there is Birmingham City Council which, as noted above, has often pre-empted the Thatcher government's agenda for urban regeneration and has, itself, established quasi-autonomous agencies and partnerships.

The next step is to illustrate how regeneration policies have evolved in Birmingham. The present phase of development activity dates from the early 1980s. The City sought to develop a remedial strategy in response to the catastrophic industrial decline of the preceding decade, and was strongly influenced by the experience of cities on the east coast of the United States (Loftman and Nevin 1992; Wright 1994) which constructed 'flagship' projects and developed business tourism initiatives. Accordingly, in 1983, Birmingham City Council voted to develop Britain's first convention centre, and a number of related projects (The National Indoor Arena, Symphony Hall and the Hyatt Hotel) in the city centre. This development strategy was executed in a closed, corporatist manner. Indeed, it was not until 1992 (*after* the completion of the projects) that public consultations were conducted (Loftman and Nevin 1992). The total cost of the development package was some £276 million, part of which was met by a £40 million grant from the European Commission and part by Birmingham City Council and the National Exhibition Centre Ltd (a joint venture between the Council and the Chamber of Commerce). Development costs were, therefore, substantially underwritten by the public sector, and funds were apparently diverted from other activities including housing and education (Loftman and Nevin 1992).

In March 1988, the City Council and the Birmingham City Action Team convened the 'Birmingham City Centre Challenge Symposium', known as the 'Highbury Initiative'. The symposium included representatives from local and national government plus participants of the private and voluntary sectors. It proposed a programme of pedestrianising Birmingham city centre and down-grading the city's inner ring road. More importantly, for our purposes, it resulted in the creation of Birmingham City 2000, a private sector umbrella organisation, representing some 150 financial and property sector firms within the City, which exists to promote a boosterist ethos within Birmingham. City 2000's interests were, therefore, synonymous with those of the City Council at the time. A second symposium involving similar interests was held in September 1989 and resulted in the establishment of another key organisation. The Birmingham Marketing Partnership was formed to further the promotion of Birmingham as a centre for business tourism through its slogan 'Birmingham: Europe's Meeting Place'. The Birmingham Marketing Partnership was the brainchild of City 2000, and its board comprises representatives of the Council, the Chamber of Commerce, City 2000, Birmingham Airport, British Airways, the Midland Association of Restaurants, Caterers and Hotels, Midlands Independent Newspapers, NEC Limited and the West Midlands Development Agency.

Regeneration activities in Birmingham have also focused on districts beyond the city centre. In 1986 the City Council designated East Birmingham as a regeneration area and, with the support of the Chamber of Commerce, persuaded the Environment Secretary against imposing an Urban Development Corporation (Cherry 1994: 208). Subsequently, in 1987, the Birmingham Heartlands initiative (a joint property development project) was established in the area by the City Council, the Chamber and five leading building companies. Three of these firms were locally based (Bryant, RM Douglas and Gallifords) and two (Tarmac and Wimpey) were national concerns (Carley 1991: 107). However, the initiative became difficult to sustain due to the recession and the failure of a City Challenge bid for the area, and central government assistance was sought. The Birmingham Heartlands Development Corporation (a UDC) was duly established in May 1992 but continues to work closely with the City Council.

Alongside boosterism the Council has sought to engage local communities in policy and services through a series of area offices and consultative committees around which council–community networks have been fostered. The boosterist ethos that characterised Birmingham during the late 1980s and early 1990s has moderated somewhat since the election, in 1993, of a new leadership committed to social and community services. However, the Council remains a fully committed member of the Birmingham Marketing Partnership and responded enthusiastically to the government's City Pride initiative, producing with its partners the first Prospectus in 1994.

The core partners of Birmingham City Pride are the Council, the Chamber, City 2000, the TEC and the Voluntary Service Council. The fundamental objective of the City Pride Prospectus is to halt the out-migration of businesses and professional workers by 2005. To this extent, it represents a continuity with the boosterist ethos that characterised Birmingham's immediate past. However, the Prospectus also stresses the need to tackle deprivation in the city. It is possible to pursue the apparently conflicting goals of wealth creation and distribution through City Pride because it is not supported by specific government funding commitments; divisive policy decisions can, therefore, be deferred (though not indefinitely). City Pride, by its very nature, enables Birmingham to project a 'one city, many people' message (Hall *et al.* 1995: 110).

THE FORM AND DIRECTION OF URBAN GOVERNANCE

There is no single policy on the part of local agencies, or indeed the City Council itself, towards the regeneration of Birmingham, but a range of policies related to different needs which together constitute what might be called the *direction* of urban governance. Nevertheless, it is possible to identify a surprisingly persistent strategy and vision on the part of the Council and other bodies throughout most of the 1980s and into the 1990s. This vision was born in response to the shock of decline of the previously vigorous Birmingham economy during the 1970s. It was developed and taken forward in a neo-corporatist manner by a relatively small number of politicians, officers and co-optees. It was driven by the desire to restore prestige and civic pride to the city and its residents, and to boost the city's position as a location for events and for inward investment. As such it constituted a distinctly *'civic' hegemonic project*, led by the City Council rather than the private sector, and harnessed to a *boosterist accumulation strategy* (Bonefeld 1986: 111). Formulated in the mid-1980s, this strategy in many respects prefigured the shift at national level towards place-marketing. Although broadly consistent with the neo-liberal thrust of Thatcherism, it grew from different soil and contradicts neo-liberalism in its reliance upon local state sponsorship and investment (cf. Peck 1995). There has, since 1993, been an attempt by the majority party in the City Council to shift the emphasis towards community needs and towards education, housing and social services. This change has brought a greater stress upon what might be called the 'one Birmingham' strand of the Council's message. But whilst changing the flavour of Council policies, strengthening their appeal to Labour Party activists and to working-class residents, the strategies of civic pride and boosterism appear to remain in place.

Recent experience in Birmingham also illustrates, however, two important trends in the *form* of urban governance – the emergence of a complex web of urban regeneration agencies, and the growth of 'privatism' – that might appear to contradict the civic project. The urban governance apparatus now contains informal networks between people and agencies as well as formal partnerships between public and private (and to a lesser extent voluntary) sector bodies. In some cases it includes secondary partnerships, in which one or more component agency is itself already a partnership. Despite appearances to the contrary, however, these networks are still constituted by and indeed centred upon the state, or rather upon an increasingly partialised state system in which there is separate but related involvement of several territorial levels. The second key trend in urban governance is the growth of 'privatism', involving the proliferation of non-elected quangos that emulate private enterprise, and the incorporation of a set of private companies and business associations into the development of urban policy. Each of these trends – which together comprise the neo-corporatism of contemporary governance – has since the 1980s been driven by central government. But each was also embraced spontaneously by the City Council in the mid-1980s and has been pursued vigorously since then as part of its own restructuring strategy for the local state. This strategy has sought to mobilise wider business opinion in support of a local hegemonic project based on civic pride and boosterism, and to manage relations with central government and Europe. It has sought to forestall or to reduce the resistance of local residents through an identification with Birmingham and through the promise of jobs and services, a strand of policy which has been re-emphasised since 1993. Despite recent changes this new apparatus of local governance remains in place, and the process of reforming urban regeneration policy is now constrained by the existence of the networked, privatised local state form.

Neo-Gramscian state theory does therefore provide a useful basis for interpreting the restructuring of the local state. But there remain several unanswered questions within this framework concerning, for instance, the relationship between the form and direction of urban governance – questions that are raised by regime theory. The original development of the civic project and of boosterism in Birmingham reflected a desire on the part of key actors within and beyond the City Council to redress economic decline and the associated loss of prestige. In this context the restructuring strategy for the local state was devised not only to build support for the civic project but also to build *the capacity for local governance* in the pursuit of this project within a city such as Birmingham, against a background of central government pressure. The Council's influence, and the direction of regeneration policy, is now constrained and channelled by the form of this regime and the capacity for local governance which it establishes. Recent adjustments to City Council policies reflect changes in the political balance of the Council, which together with its partners from the private sector constitutes the *governing regime* in urban regeneration activities. These adjustments may be expected to produce further changes in the structure of urban governance. To understand both the direction of urban regeneration policy and the (re)form of urban governance it is therefore necessary, as regime theory suggests, to investigate the intermediation of these through the political process, to examine the changing political balance of the regime that sustains and is sustained by the institutional ensemble, and the capacity this provides for urban governance which is more or less effective at meeting the needs of capital.

CONCLUSIONS

Conclusions may be derived from this case study regarding the relative strengths and weaknesses of our rival theoretical positions. Neo-Gramscian theory provides a cogent structural framework within which to locate the capitalist state, a framework that is largely missing from regime theory. It also addresses in a more adequate fashion the formal properties of the state (modes of representation, of intervention, of articulation as an ensemble of institutions), properties which underpin and constrain the state's activities. Finally, it introduces a novel set of dynamic concepts, such as hegemonic project and accumulation strategy, which help us to specify the direction of urban governance. But paradoxically neo-Gramscian theory tends in practice to play down the significance of political processes such as coalition building between factions or agencies, and neglects the important practical question of creating the organisational capacity and resources to govern effectively in the interests of capital. Signs of this lacuna may perhaps be detected in the failure to prioritise empirical analysis of the relationship between hegemonic projects and accumulation strategies, or the relationship between these and the formal properties of the state as an institutional ensemble.

Neo-Gramscian theory has not yet furnished an adequate account of the origins of projects or strategies or the articulation of institutional forms and policy directions in urban governance. The foregoing case study, though limited in scope, suggests that one way around this difficulty is to draw upon the lessons of regime theory. A stronger emphasis upon political dynamics would help neo-Gramscian theory to pinpoint the origins and agents of hegemonic projects and accumulation strategies and, in particular, to illustrate the way in which politics mediates between strategies and structures, between the direction and form of urban governance.

Neo-Gramscian theory provides a powerful overall framework for understanding urban governance. But this approach can usefully be developed and extended by addressing the issues raised by regime theory, its demonstration that politics matters, its concern with capacity building and with the investigation of case studies. Our understanding of the locally networked state, and of the patterns that are summarised under the broad headings of 'Fordist' and 'post-Fordist', can be advanced by opening a dialogue between neo-Marxism and neo-pluralism.

10

URBAN PARTNERSHIPS, ECONOMIC REGENERATION AND THE 'HEALTHY CITY'

Mike Sheaff

URBAN POLICY AND SOCIAL POLARISATION

After years of widening social divisions within the city, reliance upon the market as the prime mechanism for urban regeneration has been tempered by a new interest in local partnerships. Simultaneously, the manifest failure of the poorest groups in society to benefit from wealth expansion in the 1980s (e.g. Joseph Rowntree Foundation 1995), has prompted renewed debates over the compatibility of economic growth, social justice and social inclusion. Health status has taken a prominent position in some of these, as in the statement that, 'in a just society, everyone should be able to enjoy the best possible health' (Commission on Social Justice 1994: 285). This is frequently accompanied by a readiness to accept evidence that there is a causal relationship between deprivation and health.

It is not my intention to interpret the character of such a relationship, although that there is one is implicit in much of what is said. Analysis in this area has attracted important contributions (e.g. Blaxter 1990), but much remains controversial, open to variant interpretations, and consequently ambivalent for policy formation. Policy must however be premised upon some understanding of the relationship between the economic, social and personal spheres. How this is interpreted, and the discourses through which it is expressed, forms the underlying theme for this chapter.

The city has long been an important focus for understanding health and disease. From Edwin Chadwick and the early sanitary reformers, to more recent initiatives under the 'healthy city' programme, they have also been important sites for intervention. This has been expressed in the rationale for the healthy cities project in the following terms: 'Cities, as politically accountable and local units of population with the power to determine or influence policy in many of the areas of day-to-day life which affect health, were a very practical level at which to operate' (Ashton 1988).

If cities enjoy sufficient autonomy to make policy intervention effective, they also provide a context which participants can find meaningful. For Castells:

> The labour movement generated by the capitalist mode of production has largely lost its capacity to control the economy ... and the labour process and the welfare state are increasingly out of the control of the labour movement that was the key social actor of the class struggle of the last hundred years ... People ... may be unable to control the international flows of capital, but they can impose conditions on any multinational wishing to set up in their community ... when people find themselves unable to control the world, they simply shrink the world to the size of their community.
>
> (Castells 1983: 329–31)

In this view the city becomes a locus for social and political engagement because its spatial boundaries appear to provide a sufficiently manageable context for practical outcomes to be realised. Equally, a city is not a unitary phenomenon; indeed, urban regeneration strategies have potentially reinforced social and spatial cleavages from the outset through the delineation of discrete 'inner city' boundaries. This has been an important and long-standing element of government policy, although its significance and meaning has changed with other shifts in urban policy since the late 1980s.

Of these shifts, three have had a particular impact on framing the relationship between economic and social objectives. The first has been the increased emphasis upon economic objectives, with a concomitant reduction in the role of social and environmental schemes. Associated with this, competition between cities over anticipated outcomes began to replace needs-based systems of assessment for resource allocation purposes.

Secondly, local authorities found themselves playing a new role in these processes. Expectations that they enter into 'partnerships', particularly with the private sector, as in City Challenge, Urban Partnership and subsequently the Single Regeneration Budget, followed the introduction of government appointed bodies, notably Development Corporations, which were granted power over many traditional local authority responsibilities within designated areas. Thirdly, as in several other areas of government policy, greater emphasis came to be placed upon self-help, personal responsibility and individualism counteracting a more 'collectivist' culture.

Tensions and contradictions between economically oriented urban regeneration strategies and health and social objectives arise independently of the city but find their expression within particular social settings. A local study provides an opportunity to consider connections between economic and social objectives on the one hand, with national and local relationships on the other.

This chapter considers some experiences in the city of Plymouth, predominantly focusing upon the relationship between urban partnerships, economic regeneration and the 'healthy city'. It begins by locating the latter within a broader health promotion context, before going on to describe developments in Plymouth since the late 1980s. The final section considers some of the ways in which both health and economic behaviour may relate to wider discourses, notably those around claims concerning 'rights' and 'duties'.

HEALTH PROMOTION AND 'HEALTHY CITIES'

The heterogeneity of health promotion joins a diverse array of practices in its name, and several means of interpreting similarities and differences are available (see Bunton *et al.* 1995). One aspect is the 'collective–individual' continuum (Davison and Davey-Smith 1995), within which the healthy city project has affinities with the 'new public health' perspective: less collectivist than Fabian or Marxist perspectives, but not as individualist as either 'Health of the Nation' or, especially, 'free-market' perspectives.

Important though this is, the 'collective–individual' continuum is only one relevant dimension, as is acknowledged by Beattie (1991) in his two-dimensional typology incorporating the focus (individual–collective) and mode (authoritative–negotiated) of intervention (see Figure 10.1).

Beattie locates the healthy city project within the 'legislative action for health' tradition, concerned with the development of 'healthy public policies'. As one early British advocate of the project explained, it was based on a recognition of, 'the necessity for social as well as individual action and for explicit policy with legislation where appropriate' (Ashton 1988). However, Beattie notes that support came mainly from Labour authorities, several of which were dismantled in 1986 while others were hit by capping restrictions. What is more, whereas the model being espoused attended to issues of equity, this was a period when the government sought 'to forestall

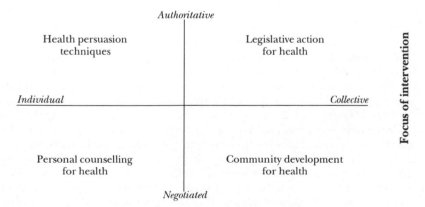

Figure 10.1 Alternative models of health promotion strategies
Source: Beattie (1991)

and eliminate unwelcome public attention to health inequalities' (Beattie 1991: 173). Elsewhere, the assessment of one American-based initiator of the project was that 'The temptation in many programmes has been to avoid the healthy public policy issues' (Duhl 1992).

Moreover, critics of this kind of focus were not restricted to the right. Others saw it as a form of 'collectivist authoritarianism', lacking a necessary wider community engagement. In contrast to a more traditional 'personal counselling for health', with its emphasis on personal autonomy, self-determination and 'self-empowerment', this view stressed 'community development for health' through 'self-organisation and mutual assistance within groups of like-minded people' (Beattie 1991: 176).

Consequently, since its launch in Lisbon in 1986, the healthy city initiative has been far from uniform. Indeed, one of the original objectives made clear an intention to seek models of good practice which would provide 'a variety of entry points to action depending on the city's perceived priorities' (Ashton 1992). These might range from major environmental action to support for individual lifestyle changes. To some extent, this all-embracing approach appears to re-introduce the 'collective–individual' continuum as the key category, although another aspect of this is the scope for constructing health in terms of 'rights' or 'duties'.

The relationship between rights and duties is a familiar one in the sociology of health, most obviously in the Parsonian sick-role. Of relevance here is its extension in the 'late modern regime', where it has been suggested: 'The contemporary citizen is increasingly attributed with responsibilities to ceaselessly maintain and improve her or his own health' (Bunton and Burrows 1995: 208). In many ways this accords with much conventional health promotion in which personal responsibilities tran-scend notions of health as a right, and individual lifestyle rather than the social environment provides the focus for intervention.

Although the healthy city initiative adopted a very different perspective, a renewed emphasis upon personal responsibilities is emerging within current dominant political discourse, as in Tony Blair's claim that the 'clear dividing line in British politics ... [is] the notion of duty ... the rights we receive should reflect the duties we owe' (Blair 1995).

Re-evaluating the traditional rights-based discourse of the left reflects a broader reassessment of the relationship between the individual and society, including post-war models of health and welfare services. However, although 'bureaucratic paternalism' must bear its share of responsibility for disempowering individuals, the view that rights are contingent upon personal behaviour can evolve into a far uglier form of authoritarianism. As the founding programme of the Nazi party clearly identified, personal duty can become the means of achieving the goals of the state: 'The state must apply itself to raising the standard of health ... and increasing bodily efficiency by legally obligatory gymnastics and sports, and by extensive use of clubs engaged in the physical training of the young' (quoted in Carpenter 1980).

The objective of 'better health' is thus a highly malleable one, with its distinguishing features being fashioned by the discourses through which it is expressed. In this the healthy city project has potentially a significant role to play, although not independently of other social processes within the city. The following account of experiences in Plymouth, describing aspects of urban regeneration and the healthy city initiative, illustrates some of the competing pressures which confront cities.

PLYMOUTH, URBAN REGENERATION AND THE 'HEALTHY CITY'

Using data drawn from the 1981 census, Levitt (1986) argued that Plymouth was not a deprived city when compared to England as a whole. Even on this data, however, it could be shown that, when disaggregated, 'certain areas of Plymouth, on certain indicators, are highly deprived compared to the national average' (Dunkerley 1991: 175–6; see also Abbott 1988).

In any event, by the second half of the 1980s irresistible change came as centuries of naval dominance were brought to an end. This had a dual significance. The Admiralty had historically influenced the broader character of the local economy, with some evidence indicating it had discouraged more diverse employment (Chalkley and Goodridge 1991: 79–80), but while undermining scope for this to continue the more immediate impact of naval decline was upon employment within Devonport dockyard.

In 1961 the dockyard employed nearly 19,000 civilian workers, representing almost one in five of all local jobs. A gradual decline occurred during the following two decades, although by 1981 employment was still over 15,000. The decline soon accelerated however, and by the later years of the decade little more than 10,000 dockyard jobs remained. In addition, alternative sources of employment – particularly in 'producer services' such as banking, insurance, finance and other business services – were not growing as elsewhere (by 3 per cent in Plymouth compared to 15 per cent in the UK as a whole from 1984–7). The result was that Plymouth became the only major town in the South West to experience a net fall in employment in the middle 1980s (Bishop 1988).

The city became an 'Urban Priority Area' (UPA) in 1987, with Urban Programme funding rising from an initial £433,000 in 1987/8 to £1,267,000 by 1990/1. However, this failed to halt economic decline. Employment in the dockyard plummeted to around 5,000 as the city's rate of unemployment rose faster than in any of the other fifty-seven UPAs.

Using 1991 census data, the Department of Environment's newly introduced measure of deprivation, the 'Index of Local Conditions' (ILC) (Department of Environment 1994), ranked Plymouth forty-second out of 360 districts, but twelfth in terms of the severity of disadvantage in the worst wards. Notwithstanding the difficulties associated with such indices, the consequences of economic decline in the 1980s are readily apparent. This was reflected in the city's Single Regeneration Budget (SRB) bid which described the priority area as largely corresponding with:

the city's three worst wards, as identified in the DoE's Index of Local Conditions, which on a national ranking indicates that the area contains a greater intensity of deprivation than any other local authority outside London and Birmingham.

(Plymouth 2000 Partnership 1994)

Although historical constraints on economic diversification were being weakened through dockyard decline, new curbs on local autonomy came with government urban policy requirements. One obvious example of this has been the encouragement of a discrete spatial focus for economic regeneration. Boundaries have not always been coterminous – with those of the Task Force, the Development Corporation and the SRB priority areas being somewhat different – but together they form a distinct area which incorporates the three most deprived wards in the city.

One result is that many areas of deprivation fall outside of this 'inner city' boundary. Six of Plymouth's twenty wards in the city account for 41 per cent of households in the city without a car, 42 per cent of the city's unemployed, 50 per cent of children in low income households and 64 per cent of 'unsuitable accommodation' (each of these are indicators used in the ILC). The area covered by these six wards extends considerably beyond the SRB priority area, outwards towards the north and west fringes of the city. In several respects, the spatial distribution of deprivation reflects an east–west divide across the city rather than a concentration within a distinctive 'inner city'.

An emphasis on spatial location may divert attention from the social processes involved in regeneration towards a focus on pieces of land, although to some extent this tendency has been tempered by newer elements of government policy. This is evident in the encouragement of local partnerships, but also in the desire to facilitate a more entrepreneurial culture. Each of these has in turn been influenced by the increased economic focus.

The local partnership taking responsibility for determining urban regeneration, 'Plymouth 2000', is a tripartite one, embracing the local authority, the 'private sector' and the 'community'. In practice, the private sector, and especially the 'community' are sufficiently heterogeneous to make direct representation difficult to achieve. Three closely related consequences flow from this. First, central directive has been a highly significant influence upon development proposals; secondly, those sections of the private sector perceiving advantage in joining the partnership are most likely to utilise the opportunity; and thirdly, a relatively undeveloped community sector has found itself in a weaker position than other elements of the partnership. More significantly, the expectation that urban funding is used to attract other money puts local community groups at a distinct disadvantage. Efforts to strengthen community influence in the partnership have to confront these inherent power imbalances.

It is also noteworthy that partnership arrangements are required to administer £950,000 in the first year of SRB funding, even though this is considerably less than the £1.25 million Urban Programme funding received by the city in 1990/1. At the same time, the Development Corporation and Task Force are not subject to the same obligations but do experience more direct central control.

The other new element in government policy, the enhancement of individual responsibility, has also confronted difficulties. In part these arise from the accumulated impact of three centuries of naval dominance, which hardly created a flourishing environment for a strong entrepreneurial culture. Intentions to overcome this are most evident in proposals from the Task Force which, in a list of local 'weaknesses', identified: 'Endemic parochialism and lack of confidence among local people. Initiative and energy are low and business culture is lacking' (Plymouth Task Force 1995).

Several initiatives have been encouraged to stimulate self-employment and small business ventures. Alongside these have been attempts to develop 'community enterprise', through community economic development trusts, co-operatives, credit unions and the like. The differences between these are considerable, even though each represents a response to the call for a more entrepreneurial culture in which individual, or small-group, endeavour replaces traditional employment relations and expectations.

This sketch of aspects of economic regeneration is inadequate to convey the full character of current developments, but provides a context for appreciating the bifurcation of 'economic' and 'social' policy spheres. To a degree this separation mirrors shifting organisational areas of engagement, particularly those of local government and the health service.

Plymouth was declared as a 'healthy city' by the city council in 1989, although by 1991, when political control of the council passed from Conservative to Labour, an officer's report noted, 'little real progress has been made over the last two years'. A proposal to create two new posts to take the project forward subsequently foundered as the city experienced a reduction in its Standard Spending Assessment. Ironically, in the very same year the local health authority acknowledged that an additional £2 million being made available to it, 'is justified by recognition of the needs of those in Plymouth living in areas of social and economic deprivation and of the substantial number in the lower income groups' (Plymouth Health Authority 1992). These centrally determined resource issues were significant in shifting some of the initiative from local government to the health service.

In May 1992, for example, the health authority introduced a project to pilot new health schemes in St Peter's ward, which has the highest levels of deprivation in the city and the worst health status. But however innovative these might be, they inevitably reflect areas of health service involvement rather than those of local government, such as housing and employment, and as such tend to avoid some of the 'healthy public policy' issues. Despite opportunities for developing a complementary relationship between economic and health initiatives, the separate organisational arrangements around funding sources and regimes has meant responses to deprivation have been substantially divorced from one another.

At the same time, national policy frameworks can have a powerful impact on the determination of local priorities. This is illustrated in Plymouth's receipt of £1.8 million capital funding under the 'Urban

Partnership' programme in 1993/4 for road and parking improvements. For this the government required evidence of private sector support, but more tangibly demanded that the city council match it with £1.8 million from capital receipts, which were then subject to a temporary 'relaxation' of restrictions.

In contrast, Plymouth's City Challenge bid had sought £7 million for housing improvements, but this was unsuccessful and a more modest £1.3 million was sought in the SRB bid. However, due to limits upon the city's capital programme, it was not possible to match even this and no housing schemes were included in the first year of the SRB programme. Given the well-documented association between housing and health (and between traffic and health for that matter), the priorities encouraged by government policy are illuminating.

A reduction in the importance of social and community development is evident in other comparisons between the City Challenge and SRB submissions. Against a £4.4 million bid in the City Challenge submission for projects intended to 'enhance community life and improve social fabric' (of which £533,000 was identified for specifically health-related projects), £1.3 million was sought in the SRB submission for those designed to 'enhance the quality of life of local people, including their health and cultural and sports opportunities' (of which £200,000 was for health-related projects).

Despite all this, with additional deprivation-related funding available to the health service came an opportunity for several projects, which might previously have sought Urban Programme money, to secure financial support. This may have served to reduce conflict over diminishing resources available through urban regeneration funding, even if the result has been to further reinforce a division between the 'economic' and the 'social' and the shift from local government to the health service.

A need for closer inter-organisational co-operation for the healthy city project was recognised in 1993 with the establishment of an officer-based steering group, including city council and health service staff. However, boundaries do not solely arise between organisations. Professional disciplines and departments, whether in the health service or local government, reflect and reinforce variant approaches towards the relationship between health objectives and other aspects of service delivery and management.

One factor contributing to these differences is the way in which health is conceived in relation to rights and duties. For example, the 'Healthy Plymouth charter' has formally adopted an emphasis upon rights, although somewhat ambiguously seeks to avoid a dichotomy with personal duty by expressing a commitment to: 'The right to health: recognising that health is a basic human right, the responsibility for which is both social and individual' (Healthy Plymouth 1994). Interestingly, in later versions of this document the word 'individual' was replaced with 'organisational'.

The charter reflects the all-encompassing approach of the Lisbon conference, and also implicitly requires an equally wide range of participants. In this connection it was soon acknowledged that the officer-based steering group was too narrow and its composition was broadened to include a majority of members from community organisations. Further moves towards a partnership approach are reflected in the creation of a wider-based Healthy Plymouth Forum, open to all organisations supporting the charter. Although several features of the project correspond with the community development for health model, other pressures work in different directions. In particular, evaluation requirements of funding agencies raise greater difficulties for longer-term projects, such as those using a community development approach, than those for which changes in individual behaviour can be more readily identified. This issue may come to have growing importance because of continued restrictions on local government resources, even though an element of SRB money has been identified for the healthy city project.

This money comes under the overall control of the primarily economically focused SRB partnership which is substantially independent of the partnership around the healthy city initiative. In both cases there is genuine evidence of a broadening of involvement beyond traditional structures, but the potential appears for the creation of two rather distinct sets of 'partners', focused around 'economic' and 'social' spheres respectively.

This may reflect difficulties of going beyond the establishment of a partnership capable of endorsing a set of specific development proposals for a distinct spatial area. It is much harder to achieve a broad consensus around wider policy objectives. An illustration of the potential difficulties came in a survey of city centre employers conducted by Plymouth Business School in 1994 which noted:

> the majority of respondents do not feel able to either revise recruitment practices to give priority to minority/special need groups or participate in customised training schemes targeted at specific groups such as inner city unemployed persons.
>
> (Chaston and Mangles, n.d.: 15)

If the healthy city project is to embrace 'public policies' then issues such as employment can hardly be neglected, for whatever the precise causal processes the close association between unemployment and poor health status is undeniable (e.g. Bartley 1994). And yet major partners within the new urban policy-making processes may be less willing to accept some of the consequences of this. The possibility arises of a divergence between urban groups around a private sector/economic axis on the one hand and a public service/social axis on the other, with many points of tension between them. Alternatively, new routes to reconciliation may emerge and possible forms these may take are explored in the final section.

HEALTH, THE ECONOMY AND POWER IN THE CITY

Despite an incipient fragmentation of economic and social policy initiatives, a potentially unifying theme has been a shift from what Beattie described in health promotion strategies as 'authoritative' to 'negotiated' styles (Beattie 1991). A similar framework can be applied to economic development strategies, allowing parallels to be drawn between community development for health and community economic development, or between legislative action for health and traditional economic planning strategies.

A rather more theorised version of the 'authoritative–negotiated' dimension contrasts modernist and post-modernist paradigms for healthy city projects. The modernist project, which envisages a 'superior rationalist solution to a set of hitherto insuperable problems', is challenged by 'the truly post-modern conception of healthy cities ... with its emphasis on the values of locality and community, aestheticism, relativism and private behaviour' (Kelly *et al.* 1993: 166).

However, as experiences in Plymouth indicate, a simple dualism cannot accommodate the complexities and subtleties involved. Partly this is because the modernist project itself incorporated alternative ways of conceptualising the city. From a belief in an 'invisible hand' ordering its complex arrangements, these extended through the 'medical paradigm' of Chadwick and others to Engels's view of the city located within wider social relations of production (Donald 1992).

The second of these paradigms, which asserted the power of human intelligence to diagnose and cure urban ills, gained the greater influence, although the idea that the market offers a better mechanism for regulation has been more evident recently. The idea of the city as a total system is replaced by one in which urban spaces became parcels of land (Donald 1992).

Despite such differentiation, modernity is undoubtedly characterised by a search for systemic solutions to the problem of achieving social order, integration and equilibrium. Whether planning or the market provides the mechanism for regulation, each assumes harmony to be a realisable objective. Such optimism may be naive, but the alternative prospect of urban disintegration and decay seems far more threatening, bringing to mind Abrams's image of 'The Hobbesian quality of urban life – a war of all against all contained within a continued and precarious domination' (Abrams 1978: 33).

People may want to 'shrink the world to the size of their community' (Castells 1983: 331), but local strategies cannot be entirely autonomous, as is evident in the greater acceptance of the exigencies of the capitalist market in local economic strategies compared to a decade ago. But the sheer failure of market mechanisms successfully to regenerate cities has prompted a renewed search for alternatives. New urban partnerships, seeking social and economic order while avoiding the perceived excesses of bureaucratic planning and unfettered markets, nevertheless reflect rather than replace prevailing power relations. For even though greater self-reliance and personal responsibility may extend the economic and social participation of individuals, they do little to alter the social forces within which this occurs. As Donnison noted in his account of Glasgow, 'policies which assume that stricken cities and their most deprived areas can, with a little help, solve their own problems are bound to fail' (Donnison 1987: 273).

It is in the context of prevailing power relations that the earlier distinction between health being considered as a right or duty gains significance. More specifically, where it is viewed as a right it is likely that equity will be an important goal. This is incorporated into the Plymouth healthy city charter, as elsewhere within healthy cities, marking it apart from more individualistic and market-oriented alternatives. The goal of equity, however, implies a need for processes of observation, measurement and regulation: that is, forms of social surveillance which may themselves conflict with individual rights. This is the contradiction described by Turner (1987) as the 'Foucault paradox' and implicit in attempts to reduce health inequalities.

Challenges to 'authoritative' approaches may reflect a necessary rejection of unwarranted bureaucratic or professional control systems – and post-modern celebration of diversity may provide a welcome alternative to drab uniformity – but there is another side to all of this. This is the risk of legitimising the *status quo* and the unequal distribution of power and resources which it sustains.

Power operates at many different levels but if it is treated as an undifferentiated and unitary concept then its particular meaning in specific social contexts can go unacknowledged. Governments, local authorities, markets and partnerships do not operate in identical ways. They reflect differing social interests, sometimes of a conflicting character, which are almost invariably grounded within imbalances of power. Thus it would be mistaken to regard urban partnerships with a kind of naive pluralism which assumes they incorporate a wide diversity of local interests, each balanced in social strength and able to negotiate freely. The reality is very obviously different, although 'structural' inequalities can be strengthened or weakened by the form that social dialogue takes within the city.

Recent debates about the so-called underclass demonstrate the continuing capacity for explanations of social phenomena in terms of individual or group psychological characteristics to gain currency. Where this is accompanied by the prioritisation of personal duty, the prospect emerges of exacerbated local conflict as certain groups are identified as worthy of blame. Whether family poverty, and accompanying childhood illness, is attributed to the growth of lone-parenthood – or whether the target is the long-term unemployed, council tenants or whoever – opportunities will always exist to absolve more powerful social actors of culpability. An important question for the healthy cities project is whether it is capable of bringing poverty, inequality and exclusion to the centre of urban policy.

Several practical implications flow from this. One concerns striking the optimum balance between independence and incorporation of healthy city projects and urban regeneration strategies and partnerships. Tensions between the 'economic' and the 'social' – and between the spheres of production and reproduction – also have important consequences for understanding the relationship of gender and urban social processes, an aspect beyond the scope of this chapter. It has been around issues concerning health, housing, social and other public services that many urban movements have arisen. In whatever ways these may develop in the future, the claims to which they give rise are unlikely to be satisfied by solutions reliant upon either personal responsibility or market forces.

In their place, principles of rights, equity and justice may achieve a renewed relevance. Because their meaning is open to dispute, itself reflective of conflicting social interests, and because they are fundamentally relational claims, they may presage a social vision for the city in ways unavailable to more individualistic solutions. The language and symbols which are used can themselves prefigure different social relations, giving rise to alternative conceptions of how the city might be. In this, unravelling the 'specific complexes of domination in which particular cities are embedded' (Abrams 1978: 33) represents an essential starting point for an analysis of urban regeneration. For things to be made better, power imbalances arising both within and outside of the city must be challenged.

11

POLICING LATE MODERNITY

Changing strategies of crime management in contemporary Britain

Gordon Hughes

> The term '*crime prevention*' is often narrowly interpreted and this reinforces the view that it is solely the responsibility of the police. On the other hand, the term '*community safety*', is open to wider interpretation and could encourage greater participation from all sections of the community in the fight against crime.
>
> (Home Office 1991)

INTRODUCTION

The above statement provides us with a typically vague definition of community safety from the most influential report to date in Britain on the potential significance of the concept for crime management strategies. This chapter is based largely on current research on one such strategy in an English Midlands county, 'Middleshire'. A key aim is to contextualise the specific policy processes at work in the rural/urban mix of 'Middleshire' in terms of the points of both convergence and divergence between developments in this locality and the broader trends on crime management emanating from the central state. However, the scope of this chapter is restricted to what may be termed routine policing and crime prevention. It does not comment on 'paramilitary policing' (Jefferson 1990) nor on international trends in policing in the context of 'Fortress Europe' (McLaughlin 1994), although I would suggest that there is some evidence of a latter-day 'convergence thesis' in discourses on crime prevention and community policing around the world.

Much contemporary research into the 'policy process' has emphasised the strong possibility of a 'gap' between the stage of policy formulation at the centre and that of policy implementation at the level of subnational government (Marsh and Rhodes 1992). This chapter will explore this crucial research issue and, in the process, critique two dominant sociological interpretations of policing/crime prevention trends, namely Radical Totalitarianism and Sceptical Pluralism, which are neglectful of local, countervailing forces at work in this contested terrain.

Before this, I outline in brief some of the major policy developments in 'routine' policing, crime prevention and consultation/accountability issues during the last two decades from central government in Britain. All this is in advance of the third section which focuses on local trends and recent developments in the county of 'Middleshire' which may point to a more complex and contested terrain on law and order matters than is often assumed in the literature on national trends.

THE WIDER PICTURE: THE NATIONAL POLITICS OF LAW AND ORDER AND 'COMMUNITY SAFETY'

During the last two decades, the problem of law and order may be said to have held centre stage in British politics. From being an issue marked by cross-party consensus, policing and the 'management' of crime in Britain have been thoroughly politicised since the 1970s (Reiner 1992). It would not be appropriate to enter into this whole debate here. Instead, the more modest purpose of this section is to place local developments regarding 'community safety' in the context of the wider *structuring and constraining but not necessarily determining* initiatives and legislation emanating from recent national government policy. The actual impact of central government diktats on 'sub-national government' (Gray 1993) should not be read as one-way domination from the centre with no room for manoeuvre and negotiation but nor can national pressures be ignored in any evaluation of local and 'subnational' policies and strategies on crime management.

Home Office concerns about the costs of policing

In recent years, the government litany of the three 'E's – economy, efficiency and effectiveness – together with the ideology of managerialism, has come to affect the organisation and operational work of the police (McLaughlin and Muncie 1994). 'Policing by objectives' has now become the established canon of modern policing in Britain and elsewhere (Goldstein 1990; Reiner 1994), further evidence of convergent, institutional trends in the era of 'late modernity' (Giddens 1991). Of particular importance to the fate of community safety initiatives is the recent decision by the British government to establish measurable, national objectives for policing. These may marginalise yet further social crime prevention strategies, given the difficulty of 'measuring' their success in terms of readily quantifiable performance indicators. The future mandate of the British police may be much more focused on quasi-militaristic public order control and serious crime investigation at the cost of the 'social service' dimension to British policing. In the current situation of uncertainty, the British police appears, almost for the first time in its history, to be a public service desperate for allies outside of central government.

Home Office initiatives on 'partnerships against crime' and 'community safety'

At the same time as we have witnessed pressure for the police to be more business-like and focused in their activities, the last decade has also seen a growing concern in the Home Office for the police and other agencies of social control to work together and form 'partnerships' with the public. In passing, it should be noted that there is a seeming contradiction between this drive towards 'community policing' and 'community safety' and the developments both noted immediately above and in the Home Secretary's 'get tough on crime' and 'prisons work' statements in 1994 and 1995, inspired by the current American policy drift to penal retribution (Rose 1995). Jones et al. (1994) may be correct in their thesis that recent years have seen the rise of a new paradigm regarding crime prevention. The view that the only proper response to crime is punishment is replaced in academic and official circles by the belief that retribution and punishment will not reduce the aggregate level of crime, and so the reduction of crime must be seen as a separate objective from the punishment of offenders. Out of this paradigm shift emerges the current discourse on crime prevention/ community safety. However, Jones et al. go on to argue that this way of thinking has had comparatively little influence on popular culture and '[p]oliticians of all parties find it easy and convenient to appeal to the old way of thinking' (Jones et al. 1994: 302–3). Thus, alongside the new discourse on crime prevention, the old approach continues to be a central plank of law and order politics in Britain.

To return to the discourse on partnership, such partnerships between the police, the public and other agencies are, arguably, part of what has been termed the 'Government's accountability package' (Morgan 1992). In effect, this package has bypassed any democratic structures of accountability and, instead, 'espoused a model of police accountability as stewardship with the police consulting more widely before taking decisions and providing fuller ex post facto explanations of events' (Morgan and Swift 1988: 427).

The key developmental stages to this 'partnership' initiative will be briefly outlined in chronological sequence. The 1984 Joint Circular on 'Crime Prevention' may be seen as a watershed, given its emphasis on the principle that crime prevention must be accepted as a significant and integral goal of public policy, both centrally and locally (Home Office 1984). In this circular, particular stress is placed on the need for a co-ordinated approach and joint strategies involving partnerships against crime. Although more often rhetoric than reality around the country (NACRO 1991; Jones et al. 1994), the idea of 'partnership' had clearly arrived.

By the end of the decade, the circular *Tackling Crime* (Home Office 1989) showed the further development of the partnership and community orientation to crime prevention in the Home Office. Particular attention was given in the circular to the problem of co-ordination, or rather the lack of it, between agencies which made up the criminal justice system. This circular led the way for what was to prove the key inspiration for much of the subsequent local government social crime prevention schemes of the 1990s – namely, the so-called Morgan Report of 1991.

The main thrust of the Morgan Report is that the concept of 'crime prevention' is somewhat limiting in scope and has generally been police-driven, with other agencies having only a marginal stake in it. Effectively community safety as a guiding idea is heralded as a way of moving beyond a 'situational' definition of crime prevention to a broader 'social' definition of crime prevention. Whilst acknowledging that the case for a partnership approach is hardly tested, Morgan notes strangely that the case for partnership is 'virtually unchallenged'. Crime prevention at the time of the report was seen as a peripheral issue to the major agencies and a 'truly core activity for none of them' (Home Office 1991: 3).

The Morgan Report then goes on to suggest that the local authority is 'the natural focus for coordinating, in collaboration with the police, the broad range of activities directed at improving community safety ... Any meaningful local structure for crime prevention must relate to the local democratic structure' (Home Office 1991: 4). Morgan thus supports the notion that local authorities be given the statutory duty to co-ordinate crime prevention/community safety strategies for their locality. The report also argues that sufficient resources to make this change must be forth-coming from central government. In passing, we may note that the recommendations regarding both local authorities' statutory role and resourcing have not been taken up by central government.

Like many reports in the past, the Morgan Report has been shelved by government or, at best, used quite selectively. This is not, however, to deny its significant effect on local authorities, including Middleshire, since its publication. It may be noted that the Morgan Report comes across for the most part as a report written by officers for officers. In particular, the discussion of how these officer groups relate to issues of democratic accountability is cursory in nature. In particular, the role of the Police Authority in community safety is largely noticeable by its absence in the report.

It was suggested above that central government has been selective in its use of the Morgan Report. In explicit terms, no further mention has been made of it in subsequent circulars from the Home Office. However, the language and rhetoric of both partnership and community safety are very prominent in the most recent pamphlet on crime prevention (Home Office 1994). If taken seriously, the pamphlet seems to be calling for what may be inelegantly termed 'the citizenisation of crime control'. Once more, there is an appeal to the much vaunted but ill-defined 'active citizen' to play a key role in both surveillance and policing. The implications for professional policing with a clear legal mandate are potentially worrying. This noted, the pamphlet confidently asserts that 'the power of partnerships in beating crime' is proved but no convincing evidence, other than a few highly selective examples, is given. Undaunted, three complementary partner-ships are presented as initiatives to be launched nationally in 1995: the already well-established Neighbourhood Watch Schemes, Street Watch and

Neighbourhood Constables. It is Street Watch which is the most contentious, and, in some eyes, humorous and ill-conceived 'community
partnership'. The catchword, according to the pamphlet, is 'vigilant' –
although critics may fear that an extra 'e' on the end of vigilant is a great
risk. The vagueness of the scheme is perhaps best captured in the Home
Secretary's 'soundbite' that the work involves 'walking with a purpose'.
Perhaps the most telling feature of this latest Home Office initiative is that
all the schemes are voluntary and low cost.

The future of police authorities and consultation with the public

As a result of the debates surrounding the eventual Police and Magistrates'
Courts Act (1994), there has been much uncertainty about the future role
and make-up of police authorities. The fear of what is now often called 'the
democratic deficit' (McLaughlin 1994), epitomised by the appointment of
non-elected individuals to sit on 'quangos' and other democratically
unaccountable bodies, has been to the fore in public debate (see Reiner
and Spencer 1993). In particular, the original proposals for the restructuring of police authority membership to tip the balance firmly in the
direction of Home Secretary-approved appointees appear to have cast an
important shadow over local policing and consultative arrangements across
the country, to which I shall return below.

The Police and Magistrates' Act has the stated aim of creating more
powerful and business-like police authorities which will give more leadership to the local police service. This greater autonomy is in turn balanced
by the police authority now having the statutory responsibility for the
performance of the force. It is widely recognised that police authorities in
the past have been somewhat toothless and ineffective, in part due to the
calibre of the membership and also because of Home Office domination
(Morgan and Swift 1987; Jones *et al.* 1994). Viewed positively, the current
changes may help invigorate local democratic influence over policing
policy. From April 1995, police authorities are responsible for the establishment of the local policing plan, which in turn will be the basis of local
accountability. Of particular importance here, consultation with the public
will be a crucial formal concern of the police authorities. A particular
emphasis, then, is on the question of how to improve accountability by
improving local consultation with the public. Local developments in
Middleshire and elsewhere, with regard to policing and crime prevention
initiatives, cannot be understood outside of this wider national context of
the debate on police accountability.

A BRIEF EXCURSUS ON TWO SOCIOLOGICAL ORTHODOXIES ON 'COMMUNITY' INITIATIVES IN CRIME CONTROL

The broad-brush sketch of 'community'-based crime control initiatives
outlined above has been descriptive in character. This is not to imply that

such developments in the 'crime control industry' (Christie 1993) have been immune from sociological analysis. Indeed, two perspectives are worthy of further comment and appraisal. I term the two major orthodoxies 'Radical Totalitarianism' (see also Ericson 1994) and 'Sceptical Pluralism'.

Radical Totalitarianism and the 'surveillance society'

Radical Totalitarianism is a body of work associated with the authors of a radical disposition, particularly influenced by both Marxism and, increasingly, Foucauldian theory (see Foucault 1977; Cohen 1985; Davis 1992 and Poster 1990, among others). What unites this body of work is a shared concern over the broad trends at work in social control whereby the late twentieth-century period is witnessing an evermore penetrative, all-seeing 'panoptical' system of social surveillance. Such developments as community policing and community safety schemes are but specific manifestations of this broader, globalising process.

Accordingly, the 'partnerships' described above would be viewed as but one manifestation of the immersion of civil society in the ever-expanding social control machine, thus confirming the grand thesis of the 'extension of social control'. Community safety, I would suggest, would be seen by such theorists as an ideological category which offers us a dystopian vision of an authoritarian or neo-fascist communitarianism. In turn, the appeal to community in the context of the penetrative social control machine feeds off, and contributes to, a further chilling of the climate of 'risk' and 'danger'.

The attractions of this grand theory are hard to resist. Glimpses of dystopia have a powerful appeal, not least to intellectuals who, doubtless, gain vicarious pleasure from being on the 'edge', compared to the supposedly slumbering masses. With the coming *fin de siècle*, the concern over an apparently growing anomie, together with the onward march of impersonal control processes, is not confined to radical criminology (see Reiner 1994: 757). It would indeed be ill-conceived to write off the analysis offered by Radical Totalitarianism. However, there are some difficulties with the radical approach to social control initiatives which limit its salience to the sociological study of such specific examples as the emergent community safety initiatives in a county like Middleshire. First, there is the problem of theoretical foreclosure, associated with the grand theories of Marxism and Foucauldian discourse analysis, whereby the answers to questions are already known without recourse to empirical testing. There is also little scope for the specifics of locality and difference in such broad deterministic theorising as is found in Radical Totalitarianism. The grand design offered by radical totalitarian theory may thus both exaggerate the dystopian tendencies at work and the power of the intrusive social control machine, whilst simultaneously underestimating the scope for local resistances, manoeuvring and negotiation from countervailing alliances in particular localities. Put briefly, the present and the future may be more open-ended and complex than implied in the radical totalitarian vision of trends in social control, including that of crime prevention.

Sceptical Pluralism

Most mainstream sociological research on crime prevention is both sceptical about the achievements of such policy and practice initiatives and avoids any strict adherence to a monocausal theory, preferring the appeal of an unspoken pluralist approach for the interpretation of these trends. The body of work is empirically driven and speaks with a fairly uniform voice of scepticism, if not impossibilism, about both British and international trends in crime prevention, community policing and consultation (see, for example, Bottoms 1990; Jones *et al.* 1994; Morgan 1992; Pease 1994; Weatheritt 1986). According to this perspective, the achievements of community policing are very limited to date, with success largely rhetorical in character rather than tangible. On crime prevention initiatives, certain commentators such as Bottoms and Pease do highlight the tangible achievements of primary prevention in particular, but, again, the overall message is that crime prevention of a more ambitious 'social' kind remains both marginal to the work of most agencies and unproven as a success. An even clearer message is conveyed about police consultation with the community on crime and policing. On this front, the academic 'audit' gives an unambiguous thumbs-down, with Scarman's consultative committees pronounced as mere 'talking shops' of a very unrepresentative nature. Little comment has been made, as yet, on the idea and practice of community safety. Pease, perhaps, speaks for this tradition in his recent critical aside on the Morgan Committee's promotion of the term community safety as a replacement for the concept of crime prevention: 'The extreme vagueness of the Morgan Committee's definition of community safety gives little confidence that a revised definition will prove a satisfactory focus for the work' (Pease 1994: 687).

In many ways, it is difficult to dissent from this overall negative verdict which emanates from the sceptical pluralist tradition of research. However, this national, and international, picture may, like that of Radical Totalitarianism's globalising theory, inevitably underplay certain specific local developments which may presage trends of a potentially important kind. Comments, such as Pease's above, may also underestimate the radical potential of such notions as community safety when they are appropriated by local networks in opposition to, or at least in negotiation with, central government's strategies of crime management. Accordingly, Pease's verdict on the term 'community safety' may itself be flawed in that it neglects how such a vague and seemingly empty idea may have potential to be 'filled' with radical proposals which the 'centre' may find difficult to manage and control.

I will now attempt to build on the work of this sceptical pluralist tradition by arguing for the importance of studying subnational government initiatives, within the context of specific localities with their own traditions and histories.

LOCAL ALLIANCES AND CONFLICTS OVER COMMUNITY SAFETY AND ACCOUNTABILITY IN MIDDLESHIRE

The research findings summarised in this chapter are based on a study of policy formulation and implementation in an English Midlands county, Middleshire, from 1991 to the present day. They cast light on both the conflicts and alliances involving local 'policy networks' and the 'local governmental inner circle' with regard to the interwoven issues of community safety, crime prevention and democratic accountability of public service deliverers.

The current situation in Middleshire (April 1995) would appear to be something of a cease-fire. A compromise has been reached whereby a progressive managerialism (associated with officers committed to multi-agency corporatism) is uneasily merged with social democratic communitarianism (associated with an influential elected member elite from the centre/left). However, the picture is even more complex when the machinations of all seven district authorities which make up the county are considered. In truth, the situation varies across the county, with the more rural and Conservative-led authorities resistant or obdurate towards what is at times considered either a Labour-driven policy or an example of a county council off-loading responsibilities for financial reasons. The full account of this local drama falls outside the remit of this chapter. In general terms, it should be noted that the story which unfolds from the research is not a simple one of unified local resistance to centrally developed trends but nor is it one of supine obedience to the centralist agenda.

Community safety strategy for Middleshire: an officer vision of inter-agency corporatism

Put briefly, the strategy developed in the early 1990s had four key objectives – namely, to provide a communication framework for all agencies; to assist in the integration of community initiatives; to enhance co-ordination through corporate policies; and to reduce the cost of crime. The philosophy of the strategy was clearly indebted to the Morgan Report and was largely 'social' crime-prevention-driven and sought to broaden out the notion to take on wider community issues regarding fear of crime and sense of safety. If successful, the strategy was meant to enable a co-ordinated approach to the management and amelioration of social problems and also help realise the ambition of making community safety a 'truly core activity' of all relevant agencies.

The corporate community safety structure, produced in 1993, was certainly hierarchical in nature and officer-driven. As with the Morgan Report, the Police Authority was noticeable for its absence. The top of the structure was occupied by the Interdependency Group (IDG) for Middleshire. The IDG has been in existence since 1985 following, according to its own report in 1993, the success of the multiagency juvenile bureaux for which Middleshire became famous in the 1980s. It is made up of the most senior officers involved in Criminal Justice and Community Safety, such as the Police, relevant County Council services, Probation, Courts, Crown Prosecution Service, Prison Service and, of late, the Health Authority. Its stated aim is to act as an information exchange and as a means of pooling resources when identifying the need for a joint approach to solving problems. Attendance is not delegated. Such a group would seem to be an unusual, if not unique, feature of Middleshire. Its lines of accountability are unclear and it is best viewed as an *ad hoc* corporate *and corporatist* executive group, created as a result of Home Office as well as local managerialist concerns over the lack of co-ordination between the various parts of the criminal justice system (Tuck 1991).

According to Pratt, corporatism refers to

> the tendencies to be found in advanced welfare societies whereby the capacity for conflict and disruption is reduced by means of the centralisation of policy, increased government intervention, and cooperation of various professional and interest groups into a collective whole with homogeneous aims and objectives.
>
> (Pratt 1989: 245)

This description of corporatism certainly helps us to analyse the work of such groups as the IDG and, indeed, groups 'lower' down the community safety strategy structure. Like Pratt, I remain ambivalent about any simple judgement as to either the oppressive or humane consequences of such developments.

Beneath the IDG, the strategy placed Crime Reduction/Community Safety Groups. In formal terms these groups had the task of liaising, communicating, facilitating and directing resources. Their membership was that of senior officers, with no member involvement. Their formal constitution involved the following objectives: to formulate a strategic plan for community safety within one local authority area; to provide the co-ordination of effort from relevant statutory agencies and enhance the potential of already existing measures. From these objectives certain actions were intended to follow – namely, to maintain and regularly update the community safety profile of the area and consider crime levels; to promote local interest in community safety; to ensure that community safety issues are integral to the future planning process; and to agree projects with the Action Against Crime groups and provide suitable resourcing.

Next in line down the structure sat Action Against Crime groups. These groups replaced the previous Crime Prevention Panels which were viewed as lacking focus. The terms of reference of these groups were: to consider local and national initiatives; to initiate topic and neighbourhood-based project teams; to receive reports from the latter and prioritise actions in respect of project team recommendations; and to maintain linkage with the parent Crime Reduction Group (CRG). The membership would normally include business, local councillors and the Area Police Commander. Such groups would also be expected to liaise with the local community. This structure bears close resemblance to that proposed in the Morgan Report.

The strategy then specified the role of Police/Community Consultative Committees (PCCCs) and public consultation. PCCCs and the like would assist in the identification of issues of local concern. No formal links with local democratic structures were made in this model. This view of PCCCs accords with the traditional model, since Scarman's recommendations, but not with recent Middleshire Police Authority's proposals to be discussed shortly.

The above offers a brief description of the officer-driven policy. Although complicated at first sight, highly corporatist in character and democratically flawed due to the lack of recognition of the Police Authority role, there may be much to recommend in this attempt at a co-ordinated and local government-led strategy of crime prevention/community safety. According to some of the participants, it envisaged a key 'enabling authority' role (Stewart 1986) for local government which may offer one positive antidote to the threat of local government withering on the vine. The strategy was also driven by the recognition that criminal justice agencies alone are unable to make much impact on crime levels. However, the prospects for the smooth implementation of this multi-agency corporate strategy in 1994 were to be drastically affected by the rather different 'vision' and concerns of an alliance of some crucial 'elected' players in the Police Authority.

Changes in community consultation in Middleshire in the mid-1990s: the politicised response to fears of the 'democratic deficit'

Arising out of the expressed concerns over the 'democratic deficit' regarding the future of police authorities and the need to improve consultation, the Chair of the Middleshire Police Authority proposed and succeeded in gaining the agreement of all members of the Police Authority for a radical restructuring of consultative arrangements whose impact was quite profound on the Community Safety Strategy for the county. Drawing explicitly on Brighton Borough Council's model of a 'Police and Public Safety sub-committee' and discussions arising out of seminars organised by the Association of County Councils, the Middleshire Police Authority decided in Spring 1994 to devolve PCCC arrangements down to the district authority level to be led by local elected councillors. The suggested organisation of the new Community Safety Committees is as follows. The groups would have elected councillors as the voting members with some non-voting 'co-opted' representatives, relevant district and county officers together with the appropriate senior police officer(s). Two police authority members would act as observers and report back to the police authority. It would seem that much of the impetus for this unusual arrangement, in national terms, arose out of the combined concern to invigorate *quite self-consciously* the democratic input into the previously rather dormant and unrepresentative PCCCs, to link these arrangements to resource centres at the district level and to give local government an axial role in community safety initiatives, given the backdrop of the Local Government Review and Police and Magistrates' Courts legislation.

It is, as yet, early days in the life of the new arrangements for consultation between the police, other relevant public agencies and the public in Middleshire. The seven district authorities which make up the county are themselves distinct localities with differing traditions, political allegiances and needs which cannot be ignored. Such differences are reflected in the differential response to implementing new consultative arrangements from the county-wide and perceived Labour-driven initiative from the Police Authority. The once calm lily pond of PCCCs in this county is currently choppy, and for some, shark-infested.

The uneven nature of the 'take up' from the various district authorities of the Police Authority's social democratically informed policy regarding the merging of community safety and consultative initiatives under the auspices of local lines of formal democratic accountability reflects the conflicts and alliances at work at both the district/borough and county council tiers of the local state. Any detailed discussion of this complex picture would require a separate research paper. It does, none the less, confirm the importance of local and comparative research on policing trends and crime prevention measures, albeit with a recognition of the crucial national and international trends and pressures at work.

Community safety as a late modern movement?

As it currently stands, consultation with, and participation of, the public in Middleshire on community safety initiatives remains very limited, as the key participants are well aware. Although there is scope for increasing the level of public participation with localised and targeted meetings, the key players – arguably 'knowledge brokers' in this specialist area of activity (Ericson 1994: 151) – are not too ambitious in their hopes for popular involvement in issues which most people will happily leave to 'professionals and politicians'. Given the sheer size and complexity of our society, any hope of a return to the direct participation of the citizenry in the democratic process on Athenian lines (Day and Klein 1987) is pure 'pie in the sky' thinking, even if dressed up in the market language of the consumer. The involvement of the citizen is a much-lauded goal in public policy but it may seriously overestimate loyalty and obligation to place. As Giddens notes, '[i]n the sense of an embedded affinity to place, community has indeed largely been destroyed' (Giddens 1991: 256). It would again be misguided to view any community safety strategy, however well-conceived and imple-mented, as a panacea for such historical shifts. Such sociological insights are not lost on both the officers of public service agencies and a small but influential minority of elected councillors who were interviewed. Indeed, the research participants' 'discourses' on crime prevention are, to para-phrase Giddens again, theorised by the lay agent in ways pervaded by sociological thinking (Giddens 1991: 43). There is not the space in this chapter to develop these issues regarding the interface of lay and academic sociological accounts of the world (see Hughes 1994: 263–8). Suffice to say, during the research process I was struck by the regularity with which research participants appropriated sociological concepts within their behaviour and reflections on current policy and practice in their orbit of specialism. Concepts such as 'net-widening', 'democratic deficit', 'asymmetries of power and knowledge' between the public and specialist services (versus the cult of partnership) were employed routinely by some of the research participants and again challenged the patronising image of lay participants which is often prevalent in academic commentaries. Thus, reflecting back on the old PCCC arrangements in his locality, a local authority officer was of similar opinion to that purveyed in much sociological commentary: indeed, sociological insights seem close to the 'common sense' of some of the research participants interviewed:

> there had been very little thought given to what they [PCCCs] were there for. Very little came out of the meetings. It wasn't community consultation . . . certain members of the public and crime prevention group member types came along. There was one voluntary sector person but she wasn't representing anybody but herself. The extent to which there was any communication with the wider public was very limited.

However, it did appear to this researcher that the very looseness and emptiness of the concept of community safety – itself a source of criticism from sceptical pluralists such as Pease (1994) and a 'free-floating signifier' in McLaughlin's view (McLaughlin 1994) – offers the opportunity for creative ideological appropriation by local, progressive alliances and networks which could challenge centralist tendencies. As a backlash to the numbing mundanity of managerially driven strategies on crime management, is it fanciful to view the appeal of the idea of community safety to radical and social democratic communitarians as a means of rekindling concerns over social solidarity and collective control over the wider social environment? (See also Tuck's (1991) self-consciously utopian meditation on 'joint communal living' and its potential lessons for criminal justice.) The situation appears fluid and although the contest between localities and the central state is profoundly uneven, the hegemonic capacity of the post-Thatcherite agenda on law and order should not be overestimated in the manner that radical totalitarians are apt to do. In the words of one chief executive officer from a Labour-controlled borough with a high level of deprivation, the looseness of the meaning of the concept of community safety was not necessarily a barrier to its creative use in local politics:

> I don't know what it means. All I can say is it means whatever you want it to mean in your particular setting and to us I suppose it means a fairly broad sort of thing to do with the quality of life in relation to the way people feel . . . Do they feel safe or do they feel intimidated about what's happening around them that's detracting from the quality of life . . . I think it is for us to define what is meant by safety.

A big question facing such policy initiatives as the revised Community Safety Strategy for Middleshire in this era of the audit is how do you measure its success? The most obvious measure would be that of a reduction in crime and a concomitant increase in security and safety among

Middleshire people. This difficult issue is certainly not amenable to measurement in any short-term manner, again as acknowledged by the participants in this research. Given the complex mixture of demographic, cultural and technological factors which come into play in any explanation of the shifts in the sense of (in)security and in the material reality of crime and disorder, the chances of ever 'measuring' in a quantifiable manner the impact of a community safety/crime prevention strategy on these phenomena is difficult to envisage. However, a more reasonable 'test' may be to ask how do the 'good intentions' associated with inter-agency-driven community safety work end up as tangible, practical and anti-despotic outcomes. On this question, the research to date is able to point to some tangible outcomes across the county, albeit unevenly spread at this early point in the implementation phase. Community safety, with its emphasis on an inter-agency approach to the social problems of crime and insecurity, is now clearly part of the agenda of the public services in Middleshire. Under the umbrella of this new rallying call, some significant policy and practice initiatives are emergent; for example, with regard to the problems of domestic violence and the diversion of offenders from custody. Community safety initiatives are not part of a popular movement but may be best understood as a policy network of knowledge brokers, whose actions may make some difference. If successful, the current developments may improve both the effectiveness of public service delivery in this broad policy area and also inject some much needed impetus into the local democratic process.

12

POVERTY AND PARTNERSHIP IN THE THIRD EUROPEAN POVERTY PROGRAMME

The Liverpool case

Robert Moore

ANTI-POVERTY STRATEGIES

Poverty Three addressed issues concerning the economic and political integration of over 12 per cent of the European population before the unification of Germany. The European Community had a population of 350 million of whom 44 million were deemed to be living in poverty, defined as less than 50 per cent of average earnings. This population is today estimated to be 52 million.

The poor were not consuming the goods that European manufacturers were producing. Even if consumer-led recovery was to be based on imports, the poor were not contributing to the generation of wealth through consumption. They were, however, consuming tax revenues through social security and other benefits (Commission of the European Communities 1993a: ch. 9). This form of consumption was regarded as a burden on the state, corporations and taxpayers. Apart from any humane concern, poverty was a drain on investment and production (see Hutton 1992). Beyond this there lay a concern with the social and political marginalisation of the poor and the threat posed to social order (Commission of the European Communities 1993b: 20–1).

The question of the single European market was also an important background element to the Third Poverty Programme, 'social exclusion is not only a problem of injustice, or a problem of human rights, but can also place a brake on economic integration' (Quinton 1990).

The Third Poverty Programme addressed an agenda current throughout the UK.[1] During the 1980s the Child Poverty Action Group and other pressure groups, Mrs Thatcher's 'moaning minnies', had drawn attention to rising poverty and inequality and the part played by taxation and welfare policies in reinforcing them. The churches also kept poverty on the agenda, through *Faith in the City* and *Living Faith in the City*. By the early 1980s poverty was no longer a problem on the margins of society. The increased unemployment that resulted from economic policy created demands for the public expenditure that the government were committed to cutting. Government was faced with steeply rising benefit bills. Later cuts in these benefits were an attempt to stem the increases in public spending, but they too had the effect of increasing poverty.

Local authorities encountered rising poverty when increasing numbers of people qualified for Housing Benefit and, at the end of the decade, many of the poorest were unable to pay their contribution to the Poll Tax. So a number of cities established committees to examine the problem of poverty. The Association of Metropolitan Authorities (AMA) created an Anti-Poverty Network through which discussion of anti-poverty strategies took place (Balloch and Jones 1990). The most striking feature of Balloch and Jones's review of local authority anti-poverty strategies is the extent to which in the 1980s local authorities were trying to cope with the effects of *government* disinvestment. Balloch and Jones cite the Cleveland study *For Richer for Poorer* which suggested that over £20 million in benefits may have been lost to the County each year. Over 5 million people in the UK lost help with rents and rates. This and the freezing of child benefit, reduced the incomes and increased the poverty of the poorest (Balloch and Jones 1990: 67). Many of these poor then became debtors to the local authorities.

In the early 1980s about 12.2 per cent of Merseyside's income was based on benefits and these benefits created one job for roughly every £106,000 of payments (Madden and Batey 1983). Without social security transfers to the local economy unemployment would have been higher (ibid.: 326). Local authorities needed more effective policies to cope with rising poverty. Notably they needed to be able to deal with indebtedness in ways that did not reduce their chances of recovering debts. However, the impact of poverty was experienced by local authority departments with different perceptions of priority groups and different approaches to the poor. It was the need for a more coherent and co-ordinated local approach to poverty that had driven local anti-poverty strategies and the collective efforts of the AMA.

THE LIVERPOOL ANTI-POVERTY STRATEGY

In the late 1980s an official wrote a report on poverty in Liverpool. A councillor sent a copy to the Prime Minister. This started an inconclusive debate with 10 Downing Street, from whence came the suggestion that Liverpool might consider applying to the forthcoming Third Poverty Programme.

Liverpool City Council were eager to pursue an initiative that promised greater prominence for poverty-related issues. The bid was made in July 1989 and a statement of intent to work in partnership was signed by representatives of the City Council, the Merseyside Community Relations Council (MCRC), the Merseyside Task Force, the churches and the Liverpool Council of Voluntary Services. By the beginning of 1990 the partnership also included the Granby Toxteth Task Force, the university and the Liverpool Health Authority. Representatives of these eight agencies were to found the Management Committee of the Liverpool Poverty Programme.

The Merseyside Task Force, which was effectively the Department of the Environment office for Merseyside, provided most of the public money for projects in Liverpool through the Urban Programme. It saw Poverty Three as a means of complementing the economic policies it was promoting. The Poverty Programme offered a means for creating a 'social' dimension to urban policies which had been developed in a political climate in which social considerations were subordinated to the economic.

The membership of the Management Committee was in part a reflection of political instability on Merseyside. The Militant Tendency had been the source of conflict with central government. This has led to the setting of an illegal rate and the disqualification of councillors. The city's Poverty sub-committee was dominated by the Militant Tendency. Central government, represented by the Merseyside Task Force, were unwilling to have funds pass to Militant control. Means had to be found to keep European funds out of the hands of the City Council and the Poverty sub-committee in particular. As a neutral party to the city's conflict the Vice-Chancellor of the University of Liverpool was asked to chair the group making the bid. He had personally committed the university to the project as an opportunity to further the university's contribution to Merseyside, in accordance with the university's mission statement. In February 1990 the partners were informed that their bid had been successful.

TOWARDS THE CONCEPT OF PARTNERSHIP

The need to establish partnership did not derive solely from responses to the poverty programme in the peculiar circumstances of Liverpool. Since the mid-1970s there had been a reappraisal of the role of local government and a recognition that it needed to be more responsive to diverse publics and to work closely with other service providers. The CDP earlier underlined the need for change when they reported that:

> The need for responsive local government and for people to participate was a constant theme of many of the official reports of the 1960s.
>
> (CDP 1977: 56)

Gyford (1991: 30–45) suggests that this was part of the breakup of the old local political order characterised by exclusive coalitions of either businessmen and the Conservative Party or trade unions and the Labour Party. Both excluded women and ethnic minorities. Both controlled highly centralised and bureaucratic administrations. The 'post-Fordist' local political order needs to be more open, with widespread pressure group and voluntary sector participation. Moreover these active groups have themselves pressed for participation in the formulation and implementation of policy. This was not unwelcome in conditions of economic decline where local government was increasingly unable to deliver the services that were expected. Partnership offered a means to tap into the knowledge and experience of the voluntary sector and to incorporate the public into policy implementation, and by implication to make them share responsibility for failures.

The changes from 1979 have also been changes made in accordance with a radical Conservative agenda. They have been part of a programme of centralisation. City councils, furthermore, were a government target because they came to embody a workable alternative agenda to the plans of the Thatcher governments, to which it was said there was no alternative.

But local government would have been a political target whether or not it was the source of an alternative agenda. Firstly, it was a major spender and able independently to raise taxes when central government was committed to reducing public spending and taxation. Secondly, the city was the location of collective provision – notably housing, education and social services – in circumstances where the government wished to eliminate collectivism and dependency.[2] Thirdly, urban administration was the locus of powerful trade unions and professions with a vested interest in the welfare state and its growth. The Conservatives were determined to 'free' Britain from trade unionism and to 'deprivilege' the professions. Unions and professions were, in Conservative eyes, a target of equal merit to the welfare state itself; in local government the three targets became one.

The idea of elected councillors tied by the reciprocity of community to a local population was, ideally, to be replaced by the cash nexus; citizens become customers and local government a series of businesses (for an introduction to these ideas see Butler et al. 1985). Commercial values were to replace social values and business was to be encouraged to bring about regeneration. But in this changed relationship is a significant change in the balance of power between the governors and the governed, because the political structure comes to reflect market inequalities rather than to offset them (Brownill 1990; Forman 1989; Moore 1992).

Labour emerged from the local elections of 1981 with control of all the metropolitan authorities and nine shire counties. In four cities electorates voted for the 'new urban left' alternatives to the Conservative vision and spending plans. In London especially, alternative strategies for economic regeneration and employment began to be put in place. In these circum-stances the problem for central government increasingly became one of *imposing* their will. There were a range of strategies open for doing this of which the most extreme would have been to abolish the vote. This is a high-risk strategy. Simpler, therefore, was to remove from local control that for which voters voted. The 1980s saw the growth of unelected quangos. Nominees from the business community were placed on the Boards of Development Corporations or seconded to Task Forces. Compulsory Competitive Tendering, local management of schools and the privatisation of services reduced local authority control. Schools 'opting out' and a series of financial measures increased central government control of local spending and services. In the case of the most recalcitrant metropolitan authorities, where voters persisted in electing councils unacceptable to central government, the final logical step was taken; namely, to abolish the authorities (Duncan and Goodwin 1988: ch. 6).

In addition to considerations of efficiency there is an ideological problem for government in squaring the reduction of local control of services and the centralisation of decision-making with the stated aim of setting the people free and making services responsive to local need. This was tackled with Citizens' Charters and by stressing the citizen's role as a consumer free to make his or her own choices. But increased centralisation of education and housing finance exacerbated *and clarified* the problem of representing local needs to the centre. In 1995 parents were brought into direct conflict with central government over education budgets. Action by parents and teachers entailed new alliances, including elected members. Local government is now less effective in shielding government from the consequences of its policies.

Local representation and partnership have been notable themes of government rhetoric from early in the 1980s, especially with the establishment of Development Corporations and Task Forces. Government's mind was also concentrated by the urban uprisings of 1981 which saw the mobilisation of some of the most marginalised and impoverished sections of urban populations. These were largely people who had historically lacked any effective representation at all. Thus, having created agencies to circumvent local elected councils, government had to create means of reincorporating local interests in the development and implementation of urban policy. 'Partnership' became the buzz-word.

ESTABLISHING PARTNERSHIPS IN LIVERPOOL

The effects of the restructuring of relations between central and local government were amplified by the 'Liverpool factor'. Relations between the Merseyside Task Force and the City Council were good at the officer level but politically weak. Relations between elected councillors and the Merseyside Development Corporation (MDC) had ceased soon after the MDC was established (National Audit Office 1990: Figure 3). Task Forces and Development Corporations were seen as central government agencies devised to circumvent local democracy and to impose the government's shift from social to economic objectives in urban policy. But they were *fait accompli*. Political opposition was mounted as a matter of principle, with little reflection upon the quality of local Liverpool democracy or the opportunities that might be afforded by the presence of local offices of central government.

In addition to being in conflict with central government, the Labour party and its own workforce, Liverpool City Council had been in dispute with the black population. It had engaged in a bitter dispute in attempting to impose a Community Relations Officer unacceptable to the black population, and its discriminatory policies in housing and employment were apparently intractable (Liverpool Black Caucus 1986; Moore 1994). By contrast the Third Poverty Programme in Liverpool (the Granby Toxteth Community Project) addressed issues of poverty, race and exclusion mainly in the Granby Ward. The achievements of this project will be reported elsewhere: the focus of this chapter is the experience of partnership.

The population of Granby have seen many projects, especially since the uprising of 1981 (see Jacobs 1992: 188). The ward had many expert opinions expressed on its problems. It had its own (DTI) Task Force. But nothing seemed to change. Meanwhile the pattern of project funding had created competition leading to local rivalry and fragmentation. Was Poverty Three to be another parachuting in of 'experts' and cash that would leave the local situation unchanged? Thus, whilst the idea of partnership was not new to the members, the Liverpool partnership had unique features: it was a partnership of old protagonists with a new forum in which their hostility and distrust could either be overcome or re-enacted.

The churches, the university and the voluntary sector did not appear to be party to the old enmities but were seen as being politically neutral and financially reliable. The university was also to be a significant funder whilst the voluntary sector, represented by Liverpool Council for Voluntary Services (LCVS), was intended to be a link to trusts and charitable funds.

The first two objectives set by the project were:

1   The establishment of a partnership of central and local government agencies, the voluntary and private sectors, and the less privileged groups, based on a joint analysis of the nature and causes of poverty, and the adoption of common objectives and targets.
2   The development of a co-ordinated and integrated anti-poverty strategy which addresses all dimensions of poverty by linking economic, social and environmental action.

In terms of implementing these objectives, three prior, practical and interrelated issues needed to be tackled. First there was the need to develop an operational definition of the task that could be taken to target groups in order, second, to establish their participation. Third, the participating target groups would then contribute to the establishment of an operational team which would work with target groups in refining, redefining and pursuing the objectives of the Project. The problem was circular; something had to be on offer to invite participation but without pre-empting likely responses. In order to get the project to this stage an operational team was needed that would be acceptable to future but as yet unconsulted participants.

Failure to break out of this circle was a feature of the first year of the Programme in Liverpool. One problem was that the Management Committee comprised senior members of the partner agencies and was too large to undertake the day-to-day development of the project. Even more importantly individuals lacked the time to attend regular meetings and work on the project between meetings. By the end of 1990 it was said that the Management Committee was not managing. The reasons for this will be expanded in the history of the Granby Toxteth Community Project, which is currently being written.

Liverpool was not unique amongst the three UK Programmes in encountering problems in establishing partnership. In Brownlow a small partnership had been established earlier but it had problems deriving from the uneven distribution of power between the partners, and questions of representativeness. In Pilton the initiative was taken by the local authority, and as a result suspicion and tension characterised the early life of the project. A major problem facing all projects was the European time-scale. There was a very short interval between the announcement of the programme and the closing of applications. Successful bidders then needed to establish projects very quickly in order to start spending substantial sums of money before the end of the first budget period. It was to be expected, therefore, that the public sector would take an early lead. But in order to win funding they had to create paper partnerships. The real partnerships would then be formed even as the first of the European money was being spent. The term 'shot-gun partnership' occurs in the discussions of the arrangements in Pilton and to some extent characterised all the local arrangements. Thus in a programme concerned with the most marginal sections of the population the time-scale ensured that the most organised sections of the localities – public and voluntary sectors – would take the lead, and then have to sell 'their' programme back to the marginalised.

Who were 'the less privileged groups' that Poverty Three was meant to address on Merseyside? It was agreed that *one* unique feature of the Liverpool project, in contrast with other EC projects, was that it addressed 'race' and poverty. Women were also identified as being especially vulnerable to poverty and marginalisation. Invitations were extended to the Afro-Asian Caribbean Standing Committee, the Consortium of Black Organisations (CBO) and the Federation of Liverpool Black Organisations (FLBO) to join the Management Committee. The Afro-Asian Caribbean Standing Committee and the FLBO never seemed to be more than shell organisations. The Consortium of Black Organisations was set up to overcome the fragmentation of minority organisations in the aftermath of 1981. Community groups go through phases of activity and quiescence; the CBO had been a powerful representative body but by 1991 it was a moribund coalition. Participation in the Third Poverty Programme, and access to funds, might have revived its fortunes, but did not do so, probably because the wider community were not convinced of the benefits of the Poverty Programme. The Management Committee never saw a constitution or membership list of the CBO, even though it was required to do so by the terms of the EC grant.

None the less the accession of local people to the project, a year after it began, was greeted with relief by the Management Committee and a six-strong operational team with strong local connections was appointed. The project was immediately redefined as a 'black' project centred on the Granby ward. This narrowing of the geographical base had, *inter alia*, the effect of making private sector participation unlikely because it excluded those parts of Liverpool's central business district that were included within the original project boundaries.

The question of the representativeness of the community members of the Management Committee was never seriously raised within the management committee, although it was raised in the wider community. Effective membership of the Management Committee was confined to (male) representatives of the Consortium of Black Organisations. It was drawn from a network centred on the local Law Centre. Whilst the Law Centre was a key agency in the locality, it is only one of many. The question of representativeness and accountability to the local community thus became a problem, and a potential weapon in the hand of partners in the statutory sector and critics of the project.

Whilst the resources available to the project may have been small compared to the budgets of central and local government in Liverpool, they were substantial in comparison with those that had previously been given to the local community. In theory they created the 'political and economic incentives for groups to cooperate' (Jacobs 1992: 160). But the original partners should not have expected the community agencies to widen the base of representation on their own volition. A community group gaining access to resources and to policy-makers has a strong incentive to pursue a policy of closure against other groups. Only outside partners could have intervened to secure wider representation, but in so doing they may have precipitated conflict within the Management Committee which they wished to avoid. Representatives of the local community (however narrowly based) faced with confrontation within the committee could have called upon outside support and threatened to extend the conflict. The perception that *this* could have been the case was important for civil servants who did not wish to jeopardise wider aspects of their Merseyside programme through conflict of the kind that had occurred in 1981. Not least, such conflict would have damaged the image of Liverpool which was being promoted by central and local government and the business community. Broader representation was thus never achieved on the Management Committee.

As university representative, the author was the most inexperienced member of the Management Committee, having only recently arrived from Aberdeen. His past experiences were thought to make him a suitable member, but it did not enable him immediately to understand specific aspects of the locality. This immediately became a problem when the university's participation was challenged by the community representatives; the university was portrayed as an agency which exploited the black community. Academics enriched themselves by doing research and writing books whilst putting nothing back into the community. The record in Liverpool is to the contrary, but a dialogue of the deaf ensued on this challenge. LCVS dropped out of the project at an early stage. The project had become a waste of time for the organisation, especially as the development of the SRB and Objective One status promised a wider scale of intervention. The Health Board was so engrossed in problems of service reorganisation that it was never able to become a fully effective partner. The MCRC was wracked by disputes. It was on its way to formal dissolution and made no serious contribution to the project as an organisation and signally failed to represent the local community in the early days of the project. Its status as representative of the local black community was challenged by black organisations. In an early flexing of community muscle, the churches' representative was forced to leave the Management Committee.

Central government officers were plainly unhappy about the representativeness of the Management Committee. They had misgivings about some of the individuals involved in the Third Poverty Programme and plainly harboured concerns about financial management, especially given that previous projects had suffered from financial irregularities. The civil servants were also subject to 'next thingism' as new schemes for inner city regeneration were developed (City Challenge, Single Regeneration Budget, Merseyside 2000) and the civil service continued its own reorganisation. Reorganising, responding and bidding became nearly full-time activities. The City Council did not achieve full political stability at any time in the life of the Third Poverty Programme but the administration was reorganised under a new chief executive. Furthermore, in both government and city offices, officials were subjected to the pressures created by the processes of 'deprivileging' and by public expenditure restrictions.

LESSONS TO BE LEARNT

Some lessons may be learnt from this early experience in Liverpool: where there is a history of projects with few tangible benefits, or where there is a history of hostility between potential partners, effective partnership becomes increasingly difficult to establish. Establishing partnership itself becomes the major problem of the project. In the Liverpool circumstances, there were disincentives for the public sector agencies to work on the question of partnership. By 1992 they were, in effect, keeping the project ticking over in a passive manner. Had Poverty Three been a project with a wider constituency and funds which formed a significant percentage of total local expenditure, then there would have been an incentive to make partnership work. Where funds are for truly new initiatives (as in the other UK projects) then a low level of pump-priming funding may be effective in stimulating local activity. But once there is a history of such activity, further small-scale funding is less likely to be effective. Early funding changes the circumstances in which future funding may take place by calling into being potentially competing interest groups and creating a history which may be a barrier to later initiatives.

Both the Task Forces and the City Council needed the participation of local people in regeneration projects in the Granby area. The project seemed to promise one means for participation. It is unlikely that the Granby Toxteth Community Project will have made a significant input to policy development, but it ensured that a local voice was heard in devising regeneration strategies for the area. Perhaps its most notable success was in articulating local fears that demolition in Granby was part of a covert scheme to destroy the black community. The demolition programme was modified as a result of the representations made by the director of the project.

The project had other successes and these have been, and will be, described in reports. A Welfare Rights Project was very successful and its results may be generalised beyond Merseyside. The project showed the benefits to individuals and the local economy that could be derived from the provision of effective advice services at the points where people made contact with an agency which might not itself be directly involved in allocating benefits. Overshadowing this successful demonstration project was the suspicion that if benefits take-up increased the Treasury would seek further reductions in benefit levels and entitlements. No amount of *local* partnership can overcome these risks.

The Welfare Rights Project raises an important question at the core of the poverty programme. However successful the project may have been in its aim of 'bending' the budgets of the big local spenders, benefits, one of the most important inputs to the locality, were decided elsewhere beyond the influence of any of the local actors. From this perspective it might be said that the Third Poverty Programme itself was marginal. It is important to note the lack of direct representation of the Department of Social Security, the UK sponsoring department for the Third Poverty Programme on the Management Committee.

A major shortcoming of the project itself was the failure to develop a strategic dimension through a systematic critique of the impacts of local, national and European policy on the locality. This had a knock-on effect in the failure to develop a locally based agency with popular support that would command the attention of the public sector in its responses to the Single Regeneration Budget and Objective One. However important it may be to get money into the local economy it is, in the longer run, more important to use one-off resources to build local capacities to contribute and respond to policy development. The benefits of such a strategy may not be immediately obvious to local people and so a balance has to be struck between local short-term and strategic needs. In conditions where community groups have traditionally competed for limited funds, this is especially difficult to manage because programmes need to show early and tangible results. 'Money in pockets', was how one activist expressed it. Project workers also need to avoid giving the impression that they are withholding public funds from the community in order to finance their own professional activities. The professionalisation and incorporation of community representatives facilitates the relationship between government agencies and the local community, but threaten to alienate the latter from its representatives (Jacobs 1992: 161, 171).

Partnership failed at crucial junctures. For example, the Granby Toxteth Task Force had promised to keep the project informed of the development of the Economic Development Trust. But, once the Task Force lost confidence in the project, it failed to do so and thus reinforced negative local attitudes to public servants. Collectively the funding partners failed to exert sufficient control to ensure timely and acceptable bids to continue important aspects of the project's work at the end of Poverty Three funding. There was no effective exit strategy. This is in sharp contrast to the other projects where teams based upon the original partnerships are continuing some of the work started by Poverty Three.

What might have been the result had the project grasped the significance of its limited life and sought to establish permanent benefits for the local community none the less?

The Single Regeneration Budget marked the end of short-term small-scale projects sponsored by a diversity of departments pursuing parallel policies. A more coherent urban policy with consolidated resources and co-ordinated management demands coherent and united responses from potential partners. The project's outcome could have been the creation of a powerful advocacy and negotiating agency for the community. The agency would have had information resources, trained capacity to evaluate policy, and the means to communicate with the local community. Such an agency could have grasped the agenda of the Single Regeneration Budget and Merseyside's Objective One Programme. This might have enabled the community to make the major budgets responsive to the needs of an excluded black community, in accordance with one of the objectives of the project.

At the end of the Third Poverty Programme Granby was left with the organisations and processes that were appropriate to the more fragmentary, and fragmentising, phase of urban policy. It could be argued that the project has contributed to this by providing training for local organisations which enabled them to compete with one another.

The obstacles to be overcome in achieving any other outcomes would have been substantial; any attempt to create what would look like a single representative agency for the community would have sparked rivalries between those who already claimed to speak for much of the community. It would have entailed creating partnership *within* the community in conditions where competition was endemic. It seems that these problems were never seriously addressed and that after 1992 they were unlikely to be addressable by the project, given official attitudes to the existing partnership.

From the point of view of the university, the experience of partnership was one of lost opportunities. For example, a survey was organised in which the analysis required by its sponsors made it virtually unusable. Had the university been involved, further analysis would have made the data useful both to the sponsors and the local community. The lack of technical capacity in local management and administration is also a problem which the university could address. Suggestions for building local research and evaluation capacity in the community by the university were rebuffed locally. The university made considerable informal inputs of census data to the project, but the project produced its own report on the census without consulting those involved in the university. The question of 'ownership' of initiatives seemed to be paramount and there was therefore a marked reluctance to be seen to be in any way dependent upon university resources. As a result access to these resources was lost.

Another failure of the university as partner was in controlling the quality of evaluation which was required at all stages of the project by the European Commission. The first evaluator had appropriate professional skills and experience and was appointed from within the university system. His presence and the Commission's requirements for evaluation were resented by certain activists and he became unable to do the job for which he was appointed. His replacement was a local activist. This had the effect of reducing the project's credibility in the eyes of the funding partners and others. The evaluation reports became the occasion for the repetition of historical resentments, with little apparent interest in accuracy or systematic analysis. Assertions made at the beginning of the project were repeated at the end, without evidence of intervening enquiry. In sum, the evaluation was that the black population could not trust the public authorities. There was no recognition of the changes that had taken place within the partner agencies and their practices or the rapidly changing circumstances in which the agencies' representatives were operating. There was, in other words, no analytic evaluation.

The first 'final' evaluation report was not submitted to the Management Committee for approval. It was printed with glossy covers and widely distributed locally. The document was repudiated by the Management Committee who refused to accept it as fulfilling the terms of the evaluation contract. In the rhetoric of community politics, the report could be said to have been a 'disempowering' document because it obscured the changing relationships between and within local agencies. The story of the report is an important indicator of the problems of partnership in an intensely conflictful inner city context. It showed that over a period of five years there had been no real meeting of minds. No one had been prepared to put him or herself into another's position, to see the institutional and interpersonal constraints within which the other works. Putting yourself in the other's shoes is an essential element both of partnership and of developing a strong bargaining position. In the Granby Toxteth Community Project, prejudgement was the order of the day. An acceptable evaluation report was produced nine months after the completion of the final year's extension to the project.

The out-turn of the Granby Toxteth Community Project was, perhaps, to underline the importance of an early objective of the project. It had been recognised from the beginning that the limited funds could bring little direct benefit to the locality. The project needed to act locally and think strategically. What was needed, firstly, was an extension of the base of the partnership. Consensus could not be built in circumstances where only one effective local partner was included. Secondly, it was necessary to build a wide range of capacities that would have made the local community an effective strategic voice in responding later to large-scale funding initiatives. The only proposal to extend the project came in the dying weeks of the project. It was for a consultancy built on the same narrow community base as the project itself. The proposal never commanded the support of the management committee and its proponents did not modify their proposal given the lack of support for it. The Granby Toxteth Community Project wound up with nearly £100,000 in its bank account.

That the exit strategy for Poverty Three should have been a priority from the beginning is illustrated by the Merseyside Objective One programme. This includes an initiative called community involvement, 'designed to help local people with the costs of setting up, designing and monitoring their own initiatives'. This is an opportunity to which the population of Granby will be less capable of responding because of the failure of the partnership in Poverty Three.

NOTES

1   The full title was Community Programme to Foster Social and Economic Integration of the Least Privileged Groups. This title derived from the refusal of the UK government to participate in any initiative using the word 'poverty'.

2   'Local government is a net to catch the unfortunate' was how Councillor Forsyth, a future Scottish Education Minister and Secretary of State for Scotland, put it.

Part IV

THE POLITICS OF EXCLUSION
AND RESISTANCE

13

DOWNTOWN REDEVELOPMENT AND COMMUNITY RESISTANCE

An international perspective

Mike Beazley, Patrick Loftman and Brendan Nevin

INTRODUCTION

The 1980s witnessed the global proliferation of prestige project and urban mega-project property developments both as a tool of local economic development and as a means of securing the physical regeneration of declining urban areas (Harvey 1988). Prestige projects are defined as large-scale, high profile, self-contained development schemes which are primarily justified as catalysts for urban regeneration (Loftman and Nevin 1995). Examples of prestige projects include convention centres, festival market-places, major office complexes and leisure and sporting facilities. Urban mega-projects are defined as much larger mixed use developments, or events, which contain prestige projects as component parts of the overall scheme. These are much more common in North America than the UK. Both types of developments are often achieved through public/private sector partnerships and massive public sector investment, with the public sector creating a conducive climate for private sector investment through subsidies, tax abatements, and loan arrangements. Such projects are predominantly located in, or adjacent to, localities which offer the greatest private sector development potential and financial returns – in most cases the central business district (CBD) or downtown area.

There is, however, a considerable body of research examining the distributional consequences of CBD-focused regeneration models, which suggests that such approaches to local economic development have concentrated on cultivating and supporting service sector interests at the expense of deprived inner urban areas and services on which dis-advantaged residents depend (Barnekov *et al.* 1989; Hambleton 1990; Neill 1991). Consequently, there have been varying degrees of resistance to these projects from impacted low income communities. Moreover, public opposition to, and community mobilisation against, such projects has in many cases been undermined by the absence of an open debate of the costs and benefits of these developments. The powerful interests in favour of the developments universally justify them to the public in terms of job creation, increased wealth generation and economic development. In contrast, those groups which oppose them often refer to the potential negative impacts such as eviction, rising land values jeopardising community-oriented development, increased traffic, and the poor quality job opportunities.

This chapter provides a brief overview of the response of deprived communities to the development of prestige projects and mega-projects near, or adjacent, to their neighbourhoods, focusing on the extent of local community resistance to such developments in three cities: Vancouver (Canada), San Francisco (USA) and Birmingham (UK). Utilising the three case study cities the chapter focuses on the extent of community participation in the development process and the success of those communities in minimising disbenefits and maximising the benefits that flow from this type of development.

PACIFIC PLACE, VANCOUVER

Vancouver is located on the Pacific Rim of North America in the Province of British Columbia, Canada. During the 1980s and 1990s, the city experienced considerable urban mega-project activity. One such development was the Pacific Place scheme facilitated by the holding of Expo '86, a World Fair that celebrated transportation as its main theme. The use of world fairs as a redevelopment tool has been well documented (Wachtel 1986; Olds 1988). The Pacific Place planning process was initiated in 1988, following the sale of the Expo site by the British Columbia provincial government to a major Hong Kong developer, Li Ka-shing, and his Vancouver-based development company Concord Pacific Developments Limited.

The Pacific Place site is located on the North Shore of False Creek and is approximately 204 acres in size. The site represents about one-sixth of Vancouver's downtown peninsula, and is currently recognised as one of the most valuable and desirable redevelopment sites in North America. The site is adjacent to the Downtown Eastside, an area of about 10,000 residents that has been designated as one of the poorest neighbourhoods in Canada. The redevelopment process for the site was launched by the holding of Expo '86, promoted by the provincial government and administered by the Expo '86 Corporation. Expo was initially resisted by the City Council, but the idea was sold to them on the basis that it would put Vancouver 'on the map', and would attract major international investment and tourism.

A central feature of Expo, and the subsequent Pacific Place redevelopment, was the building of a covered sports stadium, BC Place, costing $125 million (Canadian). Construction work on the stadium, which started in the early 1980s, coincided with a major economic recession. The result was a severe cut-back in social programmes, the abolition of fair rents, the freezing of welfare payments, and hundreds of redundancies (DERA 1987).

Moreover, the Expo Board also decided to award building contracts to non-union companies, which was seen by many trade unions and community groups as a provocative act, as there was a high level of union membership in the Vancouver construction industry. This brought about concerted resistance both from labour and community groups – and the formation of the Solidarity Coalition (an alliance of the labour and community groups) which succeeded in bringing the province within a few hours of a general strike in 1983 (Ley *et al.* 1992). Their opposition, however, was resisted by the provincial government and subsequently collapsed. The building work continued and other major development projects were added at huge public expense, including Skytrain, Canada Place, etc.; Expo '86 went ahead as scheduled.

No impact studies assessing how Vancouver's neighbourhoods would be affected by Expo, or the subsequent development, were undertaken by the City Council. Nor was there any public debate or consultation about what Vancouver citizens' goals and aspirations were for the site or the city as a whole. Instead, unilateral decisions regarding the site and Expo '86 were made in secret by the provincial government (Gutstein 1986).

Community groups based in the neighbourhoods adjacent to the Expo site asked for impact studies to be undertaken. Activists working for the Downtown Eastside Residents Association (DERA) warned the provincial government of the potential risk of housing displacement as Expo progressed. Many of the people in the Downtown Eastside had lived in hotel rooming houses, mainly on welfare benefits, for many years. These warnings, however, were ignored amidst a reluctance by the provincial government to acknowledge the potential negative impacts of major development projects.

The result of this public neglect was resident evictions. Conservative estimates suggest that between 500 and 850 long-term residents were evicted from hotel rooming accommodation in the area. Community-based housing organisations operating in the area estimated that the figure was closer to 1,000. Most alarmingly, DERA argued that a number of deaths could be directly attributed to the trauma of eviction on elderly tenants. For example, on 18 April 1986, longtime Downtown Eastside resident Olaf Solheim (aged 88 years) died six weeks after being forcibly evicted from the Patricia Hotel, his home for 62 years.

The idea of hosting Expo in Vancouver was 'sold' to the public in terms of the potential benefits it would bring to the city. In reality the World Fair cost the taxpayers of British Columbia about $1.5 billion (Canadian) to put on and it ran up a deficit of $400 million (Canadian) (DERA 1987), leading to cuts in social programmes to pay for it. Furthermore, many of the jobs generated by Expo were low paid and temporary, and many of the financial benefits in terms of contracts and franchises went to firms located outside of the city.

In 1988, the city embarked on the Pacific Place mega-project. The final development proposal for the site, approved in 1989, included 7,650 housing units, which will house up to 13,000 people (of these units 20 per cent were to be allocated for social housing units, but no mechanisms were in place to ensure that these would be provided); 2 million square feet of office development; 650,000 square feet of retail and service development; 42 acres of parkland; and hotel, cultural, recreational uses and public open space (City of Vancouver Planning Department, October 1989; City of Vancouver Planning Department, January 1990).

The plan was said to contain the largest package of public benefits ever negotiated by the City of Vancouver (City of Vancouver Planning Department, January 1990). As part of the package the developer is required to pay for the provision of parks, a continuous waterfront walkway around False Creek, shoreline improvements, circulation and utility systems, a community centre, eight day-care centres, a library, community meeting rooms, public art facilities, and bus shelters (City of Vancouver Planning Department, January 1990).

As with Expo, little impact work was undertaken. This is an omission that was freely admitted by City of Vancouver officials, although two studies were commissioned by the city from consultants. The first was from the University of British Columbia's Centre for Human Settlements (CHS) to look at the issue of low rent housing in the central area and how this would be impacted by developments like Pacific Place. The report concluded that the Pacific Place development would have a negative impact on homelessness and the stock of low income housing in the central area. However, the report's recommendations were largely ignored by the City Council. The second was a Housing and Economic Impact Study commissioned from private sector consultants called Burgess, Austin & Associates. This report was less critical of the potential impact of Pacific Place. Whilst acknowledging that 1,500 low income housing units would be lost, the report's authors argued that the development would lead to the upgrading of the low income areas adjacent to the site.

The findings of the Burgess report conflicted not only with the CHS report, but also with those of the community-based housing organisations operating in the area. These groups feared that the project would have a devastating impact on neighbourhoods like the Downtown Eastside. Fears of gentrification and potential displacement were expressed. Despite constant pleas, local community-based organisations were given no resources to demonstrate their concerns via the commissioning of their own impact assessment work.

Generally the government institutional and policy frameworks were favourably disposed to mega-project development. This made community opposition very problematic in terms of gaining political support and winning allies. There was some resistance on the City Council to Pacific Place from the Committee of Progressive Electors (COPE) councillors, but these were outnumbered by the Non-Partisan Association (NPA) – a pro-development business faction and led by a mayor who was a former property developer. This was set within a provincial and federal political context that welcomed and promoted overseas investment and that saw great financial rewards attached to mega-project developments like Pacific Place. These interests set out to market Vancouver's location on the Pacific Rim to maximise opportunity for South-East Asian investment. This was seen in very positive terms in contributing to economic growth and the future well-being of the city.

There was very little effective public participation in the planning process leading to the commencement of development on the Pacific Place site. Local community groups had from the outset attempted to input into the decision-making process relating to the Expo and Pacific Place developments, but generally to no avail. In relation to Pacific Place there were mechanisms in place to facilitate public participation (i.e., there were public meetings, exhibitions, and public hearings), at which community representatives consistently made their concerns known, but these were not acted upon. In relation to Expo, there had been concerted resistance from the community and trade unions, but this had been successfully resisted by the provincial government.

Community groups involved in the Pacific Place planning process had little access to any legal or technical support. DERA had become a knowledgeable and sophisticated campaigning body, but openly admitted that they lacked technical expertise. They had requested that the City Council fund a planner to work with them on examining the issues surrounding the mega-projects to enable them to participate more effectively. This request was denied putting them in a disadvantaged negotiating position compared with the developers and both the provincial and city governments.

DERA spearheaded much of the community resistance to Expo and the subsequent Pacific Place proposals. DERA represented the 10,000-strong, mostly low income, Downtown Eastside community that lived in the area. DERA was composed of, and controlled by, the residents themselves. They opposed the Expo evictions and have consistently campaigned against the negative impacts they feared the mega-projects would have on their neighbourhood. However, they were as consistently dismissed by the NPA majority on council as being 'too political', or being opposed to change and development. This was clearly not the case. DERA has, since Expo, become a major social housing developer and has built a number of successful housing projects in the area; they have provided an important welfare advocacy role for local residents; won a seven-year fight to provide the only recreational facility in the neighbourhood, the well-used Carnegie Centre, a library and community centre; worked in a campaign to provide a waterfront park for local residents; and dealt proactively with drug and alcohol problems in the neighbourhood. As a result of DERA's efforts the Downtown Eastside has become one of the most stable neighbourhoods in the city in the context of a rapidly changing central area.

YERBA BUENA, SAN FRANCISCO

San Francisco, like Vancouver, is also located on the Pacific Rim of North America and has experienced considerable development pressure, particularly within its downtown area. It is a city that is attractive to major developers keen to exploit its economic and locational potential. The 87-acre Yerba Buena site proved to be one such development opportunity, located in the South of Market area of the city close to its downtown and financial heart. Until the 1960s the South of Market area was largely an industrial and service commercial area, but had a substantial residential population.

Plans for redevelopment of the Yerba Buena site can be traced back to 1953, when Ben Swig, a San Francisco-based developer, put forward his redevelopment proposals for the area in his plan entitled the *San Francisco Prosperity Plan*. The plan covered four city blocks and included a convention centre, a sports stadium, high rise office buildings and parking for 7,000 cars. This plan was expanded in 1955 to include two additional city blocks and proposals for a large transportation terminal, a luxury hotel with convention facilities, an auditorium and theatre, moving sidewalks, a shopping centre, and increased parking for 16,000 cars. Swig's plan for Yerba Buena was never adopted, but it set the tone for subsequent development proposals for the area (Hartman 1974).

In 1964 the San Francisco Redevelopment Agency (SFRA) unveiled its first general plan for Yerba Buena – this led to a major confrontation over the site between development interests and the local community. A major impact of the redevelopment proposals was that in the South of Market area several thousand people (mostly retired people) would be forced out of their apartments and homes to enable demolition to occur to facilitate the plans. 'In downtown redevelopment clichés the common justification for pushing working class residents, including the elderly, off their land is that the land can be put to a "higher and better use"' (Feagin 1983: 174).

In 1970 the Executive Director of the SFRA stated the position most clearly with regard to the Yerba Buena site: 'This land is too valuable to permit poor people to park on it' (Hartman 1974: 19). Such views were commonly replicated in the San Francisco press:

> Common sense suggests that something sensible is going to have to be built here. There will be no low cost housing for the dregs of society. There is no profit in that and there is little evidence that the dregs really want to sleep in precious, clean, well lighted places. Misery loves misery, just as capitalists adore profits.
>
> (Twombly 1975)

The official justification given for the Yerba Buena development was that it would increase the city's tax base, create employment opportunities and enhance convention and tourist business – with concomitant benefits for all (Hartman 1974; Feagin 1983).

The SFRA played a key role in the Yerba Buena redevelopment from the mid-1960s onwards. The SFRA was a major renewal agency that had the power to co-ordinate private and public action and to carry out its plans and proposals with little citizen input. In the late 1960s, a series of redevelopment projects were undertaken in the area displacing about 4,000 people (mostly working-class black people and people of Japanese origin) from the area (Feagin 1983). It was estimated that over 4,000 units of housing would be demolished, but only replaced with 276 units of low income housing (Weinstein 1970).

The Yerba Buena plans were altered over the years in order to overcome the objections of numerous community groups. The developers added various amenities including public gardens, a fountain, open space, a children's centre, and other facilities (*San Francisco Weekly* 1989). By 1993, after nearly thirty years of controversy over the site, a number of developments had been completed including the Marriott Hotel (opened in 1989); The Moscone Centre (opened in 1981); ANA Hotel (opened in 1983); the Visual Arts Centre, the Museum of Modern Art and the Esplanade (a 5.5-acre garden). Development projects still to be completed include a children's centre; a retail complex; a Jewish Museum; and additional housing, hotel space and office development (*San Francisco Chronicle* 1993).

Local and federal governments supported the Yerba Buena redevelopment proposals and formed a powerful alliance with the city's larger private corporations, hotel owners and others in the convention and tourist industry, the building and construction trade unions and the newspapers and other media (Hartman 1974). The project was seen as a means of further promoting San Francisco as a major international city.

The San Francisco city government has been supportive of the corporate community and played an important facilitative role. The individuals elected and appointed to major positions in the city government overwhelmingly had links with the business community. The decision-making process relating to the Yerba Buena development was largely determined and controlled by these interests. Hartman argues:

> This involved no large-scale secret conspiracy but was a confluence of powerful and influential people acting in their class interest. The results of this elitist decision-making process are that the costs and benefits of a project presumably designed for the public good are distributed in a highly regressive manner.
>
> (Hartman 1974: 212)

While there was little formal public participation in the 'official' planning process in relation to Yerba Buena, there was considerable community activity outside this process that impacted on the development. Extensive use was made of the judiciary system in this regard, causing delay in the development. There was the 1969 Tenants and Owners in Opposition to Redevelopment (TOOR) law suit; state and federal suits were brought in 1972 by Alvin Duskin, the Sierra Club, San Francisco Tomorrow and others alleging failure to comply with the California Environmental Quality Act and National Environmental Policy Act; and there were also a number of lawsuits filed against the financing of the project. These legal actions resulted in positive outcomes: the TOOR law suit ultimately produced commitments to construct 2,200 units of permanent new and rehabilitated low rent housing units on-stream; whilst the various financing law suits stopped the development of the costly sports arena, and scaled down the convention centre subsidies (Hartman 1984).

Community opposition to the Yerba Buena plans, therefore, had resulted in a number of important concessions. However, it could be argued that these changes did not alter the fundamental basis of the development as 4,000 people were still displaced, 700 businesses were lost (with 7,600 blue-collar jobs), and a low income community destroyed (Levering and Roberts 1975).

One important factor that can be identified in explaining the ability of residents and community groups in San Francisco to challenge pro-growth development interests is the diverse and well-informed citizenry prepared to become involved in planning and development issues. There is a long history of community action in the city. Community and neighbourhood organisations in the city have had some influence on city planning and are known for the strength of their challenge to corporate interests (Barton 1985).

BIRMINGHAM

Birmingham, located in the heart of England's industrial West Midlands region, is Britain's second largest city with a population of just under one million people. During the late 1970s the city and regional economy, traditionally dependent on manufacturing industry (particularly the auto-motive and engineering sectors), was devastated by economic recession and the restructuring of industry. Between 1971 and 1987 Birmingham lost 191,000 jobs, amounting to 29 per cent of total employment in the city. In 1991 Birmingham was the poorest free-standing English city according to the government's Index of Local Conditions. In response to the city's pressing economic problems, Birmingham's ruling Labour administration in the early 1980s sought to broaden its economic base through the nurturing of service sector investment, most notably business tourism. To facilitate this process, the City Council has sought to promote a new national and international image for Birmingham and provide a framework for facilitating private sector investment within its CBD.

In this context the City Council adopted a CBD-focused model of regeneration as its primary vehicle for securing the city's economic future, promoting Birmingham as an international centre for business tourism, leisure and culture, and attracting footloose inward private sector invest-ment and jobs (Loftman and Nevin 1992). Birmingham's mega-project is focused on the Broad Street redevelopment area adjacent to the CBD. Four developments provide the focus of this strategy:

- the £180 million International Convention Centre (ICC), opened in April 1991, with a maximum conference capacity of 3,700 delegates and inclusion of a 'world class' symphony hall;
- the £60 million National Indoor Arena (NIA), built to enhance the city's position as an international centre for sport, and seating up to 12,000 people;
- the £31 million Hyatt Hotel, built as an integral part of the ICC development;
- the £250 million privately financed Brindleyplace festival marketplace scheme. Recently revised plans for the scheme include the development

of 850,000 square feet of offices, 123,000 square feet of retail space and 143 houses.

Birmingham City Council's £300 million investment in its CBD projects has been justified by local politicians largely in terms of diversifying the city's local economy, attracting mobile private investment, and putting Birmingham on the international map. However, the prime justification for Birmingham's investment in prestige projects has been the creation of jobs and the generation of an income boost to the local and regional economy. The City Council has claimed that the ICC has helped to attract £2 billion of public and private sector investment to Birmingham (Birmingham City Council 1992). Additionally, consultants commissioned by the City Council have estimated that the expenditure generated by business tourism associated with the ICC and NIA projects supports around 4,600 full-time equivalent (FTE) jobs. Of this total, however, only 1,800 FTE jobs were estimated to be filled by Birmingham residents, emphasising the extent of leakage from the city's local economy (KPMG 1993).

The perceived success of Birmingham's prestige project developments has been acclaimed by the local and national media, professional bodies (*The Planner* 1991; *Planning* 1991) and some academic commentators (Carley 1991; Martin and Pearce 1992). In the context of the widely accepted success of Birmingham's prestige projects, a climate of media, official and public optimism was created within the city which mitigated against public debate about potential negative impacts. Several criticisms of Birmingham's approach to urban regeneration have subsequently been made and are summarised below. Firstly, it is argued that many of the jobs created in the facilities and generated in the associated sectors are of low quality. In September 1991, 42 per cent of the 275 permanent jobs at the ICC and 73 per cent of the seventy-one permanent jobs at the NIA were jobs within the cleaning, catering and security occupations (Loftman and Nevin 1994).

Secondly, that disadvantaged groups in the city gained few of the benefits from Birmingham's prestige projects via the trickle-down process. For example, relatively few of the permanent staff employed in Birmingham's prestige projects were from black and minority ethnic groups. In 1992 of the 346 permanent staff employed in the ICC and NIA only 8 per cent were from black and minority ethnic groups. By comparison, these groups accounted for 17.5 per cent of the city's economically active population (Loftman and Nevin 1994).

Thirdly, that the City Council's investment in prestige project developments also resulted in the diversion of scarce public resources away from 'basic' services, such as public housing and education services, which are particularly depended on by the city's disadvantaged groups. For example, the city's education service was deprived of capital resources during the ICC and NIA construction period with capital spending falling by 60 per cent between 1984/5 and 1988/9. In addition, in 1991/2 it was estimated that £64 million was 'diverted' from education revenue support to cover the interest charges on projects such as the ICC (Loftman and Nevin 1992).

The massive diversion of capital and revenue resources from housing and education towards prestige project property developments in Birmingham will have a disproportionate long-term impact upon disadvantaged groups in Birmingham. It has been estimated that in April 1993, 81,251 homes in Birmingham were unfit for human habitation and the outstanding repair bill for the public sector housing stock was around £1.3 billion (Birmingham City Council 1993). In addition, it has been estimated that an investment of £200 million over the next five years is needed to rectify the disrepair in school buildings in the city (Birmingham Education Commission 1993).

Despite the huge physical and socio-economic impacts which the development of prestige projects have had in Birmingham, there was only limited public opposition to the developments, or an informed debate about the costs or benefits resulting from the projects, over the decade in which the policies were pursued. This lack of debate was the result of a political consensus within the city (both within the City Council and between the public and private sectors), a supportive local media, and because there was no requirement to have a public referendum on the bond issue which part-financed the developments. This can be contrasted with the more liberal freedom of information laws which exist in North America.

The political consensus emerged in Birmingham during the early 1980s around the need to pursue 'an aggressive pro-development strategy to manage the concurring problems of structural decline and cyclical downturn' (DiGaetano and Klemanski 1992: 16–17). The basic goal of this pro-development strategy was 'to promote projects that would protect the City's industrial base while facilitating the growth of downtown office and commercial sectors' (ibid.: 17).

In Birmingham, there has been little public involvement or debate concerning the development of the city's CBD-focused regeneration strategy and the formulation of the vision of Birmingham as 'the world-class City' (Kosny and Loftman 1991). The first major forum in the formulation of Birmingham's vision for the development and promotion of its CBD was the Highbury Initiative, two symposia (in 1988 and 1989) which brought together the experience of public officials, private sector interest and an international group to bear on the problems faced by the city. However, the initiative was marked by the absence of any members of the public at these meetings (The Highbury Initiative 1989).

The first major opportunity for the residents of Birmingham to have an input into the formulation of the city's urban regeneration strategy came with the preparation of the Birmingham Unitary Development Plan (UDP) in the late 1980s after construction work on the ICC and the NIA had begun. However, public involvement in the process was limited by the need to produce the plan quickly in order to comply with central government advice and provide a framework for private investment decisions. The relatively low level of public debate was reflected in the fact that only twenty-five written responses on the draft plan were received by the City Council relating to the proposals affecting the city centre area, and only seven relating to the broad strategy outlined in the report (Kosny and Loftman 1991).

The UDP was followed by a public conference 'The Future of Your City Centre' in February 1992. However, this public debate took place almost four years after the first Highbury Initiative Symposia, and once again after construction work on many city centre projects had started (for example, the city centre pedestrianisation and reconstruction of Victoria Square) or had been completed (the ICC, NIA, Hotel and Centenary Square).

Public debate of Birmingham's CBD regeneration strategy has been further constrained by the paucity of information regarding the 'real' financial costs of this strategy. Much of this information has remained on confidential council committee agendas under Sections 8 and 9 of the Local Government Act 1985. In Birmingham, therefore, it may be argued that the city's residents have had little real opportunity to influence the development of the City Council's urban regeneration strategy. Rather, a veneer of public involvement in the process was created without full access to information relating to the extent of the opportunity costs involved.

Against a backdrop of a minimalist public participation strategy relating to city centre development in general, a local political consensus, a pro-development local media and limited access to information laws, public opposition to the development of Birmingham's prestige projects was negligible. There are a number of reasons which may explain the lack of community action when compared to the two North American case studies.

Firstly, unlike in the Vancouver and San Francisco examples, there was no displacement of local residents as a *direct* result of the Birmingham developments, thus reducing the immediacy of the projects on the local people. Secondly, initial potential community resistance in a deprived council estate (Central Ladywood), located adjacent to the prestige projects, was partially offset by the City Council's utilisation of central government Estate Action funds to undertake a £13 million refurbishment of the area's housing stock. Thirdly, the manner in which Birmingham's prestige projects were funded meant that the most prominent negative impact on the most marginal groups occurred at the city level, rather than being more narrowly focused on an adjacent poor neighbourhood.

CONCLUSIONS

A major conclusion to emerge from this brief review of prestige project and mega-project activity in the three case study cities is that democratic, representative, responsible local government may seek to prioritise pro-growth interests over the needs of disadvantaged communities. Powerful forces are at work which can skew democratic decision-making processes in favour of those who control the economic and political life of the city.

Generally community groups are no match for powerful development interests and growth coalitions that exist within cities in Canada, the United States and Great Britain. In many cases the most community groups can achieve from challenging such developments is to win concessions from developers, in an attempt to make the development proposals more sensitive to community needs. The concessions gained, however, do not, in most cases, have a major bearing on the final outcome and impact of the development. Moreover, it could be argued that many of the community benefits included in the prestige and mega-project developments are often tangential to the pressing needs of the urban poor, and marginal in scale when compared with the benefits which accrue to other more affluent residents from the rest of the city or the broader region.

There appeared to have been little effective community participation in the planning processes attached to the developments in each of the three cities. In respect of the Pacific Place development, a comprehensive public participation process was set up to input community viewpoints. However, this process was not amenable to the community setting the terms of reference. The communities' input was limited to reacting to development proposals rather than being able to influence its form, nature and impact at the outset. In San Francisco, community opposition was channelled through other mechanisms outside of the planning process, and particular use was made of the courts which resulted in amendments to the plan. In both of these examples organised community resistance, often in conjunction with liberal professionals, was able to generate positive outcomes, such as commitments to provide some low income housing. However, there are still unresolved questions as to how these commitments will be honoured. In the case of Birmingham, there was a complete absence of a public debate about the costs and benefits of this type of development. The lack of publicly available information relating to the redevelopment of the city centre effectively constrained any community resistance to the regeneration proposals.

It is evident from the three case studies that the outcomes of the North American projects to date have been more brutal and socially regressive. Evictions resulted from both the Expo experience and the early days of the Yerba Buena project. No such direct negative outcome resulted in Birmingham, but potential negative impacts on low income neighbourhoods and groups are being experienced in terms of the reduction of scarce local authority resources. Vancouver and San Francisco have become the epitome of the 'entrepreneurial city' in recent years, marketing their attractive quality and their good location on the Pacific Rim. It is clear from examples such as Birmingham that local economic policy in Britain is moving in the same direction.

14

RELIGION, EDUCATION AND CITY POLITICS

A case study of community mobilisation

Wendy Ball and James A. Beckford

INTRODUCTION

A relatively new, and under-researched, dimension of the political life of British cities has emerged where sizeable communities of Muslims, Hindus, Sikhs and Jains have developed since the 1950s. These ethno-religious communities have now established their own buildings and organisations, often in networks of ties with similar communities in other cities, and have begun to explore ways of exercising political influence at least partly through the medium of religion. In other words, collective interests and identities are crystallising around actors and associations with explicitly religious significance.

The main aim of this chapter is to describe ongoing research into the processes by which political activity, at least in part, follows the contour lines of ethno-religious communities in Upton, a large, pseudonymous English city.[1] Our project is designed to assess the variable significance of religious collectivities as vehicles of political activity. To give the project a sharper focus, issues of school-level education are examined as the site on which the interaction between religious and political forces takes place.

The term 'ethno-religious' requires some discussion at this point (Wilpert 1988). Ethnicity and religion are two partially overlapping symbolic markers of collective identity (Knott 1986). The former emphasises feelings of solidarity, a common name, a shared culture, association with a shared territory of origin, and presumed descent from common ancestors (Smith 1986). The latter denotes shared beliefs and practices relative to questions of ultimate significance. The relationship between them can take different forms. In the case of groups such as Jews and Sikhs in the UK the markers are virtually coterminous, but the relationship between ethnicity and religion is more varied in the case of Muslims and Christians.

The combination of religion and ethnicity can serve as a basis for, *inter alia*, political mobilisation, social protest or campaigning activity (Modood *et al.* 1994). Our main reason for using the compound adjective 'ethno-religious' is therefore to underline the fact that local political activity sometimes follows the contours of communities which *define themselves* in terms of religion *and* ethnicity, usually in subtle and shifting combinations. Of course, the relative salience of the two terms varies from situation to situation. Moreover, finer gradations of ethnic and religious difference, which are complicated by further differentiations in terms of age, class or gender, may come into play on some occasions, but not on others. For example, differences which occasionally come between Muslims of varying ethnic background, national origins or theological tradition may nevertheless be put aside for the sake of joint participation in, say, unitary campaigns to preserve single-sex secondary schools or to challenge the existing law against blasphemy. We believe it is essential to pay special attention to the precise shades of ethnic and religious significance that actors attach to their own political activity and to that of others in particular situations.

The idea of examining the ethno-religious dimension of the politics of education at the city level arises from current debates about the changing character of politics in societies marked by ethnic diversity and conflict. There is a long tradition of inquiry into the voting behaviour, party loyalties and class identity of the communities founded by African-Caribbean and Asian migrants to the UK (Anwar 1986; Fitzgerald 1984; Layton-Henry 1984). There is also a body of knowledge about the involvement of ethnic minorities in local politics (Newton 1975; Reeves 1989). Other studies have explored the development of interest groups and other associations formed by ethnic minorities (Rex 1991; King 1993). What has so far tended to escape the attention of researchers, however, is the extent to which *religion*, either in association with or analytically separated from 'race' or ethnicity, can serve as a medium or vehicle for *local* politics in the widest sense of the term (but see Ellis 1991a, 1991b; Nielsen 1992).

Our main reasons for positioning the issue of education at the centre of the project are that it is known to be both a constant, long-running site of political struggle at local level and a topic which elicits strong responses from ethno-religious communities. As a Birmingham city councillor remarked to Newton (1975: 203), 'On education you've got a night of the long knives every night.'

Our reason for devoting an unusually large amount of attention to religion in relation to the politics of education is that it is a relatively under-researched topic which is nevertheless of increasing importance in the UK. The growing salience of the topic is partly to do with the long-term maturation of ethnic minority communities with distinctive religious traditions and partly to do with the responses of many different religious groups to a whole series of educational reforms since the 1960s.

We deliberately chose to limit the project's geographical scope to a single, large, ethnically diverse city in order to obtain a fine-grained picture of the entire range of political contributions arising from ethno-religious communities. We are confident that this is more likely to be achieved in a single location than by a necessarily less intensive study of more than one city. We also chose to analyse not only ethno-religious communities' collective involvement in the politics of education but also the other relevant actors in Upton's political life. They include elected councillors, local government officials, key personnel in the Education Department, community relations specialists, and representatives of political parties or trade unions. Our aim was to place the public debates about education in their local political context and thereby to examine the distinctiveness and relative significance of input from ethno-religious communities.

In an effort to move beyond the conventional understanding of 'local community' we wanted to capitalise on Meg Stacey's (1969) insight into 'the local social system' but to adapt her conceptualisation to the circumstances of a large, multi-ethnic and religiously diverse city. This adaptation requires greater sensitivity to (a) the fragmentary nature of the system and (b) the situational or episodic activation of the social networks. In particular, we concentrate on how and why religious factors are central to *some* mobilisations of political action but not to others, even when school-level education is selected as the sole focus of the action.

LOCAL AUTHORITY POLICIES AND RELIGIOUS DIVERSITY: RELIGIOUS EDUCATION, RACIAL EQUALITY AND COMMUNITY LIAISON

Our historical analysis[2] of the relationship between Upton Local Authority and the diverse faith communities in the city during the period 1945–95 revealed three broad foci for further exploration. They offer a framework for comparing our case study with developments in other localities with a population which is diverse in religion. There are three areas of Local Authority policy which are likely to influence how ethno-religious collectivities mobilise over educational issues. First, the provision of *religious education and collective worship* in schools elicits strong responses. Second, the *racialisation* of city politics and the development of policies for racial equality and equal opportunities impact directly on ethno-religious communities. Third, attempts by Local Authority officials and politicians to liaise with members of faith communities and to offer opportunities for *communication* of views and demands are very revealing about the local political system.

In relation to all three areas, the complex relationship between ethnicity and religious identity is a central problematic at both a theoretical and methodological level and makes it difficult to isolate the specifically *religious* dimension of city politics. From a different angle, the concepts of equal opportunities, racial equality and religious pluralism embedded in Local Authority policies may set boundaries for responding to ethno-religious demands and preferences, with potential tensions between meeting the goal of equal treatment in service delivery and respecting the religious interests of diverse groups.

Religious education and collective worship

Upton LEA's approach to religious matters and relationships with local faith communities over the post-war period has been dominated by the legal duties of all LEAs, enshrined in the 1944 Education Act concerning religion. First was the duty to provide religious education (RE) in all schools and to ensure the school day included an act of collective worship. The second requirement was to work in partnership with church schools; that is, the voluntary aided and voluntary controlled school sector. Put another way, Upton LEA never formulated a coherent and comprehensive policy for dealing with religious diversity. Instead, provision was virtually confined to meeting the expectations of schools laid down in law. They can be outlined as follows.

According to the 1944 Education Act, religious education in state schools had to be in accordance with an Agreed Syllabus developed at the LEA level through an Agreed Syllabus Conference consisting of four panels. These panels were to ensure representation of the following groups: the Church of England, the Local Authority, the teachers' associations, and other religious denominations chosen by the LEA according to the particular circumstances of the area. Whilst the Act offered LEAs scope regarding the content of religious education and in choosing which religious groups should be involved in drawing up an Agreed Syllabus, it was taken for granted at this stage that both religious education and the daily act of worship would be based on Christianity. As Parsons comments:

> The constitution of the Agreed Syllabus Conferences reflected this assumption and, significantly, made no specific provision for representatives of religions other than Christianity. Christianity clearly, it was assumed, was the historically predominant and crucial formative influence in British religious life. An undenominational Christianity, therefore, was the obvious basis for the religious worship and education of schoolchildren.
>
> (Parsons 1994: 166)

These assumptions also underpinned the continuation and consolidation of the dual system of state schools and church schools following the 1944 Education Act. As Leslie Francis claims, 'the 1944 Education Act designed an educational system appropriate for a Christian or church-related society' (1993: 159). The passing of the Education Reform Act in 1988 (and subsequent Circulars from the Department for Education) brought the issue of religious provision in schools to the forefront of political debate. The new Act reaffirmed the requirements that schools must provide religious education and hold a daily act of collective worship. However, it also went further than the earlier legislation by reducing the scope for flexibility in the interpretation of these requirements at the local level. All LEAs were required to establish a Standing Advisory Council on Religious Education (SACRE) with responsibility to review the Agreed Syllabus for RE in use in the area and with a duty to report on an annual basis. However, it is the place accorded to Christianity in the Act which is of particular concern here. As Parsons explains:

> The particular religions which were to be included in the religious education and worship provided in schools were now specified –

whereas the 1944 Act had said nothing on this point ... the requirements that the daily collective worship should be 'wholly or mainly of a broadly Christian character', and that the Agreed Syllabuses should 'reflect the fact that the religious traditions in Great Britain are in the main Christian', meant that Christianity was now *formally* and *officially* given a prominence which it had not enjoyed under the previous legislation.

(Parsons 1994: 185)

The membership of the SACREs was to consist of the same four panels referred to in relation to the Agreed Syllabus Conference in the 1944 Education Act; that is, the Church of England, the local authority, local teachers' associations and 'such Christian and other religious denominations as, in the opinion of the authority, will appropriately reflect the principal religious traditions in the area'. Whilst the criteria for membership of the fourth panel do allow for the recognition of diverse religious traditions where they are present in the area, the local authority retains the power to select them, and they will still be in a minority. Similarly, the Agreed Syllabus for RE may also take 'account of the teaching and practices of the other principal religions represented in Great Britain', but Christianity is to be given priority.

The priority accorded to Christianity in law is mirrored at the local level in Upton. In our case study, the spirit of partnership and consensus between the LEA and the local church authorities appeared to be strong in the decades following the 1944 Act. The Church of England, the Roman Catholic Church and the Free Church Council each had the right to nominate a representative to the Education Committee and they were also represented on the Local Standing Advisory Council for Religious Matters (LACRM) set up in the late 1940s. It was during this period that many voluntary aided and voluntary controlled schools for the Church of England and the Roman Catholic population were built, and the regular discussion of religious matters by the Education Committee was confined mainly to the management of this sector. The LEA was highly supportive of the need to provide denominational schools for a growing Roman Catholic school population.

We aim to explore how this apparent consensus and partnership between the LEA and the Christian Church authorities was influenced by the migration to the city during the 1950s and 1960s of people from the Caribbean and South Asia, many of whom came from different religious traditions and organisations. We want to know how far the framework which had developed for discussing religious matters shifted from the unspoken assumption that these should be confined to mainstream Christianity towards a broader based and inclusive approach. Furthermore, to what extent did the tendency to confine educational discussion over religious matters to the specific issues of religious education, collective worship and courses for teachers extend to a wider set of concerns of potential interest to religious collectivities?

Our evidence shows that, until the late 1980s, policies for Religious

Education remained largely untouched by these changes in the character of the city's population. This is remarkable, given that from the early 1970s onwards there was increasing discussion of the educational needs of ethnic minority pupils and the organisation of ethnic minority groups in the city. We consider this in more detail below.

The racialisation of city politics and the demands of ethno-religious groups

A great deal has been written about the response of LEAs to issues of 'race', ethnicity and racism and the development of policies on multicultural and anti-racist education especially since the early 1980s (Dorn 1983; Gill *et al.* 1992; Mullard 1982; Troyna 1993). Beyond the educational arena, local authorities have introduced policies on equal opportunities which include initiatives to tackle racial inequality in employment and service provision (Ball and Solomos 1990; Braham *et al.* 1992; Jenkins and Solomos 1987). The importance of political mobilisation by black and ethnic minority community groups as well as by anti-racist organisations at the local level has also been considered in this context (Cheetham 1988; Goulbourne 1987; Ramdin 1987; Reeves 1989; Solomos 1989).

These processes signify the racialisation of political debate at both local and national levels in recent decades. According to Ball and Solomos, an understanding of the local politics of 'race' requires an historical perspective for

> Over the past two decades the racialisation of local politics has undergone a number of transformations. The processes which have resulted in the racialisation of local politics are complex, and to some extent they have been determined by the specific histories of particular localities.
>
> (Ball and Solomos 1990: 6)

In Upton, from the mid-1960s onwards, meetings of the Education Committee referred more frequently to responses to the educational needs of ethnic minority children. The period from the mid-1960s to the early 1970s was one in which the LEA defined the needs of 'immigrant' children in terms of English as a Second Language support. Teachers were also encouraged to attend conferences concerned with the putative 'problems' faced by 'immigrant' children. During the early 1970s the LEA began to consider proposals for staff to be funded through Section 11 of the Local Government Act, 1966 which further encouraged a 'special needs' approach to the educational support of ethnic minority children. Upton LEA's approach corresponds closely to the assimilationist model which generally underpinned the policies and practices of schools at that time (Mullard 1982).

Our analysis reveals a slight shift in the approach of the LEA and its relationship with community groups following the reorganisation of local government in 1974, although they were still fragmented and *ad hoc*. On the one hand, for the period from the mid-1970s onwards, we found evidence of the growing mobilisation of ethnic minority community groups and communication with the LEA. The local Community Relations Council became active during this time, and membership of the LEA Education Committee was extended to a representative of 'non-Christian' religions. On the other hand, this was also the period when bidding for funds under both Section 11 and the Urban Programme acquired a momentum and became a considerable and regular part of the LEA's responsibilities. Funding under Section 11 was secured in the late 1970s to appoint a team of ESL teachers and an adviser for multicultural education, and therefore established the institutional framework within which the LEA would respond to a multi-ethnic population in the future.

Section 71 of the Race Relations Act of 1976 placed a general statutory duty on local authorities 'to eliminate unlawful racial discrimination and to promote equality of opportunity and good race relations'. Upton's Council responded by setting up an inter-departmental working party to consider a corporate approach to race relations, and its report was considered by the Education Committee in 1979. As for many other local authorities, this marked the beginning of a more co-ordinated approach to racial equality through the adoption of policies and procedures which continued during the 1980s. The City Council adopted an Equal Opportunities Statement in 1980, and in 1985 the Education Committee began to discuss whether it should prepare a policy statement on multicultural education. Further policy initiatives from both the City Council and the LEA followed after this.

The period from 1985 onwards signalled a further shift in the local politics of 'race' in the city. Whilst policy development for equal opportunities continued, it was in a context of greater pressure on the LEA in terms of new legislation and economic constraints, including the tightening of Home Office regulations concerning the allocation of Section 11 funding. A trend towards the greater mobilisation of sections of the community around educational provision can be clearly discerned in this period of constraint.

Our periodisation of the LEA's approach towards issues of 'race' and ethnicity revealed that, both in terms of the initial focus on meeting the needs of ethnic minority pupils and the subsequent shift to promotion of a policy for equal opportunities, there is an apparent reluctance to acknowledge the diversity of *religious* preferences. Despite the racialisation of city politics there has been little debate about the issue of equal treatment on religious grounds and about appropriate responses to religious diversity. It is clear from other local case studies that the question of how far to go in respecting religious diversity is one area of policy that LEAs have found particularly difficult to address.

For example, in her case study of Coventry City Council's response to Muslims and the request of one section of the community for a Muslim community centre, Ellis comments:

the early official response to the demands for a Muslim centre included an influential view against putting public funds into 'promoting the interests of any religious group or organisations', the argument being that it would 'generate sectarianism, draw scarce resources from categories of needy groups'.

(Ellis 1991a: 362)

In this context Ellis points out that it is the different groups within the Asian communities in Coventry which have pressed to gain recognition of their religious and cultural identities. Similarly, in her study of Muslims in Birmingham, Joly comments 'Muslims are remarking that there is a reticence on the part of the authorities to award grants for religious projects and some have voiced their discontent on this matter' (1987: 22). This compares with the greater willingness of the local authority to make grants for mother-tongue teaching and support for community centres. It would seem, therefore, that whilst there may be a willingness to meet certain wishes of ethnic minority groups, there is often reluctance to recognise and sponsor specifically *religious* demands.

In view of this, we will move on to consider the extent to which the various ethno-religious communities themselves have been able to propose an alternative agenda. We shall discuss this in terms of available channels of communication with the LEA.

Channels of communication: community liaison and consultation

The mobilisation of ethno-religious communities over educational issues depends partly on how far LEAs attempt to liaise with those communities and offer accessible channels for communication. Other studies have provided evidence of the limited nature of consultation exercises undertaken by Local Authorities with ethnic minority communities (Ball 1987; Ben-Tovim *et al.* 1986; Gibson 1987). With reference to communication with diverse faith communities the signs are that Local Authorities prefer to evade any focus on *religious* groupings and *religious* preferences. Instead, they prefer to use the language of 'race' and ethnicity (see, for example, Ellis 1991a, 1991b). Our evidence from Upton shows a preference by officers and councillors to approach the communication process within the context of a generalised commitment to consultation with local citizens. Community liaison is informed by the City Council's equal opportunities policy and declared commitment to tackling poverty, deprivation and discrimination. As one senior officer explained, liaison 'tends to be on a broad basis and it doesn't tend to be religious led'.

With respect to opportunities for religious *representation* on LEA committees the Church of England, Roman Catholic and Free Church authorities have enjoyed the right to send a nominee to the Education Committee since 1945. In 1974 that right was extended to a nominee for 'non-Christian' religions. This has been a source of irritation in some ethno-religious communities, however, given the obvious difficulties of nominating a single individual to represent all such groups in Upton. Following the establishment of the local SACRE, Upton Education Committee has used this forum as the mechanism for nominating that representative, now referred to as the 'representative of Asian religions'. In practice, this position has rotated between the Muslim, Hindu and Sikh members of the SACRE. However, it is fair to suggest that apart from the link with SACRE the city's strategies for communication with local faith communities are fragmented, unco-ordinated and tend to minimise the issue of *religious* identity.

ETHNO-RELIGIOUS MOBILISATION AND EDUCATIONAL POLITICS

In their case study of the local politics of 'race' in Wolverhampton, Ben-Tovim and his colleagues (1986) identify three forms of anti-racist struggle; namely 'spontaneous protest', 'pressure for community resources' and 'planned political struggle'. Applying this framework to Upton, we argue that it will be difficult for ethno-religious collectivities to pursue strategies of 'planned political struggle' as they enjoy only limited opportunities for this in terms of the existing communication process. It can be argued that the demands of ethno-religious groups take two broad forms in view of these limitations. First, there is demand for Local Authority support for self-help projects run by particular sections of the community. Here 'pressure for community resources' is the preferred form of 'struggle'. Second, there are demands that mainstream educational provision should take account of ethno-religious needs. In this case the limitations of LEA communication processes referred to above may leave 'spontaneous protest' as the only strategy available to faith communities.

Our evidence so far indicates that mobilisation has been reactive rather than proactive, is of an episodic nature and is more likely to be successful where it relates to issues of concern to a broad spectrum of ethnic groups rather than of concern to a particular religious group. We will conclude this section with an example of each kind of demand.

Requesting local authority support for a self-help project

Upton Education Committee received a request in 1992 from an organisation which provided Koranic classes to be granted free lettings at a local school. The Committee refused the request and reaffirmed its policy on this matter: whilst it was willing to provide free lettings in schools for groups to run community language classes, a fee should be charged for classes held by religious organisations. Whilst the LEA is willing to support certain forms of self-help by community groups, this example appears to support our hypothesis that it is reluctant to support specifically religious needs.

Reacting to changes in mainstream educational provision

The preference of parents from some ethno-religious groups for single-sex schools for girls became an issue of concern in the mid-1980s when the LEA was faced with the need to reorganise educational provision in a climate of declining enrolment and economic cutbacks. This review involved extensive consultation including public meetings, meetings with interested parties and written responses to its consultative documents. The proposals included several school closures, and in this context the LEA received sixty-five responses arguing the need to retain the single-sex schools in the city. In its report on the public consultation exercise, the Committee made the following comments on this issue:

> We reaffirm the principle that a truly comprehensive system should not include single sex schools and our intention to work towards all schools being mixed.
>
> However, we have taken note of the views of those who have supported retention of single sex schools in arriving at our proposals. Most of those favouring single sex provision ... do so for girls on religious grounds.

At this stage the Committee were willing to accede to parental preference, and their revised proposals included the retention of the single-sex schools. However, the comments above show clearly how the conception of equal opportunities favoured by the LEA not only fails to be clear about how this relates to religious rights and preferences but may actually be seen to be in direct conflict with the notion of separate provision on religious grounds. The issue re-emerged in 1992 when the LEA initiated public consultation on its proposal to change a single-sex secondary school for girls to a co-educational school. Whilst 26 per cent of the responses were in favour of retaining single-sex status, the LEA was still able to use the consultative exercise to argue that the majority favoured the change and it resolved to proceed with the proposal. A closer analysis of particular organisations involved in the consultation shows that there was a clear division between, on the one hand, those in favour of the transition to co-education, which comprised mainly secular educational organisations including the main teaching associations, and, on the other, those who wished to retain the single-sex status of the school, which comprised mainly ethno-religious groups from both the Muslim and Sikh communities. In addition a list of individuals from the Asian communities had been forwarded to the LEA stating that they wanted the school to consider the option of opting out of LEA control. This case provides a second example of how ethno-religious mobilisation to secure LEA recognition for religious preferences in education failed to achieve a positive response. The debate over provision of single-sex schooling for girls and the related debate over whether Muslim schools should enjoy the same right to be granted voluntary aided status enjoyed by Christian and Jewish schools (Ball and Troyna 1987; Parker-Jenkins 1991), or to use school opt-outs to create separate religious schools (Cumper 1990; Modood 1993), has gone on for many years. A decade has passed since the Swann Committee (1985) considered the case for separate religious schools. Whilst the Swann Committee acknowledged that the pressure from some ethno-religious groups to set up religious schools with voluntary aided status took place in a context in which the established churches had been able to take full advantage of the law in this area, it nevertheless rejected the case on the following grounds:

> In view of our overall aim of schools offering a full education for all our children it is hardly surprising that we cannot favour a 'solution' to the supposed 'problems' which ethnic minority communities face, which tacitly seems to accept that these 'problems' are beyond the capacity and imagination of existing schools to meet and that the only answer is therefore to provide 'alternative' schools for ethnic minority pupils thus in effect absolving existing schools from even making the attempt to reappraise and review their practices.
>
> (Swann Committee of Inquiry 1985: 510)

This response appears to gloss over the potential for conflict between the provision of education for all children in an environment which respects religious pluralism and the wishes of some parents for their children to be educated in line with their own specific religious faith (see, for example, Ashraf 1986). Our further research will provide an opportunity to explore these potential dilemmas in more detail.

CONCLUSION

We have focused this chapter on some of the obstacles which may face ethno-religious groups trying to elicit a response from local authorities to their religious preferences over school education. The preliminary findings from our research in one religiously diverse city point to the following conclusions. First, the issue of religious diversity is one area where the LEA has failed to develop a coherent policy or to ensure its channels of communication are open to the many religious groups present in the city.[3] Second, whilst reappraising educational provision in relation to the needs of ethnic minority groups and the policy on equal opportunities, the LEA has retained the power to define those needs and to avoid addressing explicitly the religious dimension of those needs. Indeed, a simplistic interpretation of the goal of offering equal treatment to all pupils can be used to rule demands for separate or different provision out of court. Drawing on the work of Bachrach and Baratz (1962), Dorn and Troyna have argued that we should take account of the '"politics of non-decisions"; that is, the exercise of power in education through the neutralisation and marginalisation of potentially contentious issues' (1982: 175). The LEA stance on religious matters appears to be a clear example of this process.

Nevertheless, it should be acknowledged that, with the establishment of the local SACRE, there is now a forum within Upton which draws together members of the main faith communities to discuss matters of religion and education in schools. How far this will help to open up channels of communication with the LEA and will be able to address issues beyond that of the Religious Education syllabus and acts of collective worship in schools remains to be seen.

Our argument in this chapter is not intended to deny the value of the racialisation of city politics and the introduction of equal opportunities policies. Indeed, we recognise that their introduction is largely a result of the campaigning activities of ethnic minority and anti-racist organisations over many years. Rather, we wish to stress that these policies and procedures tend to gloss over the most contentious and complex elements of race equality and to underplay the issue of religious difference. However, following the Rushdie affair there is growing recognition of the need to address the complex relationship between racial equality and ethno-religious identity. According to Modood (1993) it was in this context that the Commission for Racial Equality included consideration of blasphemy, incitement to religious hatred and religious discrimination in its Consultative Paper *Second Review of the Race Relations Act 1976* (1991) for 'it had to consider the issue of religion and the law when it was plain for many ethnic minorities their religious identity and the reaction of the rest of society to that identity, were of utmost importance' (Modood 1993: 513). Our continuing research in Upton aims to throw further light on these issues at the local level.

NOTES

1   We are grateful to the professional officers, elected councillors and members of the various faith communities in Upton who have generously shared their expertise and experience with us.
2   This is based on the Minutes of Upton's Education Committee and semi-structured interviews with key actors in the Local Authority and various faith communities.
3   However, a new Advisory Teacher for RE has recently implemented her commitment to breaking down the barriers between faith communities by arranging for schoolchildren to visit different places of worship and other communal resources in the city.

15

POVERTY, EXCLUDED COMMUNITIES AND LOCAL DEMOCRACY

Mike Geddes

ACKNOWLEDGEMENT

This chapter is based on a research paper written for the Commission for Local Democracy, and also draws on research on Local Strategies to Combat Poverty on Peripheral Estates funded by the Barrow and Geraldine S. Cadbury Trust. I am grateful to both for their support.

INTRODUCTION

Economic and social trends in recent years have significantly increased the numbers of those marginalised or excluded from the mainstream of representative democracy at the local level. These problems are particularly acute in areas like peripheral housing estates, where disadvantaged groups are concentrated and where physical isolation and the sparseness of community facilities reinforce social exclusion. A feature of recent disturbances on a number of such estates was the perception that they had been abandoned by the traditional representative democratic process and the institutions of local government (Campbell 1993).

This chapter outlines the growth of poverty and social exclusion in the UK, and then reviews the implications for the political participation of disadvantaged groups of a number of policy approaches to local concentrations of poverty and exclusion, from urban regeneration programmes to local anti-poverty projects and neighbourhood decentralisation initiatives by local government. It concludes that the more effective representation of excluded communities is a vital issue for local democracy.

THE GROWTH OF POVERTY AND SOCIAL EXCLUSION

The growth of poverty and social exclusion has been one of the major features of the political economy of the UK in the 1980s and the 1990s. This has been the result of four broad groups of linked factors (Mingione 1994).

Economic and industrial restructuring

The globalisation of trade and industry under the banner of the free market has been associated with successive recessions punctuated by fragile periods of economic growth; with a shift from manufacturing to service employment and a 'casino economy' of financial dealing; and with new capital-intensive production methods which have expelled workers from employment. The result has been high and long-lasting unemployment and a major increase in low-paid, part-time, temporary, casual and insecure work which means that poverty is now experienced by a significant number of those in work as well as those without jobs. Not only has the income gap between those with earnings and those dependent on benefits widened; differences in incomes from work have also grown rapidly (Joseph Rowntree Foundation 1995).

Poverty remains relatively concentrated in the economically weaker regions, and the growth of poverty in South East England, for example, has so far weakened but not eliminated such patterns (Cutler *et al.* 1994). But while traditional regional disparities still remain, unemployment and poverty are now far more widespread: in formerly prosperous as well as traditionally depressed regions; in the urban periphery as well as in the inner city; in small and medium-sized towns as well as large cities; among senior citizens and claimants in southern seaside towns as well as in old industrial areas. The implication of this is that poverty and social exclusion now pose a much more general challenge to local democracy nation-wide, not just in a limited number of specific areas.

Demographic and social change

The disappearance of many traditional male jobs and the feminisation of the workforce have been primary factors contributing to the weakening of the traditional nuclear family dependent upon the family wage of the male breadwinner. Alongside this are other trends which have attracted significant public attention: increasing homelessness; the growing numbers of lone-parent families, especially young single jobless parents; demographic trends such as the ageing of the population, resulting in growing numbers of infirm elderly people often living on fixed incomes. Together these mean that there are new social groups experiencing poverty and deprivation, creating new pressures on the supportive capacities of families and communities. Unemployment and poverty in association with social change and the cultural emphasis on individualism, consumption and competition have resulted in higher levels of crime and fear of crime, intensifying social stress especially in deprived communities (Beynon 1994).

The reshaping of the welfare system and public services

While demographic and social trends therefore place greater demands on welfare systems, the collapse of stable economic growth and high levels of unemployment have undermined the tax base of post-war welfare regimes, the 'safety net' against the worst effects of poverty, which were predicated upon the mass of the working population supporting a containable minority of dependants. Squeezed between growing demands and constrained resources, welfare systems have simultaneously undergone a turbulent period of restructuring driven by principles of privatisation, marketisation and business methods. These pressures have stretched public agencies to, and sometimes beyond, the limits of their ability to meet needs. In some places the crisis of public provision has been an important factor in community breakdown, expressed most clearly in periodic outbreaks of riot and disorder.

Changing modes of political representation

The marginalisation of poor and excluded groups has been exacerbated by the challenge which economic and social change has posed to established patterns of political representation. The decline of traditional industries in the West and the collapse of communism in the East have weakened the political parties of the left while neo-liberalism has now equally been discredited by its manifest failures. The inadequacies of the major political ideologies have contributed to the decline in public confidence in the formal political process as a whole, especially among the young. The struggle against the Criminal Justice Bill, for example, has helped to crystallise the view among many politicised young people that the mainstream political process offers little support for their campaigns or understanding of their culture. At the local level (the most likely arena of political involvement for most people) the erosion of the powers and resources of local government through centralising trends and the unelected 'new magistracy' of quangos has emptied local democracy of much of its meaning (Lamb and Geddes 1995: ch. 1).

From poverty to social exclusion?

The growth of poverty has of course not been a solely British phenomenon: poverty has increased throughout the European Union, and even more globally. Within Europe, the numbers of households in poverty grew by about 1.2 million to a total of 14 million between the mid-1970s and the mid-1980s, adding up to about 50 million people in poverty. More recently, the UK stands out with a larger growth of poverty than any other EU country, and a more rapid increase than any other 'old industrial' country (Gaffikin and Morrissey 1994a).

Many commentators see more in common between the UK and US experiences than between the UK and most other European countries, pointing to the way in which neo-liberal economic policies have accentuated the polarisation of the labour market to a greater extent than in many other European countries (Gaffikin and Morrissey 1994b). In 1979, the richest 20 per cent in the UK had a disposable income (after housing costs) of 35 per cent of the national total; but by 1989 this had grown to 41 per cent and by 1990/1 to 43 per cent. At the same time the share of the poorest 20 per cent fell from 10 per cent to 7 per cent to 6 per cent. Growing poverty in Britain is therefore associated with widening socio-economic differentials and polarisation. The previous long-term trend towards greater equality in the distribution of income has been reversed (Wilkinson 1994), and the growing gap between rich and poor is widely seen to be damaging to economic competitiveness (Dahrendorf *et al.* 1995).

The association of growing poverty with a more divided society has led to a considerable shift in the terms of policy (if not yet public) debate from the previous concept of poverty to the idea of social exclusion, which refers not only to the material deprivation of the poor but also to their inability to fully exercise their social, cultural and political rights as citizens – to employment, health, education, a minimum level of income. This takes as a starting point the existence of poverty, but goes on to explore its effects and consequences in terms of the capacity of individuals and groups to participate effectively in society. The concept of social exclusion brings with it notions of individual citizenship, rights, and obligations (Ditch 1993), which find some reflection in, for example, the perspectives on social justice and injustice adopted recently by the Commission on Social Justice (1993). But it has become particularly influential within European Union policy circles, so that for example the 1993 Green Paper on Social Policy argues that 'social exclusion ... by highlighting the flaws in the social fabric ... suggests something more than social inequality, and, concomitantly, carries with it the risk of a dual or fragmented society' (Commission of the European Communities 1993b).

While for some at least on the neo-liberal right inequality plays a positive role as a spur to growth and change, for those like the authors of the Green Paper social exclusion carries major threats to social cohesion and hence to economic prosperity.

There are some dangers in a broader – and potentially more amorphous – concept of social cohesion. It can distract our attention from the traditional concerns with low income, and the material gulf between poverty and affluence. If embracing the notion of social exclusion implied abandoning or watering down values of community, collectivity and equality, it brings obvious dangers, but there seems no compelling reason why this should be the case (Cohen 1994). Indeed, it is argued that the notion of social exclusion is helpful in recognising that disadvantage is experienced by individuals within local communities, and can be either reinforced by the degeneration of community or moderated by its network of mutual support (Room 1994). The advantages of a wider conception of social exclusion are the recognition that exclusion is a phenomenon not restricted to the lowest income groups, but that it differentially affects different social groups (young people, the elderly, single parents) and all those subject to discrimination, segregation and the weakening of traditional forms of social relationships. It points to an analysis of the causes of exclusion as a process dependent on the interplay of many factors, from the rapid pace of industrial change to the decay of some family structures, and the decline of traditional forms of solidarity and the rise of individualism.

This may make it easier to recognise poverty and marginalisation as a central component of contemporary political economy, not a residual phenomenon, a relict not yet mopped up by progress.

Political exclusion

The concept of exclusion is helpful in enabling us to recognise that problems of poverty and deprivation may be compounded by political exclusion – the isolation of poor people and communities from the mainstream of the political process, and the making of decisions about their lives elsewhere by others. This is particularly the case where geographical concentrations of poverty and deprivation exist – in inner cities, on peripheral housing estates, or in poor rural communities. Recent research shows that the concentration of intense poverty has increased during the 1980s (Green 1994). Such 'excluded communities', which can number tens of thousands of residents, are often largely composed of social groups – from single parents to the young, the old and the unemployed – who are alienated from mainstream political activity, or for whom political involvement is problematic. For single parents, child care and domestic responsibilities militate against active political involvement. Unemployment breaks the link which is crucial for many working people between the workplace and organised politics. For many poor people, even the costs of a bus fare to a community meeting can be hard to find or justify, especially if their neighbourhood has seen a succession of 'community initiatives' yielding little obvious change. Residents of poor estates can find both their neighbourhoods and the social groups to which they belong condemned and stigmatised in the local paper and the national media.

Problems of poverty, social and political exclusion have been documented in inner city areas for some considerable time now (Harrison 1983; Robson 1988). The case of more peripheral housing estates is more recent and less well documented but just as serious. On peripheral estates the sparseness of community facilities, and physical isolation compound the problems of unemployment and the ghettoisation of the poor. Many such estates were built to house the workforces of particular factories or factory estates, and as these have closed job prospects have disappeared. The initial relocation of residents to peripheral estates often broke up existing patterns of political activity and representation along with family and community networks. In 1991 outbreaks of violence and riot occurred on a number of such estates, from Cardiff to Oxford to Tyneside. In her powerful account of the causes and consequences of these events, Beatrix Campbell argues that these estates had been effectively abandoned by both the political parties and by local government and other agencies of the local state, which, in particular, had failed to support attempts – largely by women – on the estates to organise community solidarity and self-help. State agencies, Campbell suggests, don't like such neighbourhoods: they feel challenged and hurt by them, and so they disengage and become estranged from them, rather than providing the political representation and statutory services which a functioning community needs (Campbell

1993). These are disturbing questions both for officials and for traditional politicians and their parties.

Excluded communities such as peripheral estates therefore raise serious issues for democracy, and for local democracy in particular. Some of these, such as whether the national political parties can seriously address the concerns of the excluded, are beyond the scope of this chapter. Neither does it discuss those national welfare and social policies which are the primary response of the state to poverty and inequality. The concern here is with local political and policy processes, and the extent to which they offer excluded communities access to the local democratic process. Consequently the second part of the chapter assesses various locally focused initiatives, from urban regeneration projects to anti-poverty strategies and decentralisation initiatives within local government which purport to offer new approaches to the problems of excluded communities.

EMPOWERING EXCLUDED COMMUNITIES?

'Partnership with the community'?

Two concepts which today permeate discussion of the regeneration of deprived areas are 'partnership' and 'community', and unpacking the baggage which these words carry is an important objective of what follows. In the UK (Roberts *et al.* 1995), and increasingly in the European Union (Geddes 1995) the partnership approach to local area-based economic and social regeneration is now firmly established. Led by large and high-profile government programmes such as City Challenge and the more recent Single Regeneration Budget Challenge Fund, and EU programmes such as Poverty Three, the concept and practice of partnership has now percolated widely through the policy communities in both central and local government, other agencies such as Training and Enterprise Councils, and among voluntary sector agencies. Even among many of those who have their reservations about government-inspired programmes in which business is offered a leading role, there is a growing acceptance of the need to work critically but constructively within partnership frameworks to secure a variety of objectives (de Groot 1992). For local government particularly, subject to stringent resource constraints and erosion of powers and responsibilities, there now often seems little alternative to partnership.

Moreover, the involvement and 'empowerment' of local communities has now become an accepted dimension of the partnership approach. 'Partnership with the community' in local area-based regeneration and anti-poverty initiatives is becoming an important element of local governance as a preferred method of enabling local communities to voice their needs, become involved in decision-making, and to hold agencies accountable for their actions. This new 'corporatist localism', as it has recently been described (Stewart 1994), has a number of versions.

Urban regeneration

In the 1980s Conservative governments, while defeating the attempts by some Labour local authorities to pioneer 'municipal socialist' local economic policies, introduced their own innovations in the form of Enterprise Zones and Urban Development Corporations. These programmes represented an attempted privatisation of urban policy, in which large-scale government funding was used to attract private sector investment. They reflected a fairly explicit rejection by government of the ability of elected local government to promote effective urban regeneration, especially where this was seen to require collaboration with the private sector. The role of local authorities and local communities in these schemes was therefore strictly limited: local regeneration and local democracy were seen to be antagonistic.

The manifest limitations of a policy which did little more than hand 'those inner cities' to the property development industry on a plate were however increasingly obvious in the later 1980s, and governments have had to react to at least some of the criticisms. More recent urban regeneration programmes have increasingly sought to return some role to both local government and local communities in planning and implementing urban regeneration projects (Mabbott 1993).

Foremost among these has been City Challenge. Launched in 1991, by the end of the second (and last) allocation of funding in 1992 thirty-one major urban regeneration projects had been approved across the country, with a total resource allocation of £1,160 million over five years. While the nature of the competitive bidding process for City Challenge money means that many areas recognised by central government as suffering from multiple deprivation have not received funding, there is considerable overlap between the geographical spread of City Challenge projects and those areas of 'concentrated poverty' and social exclusion identified by recent research (Atkinson and Moon 1994).

Like its predecessors City Challenge remains committed to a business-led concept of urban regeneration, but has offered space for local government and local communities to participate within a partnership framework in two main ways. First, individual representatives or nominees of local authorities have been offered (and have generally accepted) places on project management structures, alongside representatives of business interests, other public bodies and quangos. Secondly, some City Challenge projects have promoted the formation of local 'community forums' as structures for neighbourhood residents to express their views, and have formed or supported Community Development Trusts or similar bodies to undertake 'community' projects funded by City Challenge monies.

However, programmes like City Challenge can confirm the marginalisation of socially excluded neighbourhoods and communities, rather than empower them in a meaningful way. Evidence from some areas suggests that the involvement of community representatives on 'partnership' structures offers only very limited control over the decisions, processes and expenditure of Boards and Executives. Even access to information may be strictly limited, and the nature of the policy processes can lead to the 'discursive marginalisation' of community representatives who are inexperienced in bureaucratic procedures (Robinson and Shaw 1991). This may not always be the case – some City Challenge projects argue that their approach has been more genuinely empowering, with strong community representation and efforts made to ensure that decision processes are open and flexible enough to enable those representatives to play a serious role. Even where such an attempt is made, though, the timetables and targets imposed by the DoE on all City Challenge projects make this difficult.

Others have suggested that the sponsorship by bodies such as City Challenge of 'community forums' and the like can create a 'tame' community, marginalising (whether or not by design) more critical voices, but at the same time undermining local government and representative local democracy by establishing a parallel and potentially competing structure of local political representation in deprived neighbourhoods (Barnes and Colenutt 1993), with apparent access to more bountiful resources than cash-strapped local councillors can offer. The danger this brings is that a growing patchwork of unco-ordinated area-based regeneration initiatives, combining local managerialism with a pseudo-democratic and participatory veneer, may undermine democratic control and accountability (Geddes and Erskine 1994; Davoudi and Healey 1995).

The main features of City Challenge are present in the current Single Regeneration Budget Challenge Fund. The essence of both programmes is that they are resource-limited rather than needs-led, emphasising competition rather than collaboration between local authorities and deprived communities, and leading to a loss of resources and hope in those areas (by far the majority of course) not funded. So although these large-scale, area-based urban regeneration programmes have been promoted as the way to both revive urban economies and deal with urban concentrations of poverty, deprivation and social exclusion, there seems little likelihood that they will have any more than a marginal effect on poverty in a few chosen areas in the foreseeable future.

Alternative proposals for urban regeneration have been made by local government. The Association of Metropolitan Authorities' pamphlet *Urban Policy: The Challenge and the Opportunity* (1993) set out an agenda whereby local government would become the lead agency for urban regeneration, with the emphasis of urban policy on equality of access for all to employment, housing, education and training, healthcare and other leisure, social and cultural facilities. Local communities would be given access to seedcorn funding for regeneration projects (Association of Metropolitan Authorities 1993). Rather similar proposals were made by the Labour Party's Cities 2020 initiative (Vaz 1993) and the Labour Planning and Environment Group (LPEG 1994). Another recent set of proposals advocates a radical change in national policy, with the creation of a National Community Regeneration Agency and the replacement of the DoE's Inner Cities Directorate by a new Directorate of Community Affairs. These changes would be intended to facilitate people-led rather than property-led regeneration schemes, empowering the community to take the lead role and bring in other partners – local government as well as the private sector – on its terms. The NCRA would be controlled by representatives of deprived communities, community development professionals and representatives of local government. It would fund local regeneration schemes through local Community Regeneration Units and a new Community Regeneration Grant which would be allocated on criteria of need, not through the competitive bidding of City Challenge (Nevin and Shiner 1993). In some versions of this kind of approach, regeneration projects would be managed not by local authorities but through a national network of 'neighbourhood trusts' which would dispense money to local groups. Holman, for example, envisages a national fund of £750 million per annum, distributed to about 250 trusts (Holman 1995).

These various proposals illustrate the current problems of formulating a modernised social democratic or centrist response to the problems of deprived neighbourhoods. Can there really be 'equal partnerships' between local communities and developers, or indeed between local communities and local authorities, let alone all three? In particular, the debate is evidence of the uneasy relationship between the representative democracy of local government, and the advocates of grassroots local community leadership. Many of the latter are suspicious of the willingness of local councils to 'forge new partnerships' with local communities except on the council's terms. Councillors question the democratic credentials of unelected 'community activists' and *ad hoc* community forums, while community leaders and representatives themselves may struggle to represent divided communities.

Local anti-poverty strategies

The above issues are ones that have been prominent in many of the local anti-poverty initiatives in different parts of the UK in recent years. Anti-poverty strategies have been developed by many local authorities, by charities (Barnardo's 1994), and in some cases by *ad hoc* partnerships of public and voluntary sector agencies (Strathclyde Poverty Alliance 1994). An important recent development has been the establishment of more effective national co-ordination and networking of local government anti-poverty initiatives, through an Anti-Poverty Unit supported by the local authority associations, and a National Local Government Forum Against Poverty which is a politically led campaigning organisation (Wheeler 1994). One important point of reference for such local initiatives has been the successive anti-poverty programmes funded by the European Community, which have supported innovative and experimental local initiatives across the member states of the Community (Benington 1989). The EC's Third Programme to Combat Poverty, 1989–94, was a transnational programme (European Commission 1994) which funded over forty local initiatives across Europe, including projects in the UK in Brownlow, Northern Ireland; Pilton, Edinburgh; Granby–Toxteth, Liverpool; and Bristol. The first three of these were area-based initiatives, but the project based in

Bristol was specifically concerned with the needs of single parents (Duffy 1994).

The Poverty Three projects were specifically concerned with combating poverty and social exclusion (in contrast to the urban regeneration focus of City Challenge and the SRB), and the programme emphasised three key concepts: partnership, participation, and a multidimensional approach to dealing with the causes of poverty and social exclusion. The empowerment of poor communities and socially excluded groups, such as single parents, has been central to the objectives of the Poverty Three projects, and the resources available from the programme (which are much more restricted than the levels of funding available through programmes such as City Challenge, and did not really permit the projects to make a major impact on the material causes of poverty) have been used by local projects as much with the process of empowerment in mind as 'hard' outcomes, although the projects have funded a wide range of activities from social and community facilities to training schemes.

In all of the projects, the aim of enhancing the capacity of socially excluded communities themselves has meant that the organisational structures of the projects have offered fuller representation to local people than we have seen to be the case in most urban regeneration projects. In Brownlow, representatives of the community and community organisations were in a majority on the Management Board. In Pilton, a leading role was played by local government and other agencies, but with very full representation of community interests. In both projects there was a considerable investment of resources, not just at the beginning but throughout the project, to broaden the representation of excluded groups, to modify the initial remit in order to reflect local demands (often at the cost of considerable conflict with the European Commission), to find ways of accommodating differences of view between different social groups within the community, and to promote effective dialogue between community and agency representatives in the partnerships.

The aim of empowering excluded communities can take a number of forms. One, as in Pilton, is to focus on the economic access of excluded groups to jobs and training. In Brownlow, where private sector employment opportunities are extremely limited, and where economic development was the responsibility of a separate agency, the Community Trust gave priority to the access of particularly deprived groups – women, the unemployed, young people – to the services provided by public agencies. In Granby–Toxteth, the strategy adopted was a response to racism and the exclusion of the black and ethnic minority communities, and emphasised political access to decision-making bodies and the control of resources, from which, indirectly, employment and access to public services might come (Duffy 1994). Not surprisingly, the Poverty Three projects have experienced different degrees of success and failure (Moore, Chapter 12, this volume). In some cases, projects have made significant steps towards their objectives of using the limited resources – of money and of time – to establish long-term processes of change in their areas and empowerment of the communities. In others obstacles to change, either within the communities themselves or in the partnership framework of agencies and organisations, have inhibited significant success.

Public services, social exclusion and local democracy

We have seen that for poor communities, excluded from commodity consumption, public services are of especial importance. Yet the extent and form of public provision in deprived neighbourhoods is often very deficient, a problem compounded by the squeeze on resources and the fragmentation of service provision through privatisation that has been the dominant feature of recent years (Robbins 1992; Varelidis *et al.* 1994). Too frequently, the local state has provided services and resources which poor communities need, but has done so in ways which confirm existing relations of power and oppression (London Edinburgh Weekend Return Group 1979).

The quality of public services is a particularly important issue for women, and especially for women in deprived and marginalised neighbourhoods and communities. Women tend to be disproportionately represented among marginalised sections of the population such as the elderly, single parents and carers. In most cases, despite the growth of female employment and male unemployment, it is women who take responsibility for co-ordinating the family's needs and securing access to goods and services, which for the disadvantaged involves time-consuming and frequently frustrating dealings with numerous public agencies. In undertaking such roles, many women suffer from low mobility, reliance on public transport, and often need to take with them, or schedule their working days around, small children. To the extent that lack of access to key services and opportunities perpetuates economic and social exclusion, in many cases women have less access and choice in critical respects than men, and women living on low incomes have poorer access than women from more prosperous or comfortable backgrounds. It is also the case that women are strongly represented as workers in public (as well as private – and privatised) service employment, in jobs at the client–provider interface, such as nursing or social work or benefits administration, but also in support occupations such as cleaning and catering. This type of employment can often mean low pay, low skill levels, poor working environments and high stress levels. For many women, therefore, the primary reality of public services is a double oppression: as both users and workers (Conroy and Flanagan 1992).

The deficiencies of local public service provision in meeting the needs of deprived communities and excluded groups such as women and ethnic minorities are now increasingly recognised by many local authorities, and a number of them are now actively grappling with the dilemmas which are posed by the combination of rising levels and intensity of poverty, increasing public expectations and a shrinking resource base. If it is the case, as research has seemed to show, that on the whole it has been the better-off who benefit more from local authority services (Bramley and

Le Grand 1992), this may mean rethinking the traditional approach of unselective universal provision. Some authorities are moving towards a more strategic approach which tries to combine a greater emphasis on charging for those who can afford to pay with targeting and subsidisation for the poor and those in need, for example through 'passport' or discount schemes (Charteris and Wheeler 1993). Some authorities are trying to take action both to make their own buildings and decision-making processes more accessible to excluded groups, and to get to grips with the growing problem of control of local public services by unaccountable and unelected quangos; for example, by opening them up to examination through 'scrutiny committees' of the council or other similar mechanisms (Kirklees MBC 1994).

Some of the most interesting of such initiatives are those which combine a number of dimensions at a local neighbourhood level: improving the delivery of public services in the area to better meet residents' priorities, through consultation with and involvement of local people; and bringing together at the local level different service providers both from different council departments and also from other public authorities (health, police) and local voluntary sector providers. In Wood End in Coventry, for example, another of the locations of disturbances in 1991, an area management initiative by the City Council in partnership with the local community has attempted with some success to recognise the complex and interrelated causes and effects of poverty, to support local community initiatives and to find better organisational arrangements and ways of working, both corporately within the authority and between public agencies (Hayden 1994).

Similar objectives underlie the growing interest on the part of a widening group of local authorities, of different types and under different party political control, in administrative or political decentralisation to an area or neighbourhood level. Recent research shows that such decentralisation initiatives can take a variety of forms and that not infrequently they exhibit some confusion between various possible objectives, which may range from improving the efficiency and/or the accountability of service provision, to empowering disadvantaged neighbourhoods or communities through a more participatory local political process, or strengthening the local representative democratic process by building closer links between councillors and their wards and electorates (Wahlberg *et al.* 1995). Decentralisation initiatives can undoubtedly pose a number of problems. By opening up new political arenas at the local level for social groups whose means of political expression may have been frustrated for a long period, they can give space to the prejudiced or parochial political allegiances which can develop among sections of excluded communities where oppression has resulted in one group of the excluded turning against another, as recently in Tower Hamlets. Decentralised neighbourhood forums can also lead to expression being given to a level of pent-up demands and needs that are beyond the ability of local agencies to respond to effectively. This means that local authorities pursuing initiatives which open up new political spaces to excluded communities must be aware of the likely results, and have formulated a strategic approach to such questions. It is surely preferable, however, that such problems should be given expression in open and democratic political arenas rather than fester as repressed needs and intensifying alienation from democratic politics. If decentralisation initiatives can 'turn grumbles into politics' (Corrigan 1994) they are making a valuable contribution to local democracy.

CONCLUSION: SOCIAL EXCLUSION, LOCAL DEMOCRACY AND THE LOCAL STATE

The challenge to local democracy to represent more fully the needs and interests of socially excluded groups could hardly be a more vital one. If democracy cannot do this, it forfeits its main progressive claim to offer something other than the market can deliver.

This chapter has reviewed a range of local initiatives which are intended to regenerate depressed areas, improve the material conditions of deprived communities, and empower the socially excluded. Some of these initiatives – the large-scale, government-controlled urban regeneration schemes – deploy substantial resources, but the regeneration processes which they set in train are frequently tangential to the needs of deprived communities, and the politics of such schemes can manipulate rather than empower them. Other initiatives are focused more directly on problems of poverty and social exclusion (not just on the areas where they are found), and these may be able to do more to refocus local policies on deprived neighbourhoods – but they are mostly constrained by limited resources and power over crucial determinants of poverty and deprivation.

Meanwhile, the fact is that many of the poor and excluded in deprived communities up and down the country remain untouched by such initiatives. If poverty and social exclusion are not to continue to limit our local democracy to the status of a privilege of the relatively affluent, there needs to be much more systematic political representation of poor communities within the democratic system. The current review of the structure of local government in England – if it is moving in any clear direction – is tilting towards larger local authorities. The political representation of poor neighbourhoods, on the other hand, suggests the need for movement in the other direction – towards the strengthening of local democracy at the grassroots, neighbourhood level, drawing on the positive features of the recent experiments in neighbourhood decentralisation and anti-poverty projects and bringing their lessons into the mainstream.

A more systematic framework for the political representation of excluded communities will be uncomfortable for local government. Poor people will use such structures to make demands of the local state which it finds difficult or even impossible to meet. Local government has two aspects: on the one hand, it is responsible to local society; it fulfils 'caring' functions; it can 'enable' or empower its citizens. If this were all, the achievement of social justice for poor communities would in principle be in the grasp of local authorities, even if it might sometimes require a very substantial shift in the emphasis and priorities of policies. But local government is also part of a wider structure of government, and of power beyond government. Its powers, duties and resources, the limits to them, and the way they are performed, reflect other interests than those of local communities. Because of this, local government often finds itself negotiating the imposition of quite other priorities, from those of a charge-capping government to those of the unelected leaders of local quangos, on its local community.

The effective political representation of the interests of poor communities will therefore often mean an ambivalent attitude by those representatives to local government, and requires a recognition by policy-makers in local authorities that local democracy must be rooted both in and against the local state.

BIBLIOGRAPHY

Abbott, P. (1988) *Material Deprivation and Health Status in the Plymouth Health District*, Plymouth: Department of Applied Social Sciences, Polytechnic South West.

Abrams, P. (1978) 'Towns and economic growth: some theories and problems', in Abrams, P. and Wrigley, E.A. (eds) *Towns in Societies: Essays in Economic History and Historical Sociology*, Cambridge: Cambridge University Press.

—— (1980) 'Social change, social networks and neighbourhood care', *Social Work Service* 22: 12–23.

Aglietta, M. (1979) *A Theory of Capitalist Regulation*, London: New Left Books.

Alcock, P. (1993) *Understanding Poverty*, London: Macmillan.

Almond, G. and Verba, S. (1965) *The Civic Culture*, Boston: Princeton University Press.

Altvater, E. (1994) 'Operationsfeld Weltmarkt oder: Die Transformation des souveränen Nationalstaats in den nationalen Wettbewerbsstaat', *Prokla* 97: 517–47.

Anderson, B. (1991) *The Imagined Community* (2nd edn), London: Verso.

Anwar, M. (1986) *Race and Politics*, London: Tavistock.

Ashraf, Syed Ali (1986) 'Preface', in Halstead, J.M., *The Case for Muslim Voluntary-Aided Schools: Some Philosophical Reflections*, Cambridge: The Islamic Academy.

Ashton, J. (1988) 'Rising to the challenge', *Health Service Journal* 98(5123).

—— (1992) 'The origins of healthy cities', in Ashton, J. (ed.) *Healthy Cities*, Buckingham: Open University Press.

Association of Metropolitan Authorities (1993) *Urban Policy: The Challenge and the Opportunity*, London: AMA.

Atkinson, R. and Moon, G. (1994) 'The City Challenge Initiative: an overview and preliminary assessment', *Regional Studies* 28(1): 94–7.

Audit Commission (1991) *Healthy Housing: The Role of Environmental Health Services*, London: HMSO.

Augur, D.A. (1993) 'Urban realities, US national policy and the Clinton administration', *Regional Studies* 27(8): 807–15.

Bachrach, P. and Baratz, M.S. (1962) 'The two faces of power', *American Political Science Review* 56: 947–52.

Bailey, N., Barker, A. and MacDonald, K. (1995) *Partnership Agencies in British Urban Policy*, London: UCL Press.

Bakshi, P., Goodwin, M., Painter, J. and Southern, A. (1995) 'Gender, race, and class in the local welfare state', *Environment and Planning A*, Special issue.

Ball, W. (1987) 'Local authority policy-making on equal opportunities: corporate provision, co-option and consultation', *Policy and Politics* 15(2): 101–10.

Ball, W. and Solomos, J. (eds) (1990) *Race and Local Politics*, London: Macmillan.

Ball, W. and Troyna, B. (1987) 'Resistance, rights and rituals: denominational schools and multicultural education', *Journal of Education Policy* 2(1): 15–25.

Ballard, R. and Ballard, C. (1977) 'The Sikhs: the development of South Asian settlements in Britain', in Watson, J.L. (ed.) *Between Two Cultures: Migrants and Minorities in Britain*, Oxford: Blackwell.

Balloch, S. and Jones, B. (1990) *Poverty and Anti-Poverty Strategy: The Local Government Response*, London: Association of Metropolitan Authorities.

Barnardo's (1994) *Challenging Disadvantage: Barnardo's Anti-Poverty Strategy*, Ilford: Barnardo's.

Barnekov, T., Boyle, R. and Rich, D. (1989) *Privatism and Urban Policy in Britain and the United States*, Oxford: Oxford University Press.

Barnes, J. and Colenutt, B. (1993) *The Urban Regeneration Agency: Property-led or Partnership-led?*, London: Docklands Consultative Committee.

Barnes, W.R. and Ledubur, L.C. (1991) 'Toward a new political economy of metropolitan regions', *Environment and Planning C: Government and Policy* 9(2): 127–41.

Bartley, M. (1994) 'Unemployment and ill-health: understanding the relationship', *Journal of Epidemiology and Community Health* 48: 333–7.

Barton, S.E. (1985) 'The neighbourhood movement in San Francisco', *Berkeley Planning Journal* 2: 85–103.

Beattie, A. (1991) 'Knowledge and control in health promotion: a test case for social policy and social theory', in Gabe, J., Calnan, M. and Bury, M. (eds) *The Sociology of the Health Service*, London: Routledge.

Beauregard, R.A. (1993) 'Descendants of ascendent cities and other urban dualities', *Journal of Urban Affairs* 15(3): 217–29.

Bell, D. (1961) 'Crime as an American way of life', in Bell, D., *The End of Ideology*, New York: Collier.

—— (1987) 'The World and the United States in 2013', *Daedalus* (Summer): 1–33.

Ben-Tovim, G., Gabriel, J., Law, I. and Stredder, K. (1986) 'A political analysis of local struggles for racial equality', in Rex, J. and Mason, D. (eds) *Theories of Race and Ethnic Relations*, Cambridge: Cambridge University Press.

Benington, J. (1989) 'Poverty, unemployment and the European Community: lessons from experience', in Dyson, K. (ed.) *Combating Long-Term Unemployment: Local/EC Relations*, London: Routledge.

Benko, G. and Lipietz, A. (1994) 'De la régulation des espaces aux espaces de régulation', in Boyer, R. and Saillard, Y. (eds) *Théorie de la Régulation. L'état des Savoirs*, Paris: La Découverte.

Best, M. (1990) *The New Competition*, Cambridge: Polity Press.

Beynon, H., Hudson, R., Lewis, J., Sadler, D. and Townsend, A. (1989) ' "It's all falling apart here": coming to terms with the future in Teesside', in Cooke, P. (ed.) *Localities: The Changing Face of Urban Britain*, London: Unwin Hyman.

Beynon, J. (1994) *Law and Order Review 1993: An Audit of Crime, Policing and Criminal Justice Issues*, Centre for the Study of Public Order, University of Leicester.

Bhachu, P. (1985) *Twice Migrants: East African Settlers in Britain*, London: Tavistock.

Bianchini, F. (1989) 'Urban renaissance', in Pimlott, B. and MacGregor, S. (eds) *Tackling the Inner Cities*, London: Routledge.

—— (1990), 'Urban renaissance? The arts and the urban regeneration process', in MacGregor, S. and Pimlott, B. (eds) *Tackling the Inner Cities*, Oxford: Clarendon Press.

—— (1991) 'Re-imagining the city', in Corner, J. and Hartley, S. (eds) *Enterprise and Heritage*, London: Routledge.

Bianchini, F. and Schwengel, H. (1991) 'Re-imagining the city', in Corner, J. and Harvey S. (eds) *Enterprise and Heritage*, London: Routledge.

Birmingham City Council (1992) *City Centre Strategy*, Birmingham: Birmingham City Council.

—— (1993) *Housing Investment Programme Strategy Statement 1993*, Birmingham: Birmingham City Council.

Birmingham Education Commission (1993) *Aiming High: The Report of the Birmingham Education Commission: Part 1*, Birmingham: Birmingham City Council.

Bishop, P. (1988) 'Dependence and diversification in the local economy of Plymouth', *Regional Studies* (November): 169–76.

Blair, T. (1995) 'The Spectator/Allied Dunbar Lecture', *The Spectator*, 25 March.

Blaxter, M. (1990) *Health and Lifestyles*, London: Routledge.

Bograd, M. (1988) 'Feminist perspectives on wife abuse: an introduction', in Yllo, K. and Bograd, M. (eds) *Feminist Perspectives on Wife Abuse*, Newbury Park, Calif.: Sage.

Boisier, S. (1994) 'Regionalization processes: past crises and current options', *CEPAL Review* 52: 177–88.

Bonefeld, W. (1986) 'The reformulation of state theory', *Capital and Class* 33: 96–127.

Booth, P. and Boyle, R. (1993) 'See Glasgow, see culture', in Bianchini, F. and Parkinson, M. (eds) *Cultural Policy and Urban Regeneration*, Manchester: Manchester University Press.

Bottoms, A. (1983) 'Some neglected features of contemporary penal systems', in Garland, D. and Young, P. (eds) *The Power to Punish*, London: Heinemann.

—— (1990) 'Crime prevention facing the 1990s', *Policing and Society* 1: 1–18.

Bottoms, A., Mawby, R.I. and Xanthos, P. (1989) 'A tale of two estates', in Downes, D. (ed.) *Crime and the City,* London: Macmillan.

Boyle, R. (1990) 'Regeneration in Glasgow: stability, collaboration, and inequity', in Judd, D. and Parkinson, M. (eds) *Leadership and Urban Regeneration,* Newbury Park, Calif.: Sage.

Braham, P., Rattansi, A. and Skellington, R. (eds) (1992) *Racism and Antiracism. Inequalities, Opportunities and Policies,* London: Sage.

Bramley, G. and Le Grand, J. (1992) *Who Uses Local Services? Striving for Equity,* London/Luton: Local Government Management Board, Belgrave Paper No. 4.

Breines, W. and Gordon, L. (1983) 'The new scholarship on family violence', *Signs* 8(3): 490–531.

Brenner, R. and Glick, M. (1991) 'The regulation approach: theory and history', *New Left Review* 188: 45–119.

Brogden, M. (1982) *The Police: Autonomy and Consent,* London: Academic Press.

Brown, C. (1984) *Black and White Britain,* London: Heinemann/PSI.

Brownill, S. (1990) *Developing London's Docklands: Another Great Planning Disaster,* London: Paul Chapman.

Brush, L. (1993) 'Violent acts and injurious outcomes in married couples: methodological issues in the national survey of families and households', in Bart, P. and Moran, E. (eds) *Violence Against Women,* Newbury Park, Calif.: Sage.

Bulmer, M. (1986a) 'Race and ethnicity', in Burgess, R. (ed.) *Key Variables in Social Investigation,* London: Routledge & Kegan Paul.

—— (1986b) *Neighbours: The Work of Phillip Abrams,* Cambridge: Cambridge University Press.

Bunton, R. and Burrows, R. (1995) 'Consumption and health in the "epidemiological" clinic of late modern medicine', in Bunton, R., Nettleton, S. and Burrows, R. (eds) *The Sociology of Health Promotion: Critical Analyses of Consumption, Lifestyle and Risk,* London: Routledge.

Bunton, R., Nettleton. S. and Burrows, R. (eds) (1995) *The Sociology of Health Promotion: Critical Analyses of Consumption, Lifestyle and Risk,* London: Routledge.

Burns, D., Hambleton, R. and Hoggett, P. (1994) *The Politics of Decentralisation,* London: Macmillan.

Burrows, J. and Loader, B. (eds) (1994) *Towards a Post-Fordist Welfare State?,* London: Routledge.

Butler, E., Pirie, M. and Young, P. (1985) *The Omega File: A Comprehensive Review of Government Functions,* London: Adam Smith Institute.

Campbell, B. (1993) *Goliath: Britain's Dangerous Places,* London: Methuen.

Carley, M. (1991) 'Business in urban regeneration partnerships: a case study of Birmingham', *Local Economy* 6(2): 100–15.

Carpenter, M. (1980) 'Left orthodoxy and the politics of health', *Capital and Class* 11.

Castells, M. (1977) *The Urban Question,* London: Edward Arnold.

—— (1983) *The City and the Grassroots: A Cross-Cultural Theory of Urban Social Movements,* London: Edward Arnold.

—— (1989) *The Informational City: Information Technology, Economic Restructuring and the Urban–Regional Process,* Oxford: Blackwell.

—— (1994) 'European cities, the informational society, and the global economy', *New Left Review* 204, March–April, 19–35.

Castells, M. and Hall, P. (1993) *Technopoles of the World,* London: Routledge.

CDP (1977) *Gilding the Ghetto,* London: CDP.

Central Manchester Development Corporation (1993a) *Manchester by Canal Boat,* Manchester.

—— (1993b) *Fun and Games in the 24 Hour City,* Manchester.

Cerny, P.G. (1990) *The Changing Architecture of Politics,* London: Sage.

Chalkley, B. and Goodridge, J. (1991) 'The 1943 plan for Plymouth: wartime vision and post-war realities', in Chalkley, B., Dunkerley, D. and Grapaios, P. (eds) *Plymouth: Maritime City in Transition,* Newton Abbot: David & Charles.

Chalkley, B., Dunkerley, D. and Grapaios, P. (eds) (1991) *Plymouth: Maritime City in Transition,* Newton Abbot: David & Charles.

Champion, S. (1990) *And God Created Manchester,* Manchester: Wordsmith.

Charteris, S. and Wheeler, R. (1993) 'Paying for service and social justice – a local authority perspective', *Local Government Policy Making* 20(1): 27–34.

Chaston, I. and Mangles, T. (n.d.) *Plymouth City Centre Project: Assessment of Economic Characteristics and Attitudes of Local Employers*, Plymouth: Management Research Centre, Plymouth Business School, University of Plymouth.

Cheetham, J. (1988) 'Ethnic associations in Britain', in Jenkins, S. (ed.) *Ethnic Associations and the Welfare State*, New York: Columbia University Press.

Cherry, G. (1994) *Birmingham: A Case Study in Geography, History and Planning*, Chichester: John Wiley.

Chisholm, M. (1990) *Regions in Recession and Resurgence*, London: Unwin Hyman.

Christie, N. (1993) *Crime Control as Industry*, London: Routledge.

Clark, M., Martin, R. and Townroe, P. (1992) *Regional Development in the 1990s*, Regional Studies Assoc., London: Jessica Kingsley Publishers.

Clarke, M. and Stewart, J. (1994) 'The local authority and the new community governance', *Local Government Studies* 20(2): 163–76.

Clarke, S. (1990) 'The crisis of Fordism or the crisis of social democracy?', *TELOS* 83.

CLES (1989) 'Making an industry of culture', *Local Work* 10 (Manchester).

Cloward, R. and Ohlin, L. (1960) *Delinquency and Opportunity*, New York: The Free Press.

Cochrane, A. (1993) *Whatever Happened to Local Government?*, Milton Keynes: Open University Press.

Cohen, A. (1955) *Delinquent Boys*, New York: The Free Press.

Cohen, G.A. (1994) 'Back to socialist basics', *New Left Review* 207: 3–16.

Cohen, P. (1979) 'Policing the working class city', in Fine, R., Kinsey, J., Lea, J., Picciotto, S. and Young, J. (eds) *Capitalism and the Rule of Law*, London: Hutchinson.

Cohen, S. (1985) *Visions of Social Control*, Cambridge: Polity Press.

Coleman, A. (1985) *Utopia on Trial*, London: Hilary Shipman.

Commission for Racial Equality (1984) *Race and Environmental Health*, London: CRE.

—— (1988) *Homelessness and Discrimination: Report of a Formal Investigation into the London Borough of Tower Hamlets*, London: CRE.

—— (1991) *Second Review of the Race Relations Act 1976: Consultative Paper*, London: CRE.

—— (1994) *Environmental Health and Racial Equality*, London: CRE.

Commission of the European Communities (1993a) *Growth, Competitiveness, Employment: The Challenges and Ways Forward into the 21st Century*, Bulletin of the EC 6/93.

—— (1993b) *European Social Policy: Options for the Union*, Directorate General for Employment, Industrial Relations and Social Affairs.

Commission on Social Justice (1993) *The Justice Gap*, London: Institute for Public Policy Research.

—— (1994) *Social Justice: Strategies for National Renewal*, London: Vintage.

Connolly, M., Ben-Tovim, G., Roberts, K. and Torkington, E. (1992) *Black Youth in Liverpool*, Culemborg, Netherlands: Giordano Bruno.

Conroy, P. and Flanagan, N. (1992) *Women and Local Community Development: Combating Disadvantage*, Dublin: European Foundation for the Improvement of Living and Working Conditions, Working Paper WP 92/26/EN.

Cornwell, J. (1984) *Hard-Earned Lives: Accounts of Health and Illness from East London*, London: Tavistock.

Corrigan, P. (1994) *Decentralisation in Islington*, Contribution to Warwick University Local Authorities Research Consortuim Conference on Promoting Local Democracy and Citizen Participation in the UK and Europe.

Cox, K. and Mair, A. (1988) 'Locality and community in the politics of local economic development', *Annals of the Association of American Geographers* 78(2): 307–25.

Cox, K.R. (1995) 'Globalization, competition and the politics of local economic development', *Urban Studies* 32(2): 213–24.

Crawford, A., Jones, T., Woodhouse, T. and Young, J. (1990) *The Second Islington Crime Survey*, Middlesex Polytechnic: Centre for Criminology.

Crook, S., Pakulski, P. and Waters, M. (1992) *Postmodernization: Change in Advanced Society*, London: Sage Publications.

Crosland, A. (1956) *The Future of Socialism*, London: Jonathan Cape.

Crow, G. and Allen, G. (1994) *Community Life: An Introduction to Local Social Relations*, New York: Harvester Wheatsheaf.

Crozier, M., Huntingdon, S. and Watanaki, J. (eds) (1975) *The Crisis of Democracy*, New York University Press.

Cumper, P. (1990) 'Muslim schools and the ERA', *New Community* 16(3): 379–89.

Currie, E. (1993) *Reckoning: Drugs, the Cities and the American Future*, New York: Hill & Wang.

Cutler, M., Newman, I. and Ward, H. (1994) *Poles Apart: The Impact of the Recession on Disadvantaged Groups in the Labour Market*, Harlow: South East Economic Development Strategy.

Dahrendorf, R. *et al.* (eds) (1995) *Wealth Creation and Social Cohesion in a Free Society*, Report of the Commission on Wealth Creation and Social Cohesion, London.

Daly, G. (1993) 'The discursive construction of economic space', *Economy and Society* 20(1): 79–102.

Damer, S. (1974) 'Wine Alley: the sociology of a dreadful enclosure', *Sociological Review* 22: 221–48.

——— (1989) *From Moorepark to 'Wine Alley': The Rise and Fall of a Glasgow Housing Scheme*, Edinburgh: Edinburgh University Press.

Dangschat, J.S. (1994) 'Concentrations of poverty in the landscapes of "boomtown" Hamburg: the creation of a new urban underclass?', *Urban Studies* 31(7): 1133–47.

Davies, H. (1993) *Partnership Papers: A First Guide to Appointed Local Executive Bodies in the West Midlands*, Birmingham: INLOGOV.

Davies, J. and Kelly, M. (eds) (1993) *Healthy Cities: Research and Practice*, London: Routledge.

Davis, M. (1990) *City of Quartz: Excavating the Future in Los Angeles*, London: Verso.

——— (1992) *City of Quartz*, New York: Vintage.

Davison, C. and Davey-Smith, G. (1995) 'The baby and the bath water: examining socio-cultural and free-market critiques of health promotion', in Bunton, R., Nettleton. S. and Burrows, R. (eds) *The Sociology of Health Promotion: Critical Analysis of Consumption, Lifestyle and Risk*, London: Routledge.

Davoudi, S. and Healey, P. (1995) 'City Challenge: sustainable process or temporary gesture?', *Environment and Planning C* 13(1): 79–96.

Day, P. and Klein, R. (1987) *Accountabilities*, London: Tavistock.

Dayha, B. (1974) 'The nature of Pakistani ethnicity in industrial cities in Britain', in Cohen, A. (ed.) *Urban Ethnicity*, London: Tavistock.

de Groot, L. (1992) 'City Challenge: competing in the urban regeneration game', *Local Economy* 7(3): 196–209.

Deakin, N. and Edwards, J. (1993) *The Enterprise Culture and the Inner City*, London: Routledge.

Dennis, F. (1988) *Behind the Frontlines*, London: Gollancz.

Department of the Environment (1993) *English House Condition Survey 1991*, London: HMSO.

——— (1994) *Index of Living Conditions*, London: Department of the Environment.

DERA (Downtown Eastside Residents Association) (1987) *Expo '86: Its Legacy to Vancouver's Downtown Eastside*, Vancouver: DERA.

DeVroey, M. (1984) 'A regulationist approach interpretation of the contemporary crisis', *Capital and Class* 23: 45–66.

DiGaetano, A. and Klemanski, J.S. (1992) *Urban Regime Capacity: A Comparison of Birmingham, England and Detroit, Michigan*, Paper presented at the 1992 Annual Meeting of the Urban Affairs Association, Cleveland, Ohio, April–May.

——— (1993) 'Urban regime capacity: a comparison of Birmingham, England and Detroit, Michigan', *Journal of Urban Affairs* 15(4): 367–84.

Ditch, J. (1993) 'Lessons from anti-poverty programmes in the European Community: the pursuit of economic and social justice', in Sinfield, A. (ed.) *Poverty, Inequality and Justice*, New Waverley Papers, Social Policy Series No. 6, University of Edinburgh.

Dobash, R.E. and Dobash, R.P. (1979) *Violence Against Wives: A Case Against the Patriarchy*, New York: The Free Press.

——— (1992) *Women, Violence and Social Change*, London: Routledge.

Docklands Forum (1993) *Race and Housing in London's Docklands*, London: Docklands Forum.

Dommergues, P. (1992) 'The strategies for international and interregional cooperation', *Ekistics* 352/3: 7–12.

Donald, J. (1992) 'Metropolis: the city as text', in Bocock, R. and Thompson, K. (eds) *Social and Cultural Forms of Modernity*, Cambridge: Polity/Open University Press.

Donnison, D. (1987) 'Conclusions', in Donnison, D. and Middleton, A. (eds) *Regenerating the Inner City: Glasgow's Experience*, London: Routledge.

Dorling, D. (1993) 'The 1991 Census data and Housing Tenure', *BURISA* 108: 5–7.

Dorn, A. (1983) 'LEA policies on multiracial education', *Multi-Ethnic Education Review* 2(2): 3–5.

Dorn, A and Troyna, B. (1982) 'Multiracial education and the politics of decision-making', *Oxford Review of Education* 8(2): 175–85.

Dorn, N., Murji, K. and South, N. (1991) *Traffickers: Drug Markets and Law Enforcement*, London: Routledge.

Downes, D. (1966) *The Delinquent Solution: A Study in Subcultural Theory*, London: Routledge & Kegan Paul.

Duchacek, I.D. (1984) 'The international dimension of subnational self-government', *Publius* 14 (Fall): 5–31.

Duffy, K. (1994) 'Poverty 3 in the UK: Final Report of the Third European Programme to Foster the Economic and Social Integration of the Least Privileged Groups (1989–1994)', UK Research and Development Unit, Local Government Centre, University of Warwick, Unpublished report to the European Commission.

Duhl, L. (1992) 'Healthy Cities: Myth or Reality', in Ashton, J. (ed.) *Healthy Cities*, Buckingham: Open University Press.

Duncan, S., and Goodwin, M. (1988) *The Local State and Uneven Development*, Cambridge: Polity Press.

Dunkerley, D. (1991) 'Population and social structure', in Chalkley, B., Dunkerley, D. and Grapaios, P. (eds) *Plymouth: Maritime City in Transition*, Newton Abbot: David & Charles.

Dunn, S. (ed.) (1994) *Managing Divided Cities*, Keele: Fulbright Papers/Ryburn.

Eisenham, P. (1972) '(Riverside), London E14', *Architectural Design* 9: 557–71.

Eisenschitz, A. and Gough, J. (1993) *The Politics of Local Economic Policy*, Basingstoke: Macmillan.

Eisinger, P.K. (1988) *The Rise of the Entrepreneurial State*, Madison: University of Wisconsin Press.

Elkin, S. (1985) 'Twentieth century urban regimes', *Journal of Urban Affairs* 7(2): 11–28.

Ellis, J. (1991a) 'Local government and community needs: a case study of Muslims in Coventry', *New Community* 17(3): 359–76.

—— (1991b) *Meeting Community Needs. A Study of Muslim Communities in Coventry*, Monographs in Ethnic Relations No. 2, CRER, University of Warwick.

Ericson, R. (1994) 'The division of expert knowledge in policing and security', *British Journal of Sociology* 45(2): 149–75.

Esser, J. and Hirsch, J. (1994) 'The crisis of Fordism and the dimensions of a "post-Fordist" regional and urban structure', in Amin, A. (ed.) *Post-Fordism: A Reader*, Oxford: Blackwell.

Ettlinger, N. (1994) 'The localization of development in comparative perspective', *Economic Geography* 70(2): 144–66.

European Commission DGV/E/2 (1994) *The Lessons of the Poverty 3 Programme*, Lille: EEIG Animation and Research.

Evans, S. (1994) 'Blacklisted', *Guardian*, 16 August.

Ewick, P. and Silbey, S.A. (1995) 'Subversive stories and hegemonic tales: toward a sociology of narrative', *Law and Society Review* 29(2): 197–226.

Fainstein, S. (1990) 'The changing world economy and urban restructuring', in Judd, D. and Parkinson, M. (eds) *Leadership and Urban Regeneration*, Newbury Park, Calif.: Sage.

—— (1991) 'Rejoinder to Cox', *Journal of Urban Affairs* 13: 285–7.

Fainstein, S., Gordon, I. and Harloe, M. (1992) *Divided Cities*, Oxford: Blackwell.

Feagin, J.R. (1983) *The Urban Real Estate Game: Playing Monopoly with Real Money*, Englewood Cliffs, N.J.: Prentice-Hall.

Feeley, M. and Simon, J. (1992) 'The new penology: notes on the emerging strategy of corrections and its implications', *Criminology* 30(4): 449–74.

—— (1994) 'Actuarial justice: the emerging new criminal law', in Nelken, D. (ed.) *The Futures of Criminology*, London: Sage Publications.

Financial Times (1989) 'NW Survey', 9 June.

Fitzgerald, M. (1984) *Political Parties and Black People*, London: Runnymede Trust.

Forman, C. (1989) *Spitalfields: A Battle for Land*, London: Hilary Shipman.
Fosler, R.S. (ed.) (1988) *The New Economic Role of American States*, New York: Oxford University Press.
——— (1992) 'State economic policy: the emerging paradigm', *Economic Development Quarterly* 6(1): 3–13.
Foster, J. (1992) 'Living with the Docklands' redevelopment: community view from the Isle of Dogs', *London Journal* 17(2): 170–82.
——— (1995) 'Informal social control and community crime prevention', *British Journal of Criminology* 35(4): 563–83.
——— (1996) ' "Island homes for island people": competition, conflict and racism in the battle over public housing on the Isle of Dogs', in Sampson, C. and South, N. (eds) *The Social Construction of Social Policy*, London: Macmillan.
——— (forthcoming) *'Cultures in Conflict: Worlds in Collision': Redeveloping a Docklands Community*, London: UCL Press.
Foster, J. and Hope, T. (1993) *Housing, Community and Crime: The Impact of the Priority Estates Project* (Home Office Research Study 131) London: HMSO.
Foucault, M. (1977) *Discipline and Punish*, London: Allen Lane.
——— (1979) *The History of Sexuality* (vol. 1), Harmondsworth: Penguin.
Francis, L. (1993) 'Church and state', in Francis, L. and Lankshear, D.W. (eds) *Christian Perspectives on Church Schools: A Reader*, Leominster: Gracewing Books.
Friedman, D. and Pawson, H. (1989) *One in Every Hundred: A Study of Households Accepted as Homeless in London*, London: London Housing Unit/London Research Centre.
Fryer, P. (1984) *Staying Power: The History of Black People in Britain*, London: Pluto.
Gaffikin, F. and Morrissey, M. (1994a) 'In pursuit of the Holy Grail: combating local poverty in an unequal society', *Local Economy* 9(2): 100–16.
——— (1994b) 'Poverty in the 1980s: a comparison of the United States and the United Kingdom', *Policy and Politics* 22(1): 43–58.
Gaffikin, F. and Warf, B. (1993) 'Urban policy and the post-Keynesian state in the United Kingdom and the United States', *International Journal of Urban and Regional Research* 17(1): 67–84.
Garland, D. (1985) *Punishment and Welfare*, Aldershot: Gower.
Geddes, M. (1995) *The Role of Partnerships in Promoting Social Cohesion*, Dublin: European Foundation for the Improvement of Living and Working Conditions.
Geddes, M. and Erskine, A. (1994) 'Poverty, the local economy and the scope for local initiative', *Local Economy* 9(2): 192–206.
Gelles, R. (1987) *Family Violence*, Newbury Park, Calif.: Sage.
——— (1993) 'Through a sociological lens: social structure and family violence', in Gelles, R. and Loseke, D. (eds) *Current Controversies on Family Violence*, Newbury Park, Calif.: Sage.
Gelles, R. and Cornell, C. (1985) *Intimate Violence in Families*, Beverly Hills, Calif.: Sage.
Gibson, D. (1987) 'Hearing and listening: a case study of the "consultation" process undertaken by a local education department and black groups', in Troyna, B. (ed.) *Racial Inequality in Education*, London: Tavistock.
Giddens, A. (1991) *The Consequences of Modernity*, Cambridge: Polity.
Gill, D., Mayor, B. and Blair, M (eds) (1992) *Racism and Education. Structures and Strategies*, London: Sage.
Girardet, H. (1992) *The Gaia Atlas of Cities: New Directions for Sustainable Urban Living*, London: Gaia.
Glasgow City Council (1991) *City Planning Aims For The Next Decade*, Glasgow: Glasgow City Council Planning Department.
Glasgow Regeneration Alliance (1993) *Shaping the Future: A Commitment to Area Regeneration*, Glasgow: Glasgow Regeneration Alliance.
Goldstein, H. (1990) *Problem Solving Policing*, New York: McGraw-Hill.
Goldthorpe, J.H., Lockwood, D., Bechhofer, F. and Platt, J. (1968) *The Affluent Worker: Industrial Attitudes and Behaviour*, Cambridge: Cambridge University Press.
Goodwin, M. (1991) 'Replacing a surplus population: the employment and housing policies of the London Docklands Development Corporation', in Allen, J. and Hamnett, C. (eds) *Housing and Labour Markets*, London: Unwin Hyman.
Goodwin, M., Duncan, S. and Halford, S. (1993) 'Regulation theory, the local state, and

the transition of urban politics', *Environment and Planning D: Society and Space* 11: 67–88.

Gottfredson, M. (1984) *Victims of Crime: The Dimensions of Risk*, London: HMSO.

Goulbourne, H. (1987) 'West Indian groups and British politics', Paper presented to the Conference on Black People and British Politics, University of Warwick, November.

Gray, C. (1993) *Government Beyond the Centre*, London: Macmillan.

Greater Manchester Council (GMC) Planning Department (1985) *Comparative Study of Conurbations*, Manchester.

Greater Manchester Low Pay Unit (GMLPU) (1993) *Employment in the NW*, Manchester.

—— (1994) *Low Pay in the North West*, Manchester.

—— (1995) *Bagatelle or Benefit?*, Manchester.

Greater Manchester Research and Information Planning Unit (GMRIPU) (1985) 'Employment changes in Greater Manchester, 1965–84', *Employment Changes in Greater Manchester*, Oldham.

Green, A.E. (1994) *The Geography of Poverty and Wealth*, Warwick: Institute for Employment Research, University of Warwick.

Greenhalgh, M. (1994) 'Cool cafe bars', *City Life* 257(9), Manchester.

Gutstein, D. (1986) 'The impact of Expo on Vancouver,' in Anderson, R. and Wachtel, E. (eds) *The Expo Story*, Madeira Park, B.C.: Harbour Publishing.

Gyford, J. (1991) *Citizens, Consumers and Councils: Local Government and the Public*, Government Beyond the Centre series, Basingstoke: Macmillan.

Habeebullah, M. and Slater, D. (1990) *Equal Access: Asian Access to Council Housing in Rochdale*, Research and Policy Paper Number 11, London: Community Development Foundation.

Habermas, J. (1976) *Legitimation Crisis*, London: Heinemann.

—— (1987) *The Theory of Communicative Action* (vol. 2), Cambridge: Polity Press.

Hall, S., Critcher, C., Jefferson, T., Clarke, J. and Roberts, B. (1978) *Policing the Crisis*, London: Macmillan.

Hall, S., Mawson, J. and Nicholson, B. (1995) 'City Pride: the Birmingham experience', *Local Economy* 10(2): 108–16.

Hambleton, R. (1990) *Urban Government in the 1990s: Lessons from the USA*, SAUS Occasional Paper 35, Bristol: University of Bristol.

Hamnett, C. (1994) 'Social polarisation in global cities: theory and evidence', *Urban Studies* 31(3).

Handelman, S. (1994) *Comrade Criminal: The Theft of the Second Russian Revolution*, London: Michael Joseph.

Hanmer, J. and Saunders, S. (1984) *Well-Founded Fear*, London: Macmillan.

Harding, A. (1991) 'The rise of urban growth coalitions UK style?', *Environment and Planning C* 9: 295–318.

—— (1994) 'Urban regimes and growth machines: towards a cross-national research agenda', *Urban Affairs Quarterly* 29(3): 356–82.

Harrison, P. (1983) *Inside the Inner City*, London: Penguin.

Hartman, C. (1974) *Yerba Buena: Land Grab and Community Resistance in San Francisco*, San Francisco: Glide Publications.

—— (1984) *The Transformation of San Francisco*, San Francisco: Rowan & Allanheld Publishers.

Harvey, D. (1977) 'The urban process under capitalism', *International Journal of Urban and Regional Research* 2: 101–31.

—— (1985) 'The geopolitics of capitalism', in Gregory, D. and Urry, J. (eds) *Social Relations and Spatial Structures*, London: Macmillan.

—— (1987) 'Flexible accumulation through urbanization: reflections on "post-modernism" in the American city', *Antipode* 19(3): 260–86.

—— (1988) 'Voodoo cities', *New Statesman and Society* 30 (September).

—— (1989a) *The Condition of Post-Modernity*, Oxford: Blackwell.

—— (1989b) 'From managerialism to entrepreneurialism: the transformation in urban governance in late capitalism', *Geografiska Annaler* 71B(1): 3–17.

Hay, C. (1996) *Re-stating Social and Political Change*, Buckingham: Open University Press.

Hayden, C. (1994) 'Partnership – sop or solution? Trying to tackle poverty through partnership in Wood End, Coventry', *Local Economy* 9(2): 153–65.

Healthy Plymouth (1994) *Healthy Plymouth: A City Fit to Live and Work In*, Plymouth: Healthy Plymouth Planning Team.

Henderson, J. and Karn, V. (1987) *Race, Class and State Housing: Inequality and the Allocation of Public Housing in Britain*, Aldershot: Gower.

Hewison, R. (1987) *The Heritage Industry*, London: Methuen.

Hindess, B. (1992) 'Power and rationality: the western concept of political community', *Alternatives* 17(2) Spring: 149–63.

Hiro, D. (1991) *Black British: White British*, London: Grafton.

Hirsch, J. (1983) 'The Fordist security state and new social movements', *Kapitalistate* 10/11: 75–87.

Hirsch, J., Esser, J., Fach, W. *et al.* (1991) *Modernisierungspolitik Heute: die Deregulationspolitiken von Regierungen und Parteien*, Frankfurt: Materialis Verlag.

Hirst, P. and Thompson, G. (1996) *Globalisation in Question: The International Economy and the Possibilities of Governance*, Cambridge: Polity Press.

Hobbs, D. (1988) *Doing The Business: Entrepreneurship, the Working Class and Detectives in the East End of London*, Oxford: Clarendon Press.

Hobsbawm, E. (1972) 'Distinctions between socio-political and other forms of crime', *Society for the Study of Labour History Bulletin* 25: 5–6.

Holman, B. (1995) 'Locals can do it for themselves', *The Guardian* 'Society', 14 June.

Holme, A. (1985) *Housing and Young Families in East London*, London: Routledge & Kegan Paul.

Home Office (1984) *Joint Circular on Crime Prevention*, London: HMSO.

—— (1989) *Tackling Crime*, London: HMSO.

—— (1991) *Safer Communities: The Local Delivery of Crime Prevention Through The Partnership Approach*, London: HMSO.

—— (1994) *Partners Against Crime*, London: HMSO.

Horsman, M. and Marshall, A. (1994) *After the Nation-State: Citizens, Tribalism, and the New World Disorder*, London: HarperCollins

Hough, M. and Mayhew, P. (1983) *The British Crime Survey: First Report*, London: HMSO.

—— (1985) *Taking Account of Crime: Key Findings from the 1984 British Crime Survey*, London: HMSO.

Hughes, G. (1994) 'Talking cop shop: a case-study of police community consultative groups in transition', *Policing and Society* 4: 253–70.

Hunter, N. (1901) *Tenement Conditions in Chicago*, Chicago, Ill.: University of Chicago Press.

Hutton, W. (1992) 'The real price of poverty', *Guardian*, 24 February.

—— (1995) *The State We're In*, London: Cape.

Jacobs, B.D. (1992) *Fractured Cities: Capitalism, Community and Empowerment in Britain and America*, London: Routledge.

Jacobs, J. (1984) *Cities and the Wealth of Nations: Principles of Economic Life*, Harmondsworth: Penguin.

Jefferson, T. (1990) *The Case Against Paramilitary Policing*, Milton Keynes: Open University Press.

Jenkins, R. (1986) *Racism and Recruitment*, Cambridge: Cambridge University Press.

Jenkins, R. and Solomos, J. (eds) (1987) *Racism and Equal Opportunity Policies in the 1980s*, Cambridge: Cambridge University Press.

Jessop, B. (1982) *The Capitalist State*, Oxford: Martin Robertson.

—— (1983a) 'The capitalist state and the rule of capital', *West European Politics* 6: 139–62.

—— (1983b) 'Accumulation strategies, state forms and hegemonic projects', *Kapitalistate* 10/11: 89–112.

—— (1990) *State Theory: Putting Capitalist States in their Place*, Cambridge: Polity Press.

—— (1993) 'Towards a Schumpeterian workfare state? Preliminary remarks on post-Fordist political economy', *Studies in Political Economy* 40: 7–39.

—— (1994a) 'Post-Fordism and the state', in Amin, A. (ed.) *Post-Fordism: A Reader*, Oxford: Blackwell.

—— (1994b) 'The transition to post-Fordism and the Schumpeterian workfare state', in Burrows, J. and Loader, B. (eds) *Towards a Post-Fordist Welfare State?*, London: Routledge.

—— (1995a) 'The nation-state: erosion or reorganization?', *Lancaster Regionalism Group Working Papers*, no. 50, Lancaster University.

—— (1995b) 'The regulation approach, governance and post Fordism: alternative perspectives on economic and political change', *Economy and Society* 24(3) August: 307–33.

Jessop, B., Bonnett, K., Bromley S. and Ling, K. (1984) 'Authoritarian populism, two nations and Thatcherism', *New Left Review* 147: 32–60

Jessop, B., Nielsen, K. and Pedersen, O.K. (1993) 'Structural competitiveness and strategic capacities: the cases of Britain, Denmark, and Sweden', in Sjöstrand, S.E. (ed.) *Institutional Change: Theory and Empirical Findings*, New York: M.E. Sharpe.

Johnson, L. (1992) *The Rebirth of Private Policing*, London: Routledge.

Joly, D. (1987) *Making a Place for Islam in British Society: Muslims in Birmingham*, Research Papers in Ethnic Relations No. 4, CRER, University of Warwick.

Jones, T. (1993) *Britain's Ethnic Minorities*, London: PSI.

Jones, T., MacLean, B. and Young, J. (1986) *The First Islington Crime Survey*, Aldershot: Gower.

Jones, T., Newburn, T. and Smith, D. (1994) *Democracy and Policing*, London: PSI.

Joseph Rowntree Foundation (1995) *Inquiry into Income and Wealth*, York: JRF.

Kantor, P. (1993) 'The dual city as political choice', *Journal of Urban Affairs* 15(3): 231–44.

Karn, V. (1977/8) 'The financing of owner occupation and its impact on ethnic minorities', *New Community* 6(1/2): 49–63.

Karn, V., Kemeny, J. and Williams, P. (1985) *Home Ownership in the Inner City: Salvation or Despair*, Aldershot: Gower.

Kasinitz, P. (ed.) (1995) *Metropolis*, London: Macmillan.

Keating, M. (1988) *The City That Refused To Die*, Aberdeen: Aberdeen University Press.

—— (1989) 'The disintegration of urban policy: Glasgow and the New Britain', *Urban Affairs Quarterly* 24 (June): 513–16.

—— (1991) *Comparative Urban Politics: Power and the City in the US, Canada, Britain and France*, London: Edward Elgar.

—— (1993) 'The politics of economic development: political change and local economic development policies in the United States, Britain, and France', *Urban Affairs Quarterly* 28(3): 373–96.

Keating, M. and Boyle, R. (1986) *Remaking Urban Scotland*, Edinburgh: Edinburgh University Press.

Kelly, L. (1988) *Surviving Sexual Violence*, Cambridge: Polity Press.

—— (1991) 'Unspeakable acts: women who abuse', *Trouble and Strife* 23: 20–2.

Kelly, M., Davies, J. and Charlton, B. (1993) 'Healthy cities: a modern problem or a postmodern solution?', in Davies, J. and Kelly, M. (eds) *Healthy Cities: Research and Practice*, London: Routledge.

Kennedy, P. (1993) *Preparing for the Twenty-First Century*, New York: Random House.

King, A.D. (1996) *Re-presenting the City: Ethnicity, Capital and Culture in the 21st-Century Metropolis*, London: Macmillan.

King, J. (1993) *Three Asian Associations in Britain*, Monograph in Ethnic Relations, CRER, University of Warwick.

Kinsey, R., Lea, J. and Young, J. (1986) *Losing the Fight Against Crime*, Oxford: Blackwell.

Kirklees MBC (1994) *The Quango Handbook: A Guide to Extra-governmental Public Services in Kirklees*, Kirklees MBC.

Kish, L. (1965) *Survey Sampling*, New York: Wiley.

Knott, K. (1986) 'Religion and identity, and the study of ethnic minority religions in Britain', *Community Religions Project Research Paper No. 3*, University of Leeds.

Kosny, M. and Loftman, P. (1991) 'Birmingham Unitary Development Plan and Toronto's City Plan 1991: Two responses to a similar problem of "world class-itis"', Paper presented to the ACSP–AESOP Joint International Congress, Oxford, July.

KPMG (1993) *The Economic Impact of the International Convention Centre, the National Indoor Arena, Symphony Hall and the National Exhibition Centre on Birmingham and the West Midlands: Main Report November 1993*, Birmingham: KPMG.

Kurz, D. (1993) 'Social science perspectives on wife abuse: current debates and future directions', in Bart, P. and Moran, E. (eds) *Violence Against Women*, Newbury Park, Calif.: Sage.

Lamb, C. and Geddes, M. (1995) *The Scope for Choice and Variety in Local Government*, London: LGC Publications.

Lash, S. and Urry, J. (1994) *Economies of Signs and Space*, London: Sage.

Layton-Henry, Z. (1984) *The Politics of Race in Britain*, London: Allen & Unwin.
Lea, J. and Young, J. (1984) *What is to be Done About Law and Order?*, London: Penguin.
Lee, R. (1989) 'Urban transformation: from problems *in* to the problem *of* the city', in Herbert, D.T. and Smith, D.M. (eds) *Social Problems and the City: New Perspectives*, Oxford: Oxford University Press.
Leeds, A. (1994) *Cities, Classes and the Social Order*, Ithaca, N.Y.: Cornell University Press.
Lefebvre, H. (1970) *La Revolution Urbaine*, Paris: Gallimard.
Leitner, H. (1989) 'Cities in pursuit of economic growth: the local state as entrepreneur', *Political Geography Quarterly* 9(2): 146–70.
Levering, B. and Roberts, J. (1975) 'Yerba Buena – cut through the smoke screen over jobs and you still find a half billion dollar price tag', *San Francisco Bay Guardian*, 9 April 1975–2 May 1975.
Levitt, I. (1986) *Report on Urban Deprivation in Plymouth*, Exeter: Diocese of Exeter.
Ley, D. *et al.* (1992) 'Time to grow up? From urban village to world city, 1966–91', in Wynn, G. and Oke, T. (eds) *Vancouver and its Regions*, Vancouver: UBC Press.
Lindblom, C. (1982) 'The market as prison', *Journal of Politics* 44: 324–36.
Liverpool Black Caucus (1986) *The Racial Politics of Militant in Liverpool*, Liverpool Black Caucus.
Lobel, K. (ed.) (1986) *Naming the Violence: Speaking Out About Lesbian Battering*, London: Seal.
Loftman, P. and Nevin, B. (1992) *Urban Regeneration and Social Equality: A Case Study of Birmingham 1986–1992*, Faculty of the Built Environment Research Paper No. 8, Birmingham: University of Central England.
—— (1994) 'Prestige project development: economic reconnaissance or economic myth? A case study of Birmingham', *Local Economy* 8(4): 307–25.
—— (1995) 'Prestige project and urban regeneration in the 1980s and 1990s, a review of the Benefits Administration', *Planning Practice and Research* 10(3/4): 299–315.
Logan, J. and Swanstrom, T. (1990) *Beyond the City Limits: Urban Policy and Economic Restructuring in Comparative Perspective*, Philadelphia, Pa.: Temple University Press.
London Edinburgh Weekend Return Group (1979) *In and Against the State*, London: Pluto.
LPEG (Labour Planning and Environment Group) (1994) *Empowering Local Communities*, London: LPEG.
Luttwak, E.N. (1990) 'From geopolitics to geo-economics', *The National Interest* 20 (Summer): 17–23.
Mabbott, J. (1993) 'City Challenge – faith, hope and charities', *Town and Country Planning*, June: 137–8.
McCarthy, T. (1978) *The Critical Theory of Jurgen Habermas*, Oxford: Blackwell.
McDowell, L. (1991) 'Life without father and Ford: the new gender order of post-Fordism', *Transactions of the Institute of British Geographers* 16(2): 400–19.
MacGregor, S. (1994) 'The semantics and politics of urban poverty', in Mangen, S. and Hantrais, L. (eds) *Polarisation and Urban Space*, Loughborough: Cross-National Research Papers.
—— (1995) *Drugs Policy, Community and the City*, Middlesex University Occasional Paper.
MacGregor, S. and Lipow, A. (eds) (1995) *The Other City: People and Politics in New York and London*, Atlantic Highlands, NJ: Humanities Press.
MacGregor, S. and Pimlott, B. (eds) (1990) *Tackling the Inner Cities*, Oxford: Clarendon Press.
MacKenzie, S. and Rose, D. (1983) 'The city of separate spheres', in Anderson, J., *Redundant Spaces*, London: Academic Press.
McLaughlin, E. (1994) *Community, Policing and Accountability*, Aldershot: Avebury.
McLaughlin, E. and Muncie, J. (1994) 'Managing the criminal justice system', in Clarke, J., Cochrane, A. and McLaughlin, E. (eds) *Managing Social Policy*, London: Sage.
Madden, M. and Batey, P. (1983) 'The modelling of demographic–economic change within the context of regional decline: analytical procedures and empirical results', *Socio-Economic Planning Science* 17: 315–28.
Manchester City Council (1994) *City Pride*, Manchester.
—— (1995) *Design Guidelines*, Manchester.
Manchester City Council Planning Department (1980a) *Housing and Urban Renewal*, Manchester.
—— (1980b) *City Centre Local Plan*, Manchester.

Mann, L. (1993) 'Domestic violence in lesbian relationships', Paper presented at the British Sociological Association Annual Conference, Essex.

Marcuse, P. (1989) 'Dual city': a muddy metaphor for a quartered city', *International Journal of Urban and Regional Research* 13(4): 697–708.

—— (1993) 'What's so new about divided cities?', *International Journal of Urban and Regional Research* 17(3): 355–65.

Marsh, D. and Rhodes, R. (1992) *Implementing Thatcherite Policies*, Milton Keynes: Open University Press.

Martin, S. and Pearce, G. (1992) 'The internationalization of local authority economic development strategies: Birmingham in the 1980s', *Regional Studies* 26(5): 499–509.

Mason, D. (1995) *Race & Ethnicity in Modern Britain*, London: Oxford University Press.

Massey, D. (1994) *Space, Place and Gender*, Cambridge: Polity Press.

Massing, H. (1992) 'The new mafia', *New York Review of Books*, 3 September.

Matthews, R. (1995) 'Crime and its consequences in England and Wales', *Annals of the American Academy of Political and Social Science* 539, May.

Mattick, P. (1969) *Marx and Keynes: The Limits of the Mixed Economy*, Boston: Porter Sargent.

May, R. and Cohen, R. (1974) 'The interaction between race and colonialism: the Liverpool race riots of 1919', *Race and Class* 16(2): 111–26.

Mayer, M. (1994) 'Post-Fordist city politics', in Amin, A. (ed.) *Post-Fordism*, Oxford: Blackwell.

Mayhew, P., Elliot, D. and Dowds, L. (1989) *1988 British Crime Survey*, London: HMSO.

Mayhew, P., Maung, N.A. and Mirrlees-Black, C. (1993) *The 1992 British Crime Survey*, London: HMSO.

Mays, J. (1954) *Growing Up in the City*, Liverpool: Liverpool University Press.

Mellor, R. (1984) *The Inner City as Periphery*, Department of Sociology, University of Manchester, Occasional Paper, No. 14.

Merton, R.K. (1957) 'Social structure and anomie', in Merton, R.K., *Social Theory and Social Structure*, New York: Free Press.

Mingione, E. (1994) *Socio-Economic Restructuring and Social Exclusion*, Paper to Conference on Cities, Enterprises and Society on the Eve of the XXIst Century, Lille: CNRS/University of Lille.

Modood, T. (1993) 'Muslim views on religious identity and racial equality', *New Community* 19(3): 513–19.

Modood, T., Beishon, S. and Virdee, S. (1994) *Changing Ethnic Identities*, London: Policy Studies Institute.

Mollenkopf, J.H. and Castells, M. (eds) (1991) *Dual City: Restructuring New York*, New York: Russell Sage Foundation.

Mooney, G. (1994) 'The Glasgow regeneration alliance: the way forward for peripheral estates?', *Regions* 192 (August): 12–19.

Mooney, J. (1993) *The Hidden Figure: Domestic Violence in North London*, Islington Council: Police and Crime Prevention Unit.

—— (1994) 'The prevalence and social distribution of domestic violence: an analysis of theory and method', Ph.D. thesis, Middlesex University.

—— (1996) 'Researching domestic violence: the North London domestic violence survey', in Lyon, S. and Morris, L. (eds) *Gender Relations in Public and Private: Changing Research Perspectives*, BSA volume, London: Macmillan.

Moore, R. (1992) 'Labour and housing markets in inner city regeneration', *New Community* 18(3): 371–86.

—— (1994) 'Crisis and compliance: the Liverpool non-discrimination notice, 1989–1994', *New Community* 20(4): 581–602.

Morgan, D. (1992) 'Talking policing', in Downes, D. (ed.) *Unravelling Criminal Justice*, London: Macmillan.

Morgan, R. and Swift, P. (1987) 'The future of police authorities', *Public Administration* 65(2): 259–76.

—— (1988) 'Magistrates and the police authorities', *Justice of the Peace*, July: 425–7.

Morris, L. (1994) *Dangerous Classes*, London: Routledge.

Mulgan, G (1990) 'The changing shape of the city', in Hall, S. and Jacques, M. (eds) *New Times: The Changing Face of Politics in the 1990s*, London: Lawrence & Wishart.

Mullard, C. (1982) 'Multiracial education in Britain: from assimilation to cultural pluralism', in Tierney, J. (ed.) *Race, Migration and Schooling*, New York: Holt, Rinehart & Winston.

Murphy, A. (1993) 'Emerging regional linkages within the European Community: challenging the dominance of the state', *Tijdschrift voor Economische en Sociale Geografie* 84(2): 103–18.

NACRO (1991) *Preventing Youth Crime*, London: NACRO.

National Audit Office (1990) *Regenerating the Inner Cities*, London: HMSO.

Neill, W. (1991) 'Motown Blues – no answer in privatised planning', *Town and Country Planning* 60(3): 86–7.

Nevin, B. and Shiner, P. (1993) 'Britain's urban problems: communities hold the key', *Local Work* 50, Manchester: Centre for Local Economic Strategies.

—— (1995) 'The Left, urban policy and community empowerment: the first steps toward a new framework for urban regeneration', *Local Economy* 10(3): 204–17.

Newton, K. (1975) *Second City Politics*, Oxford: Oxford University Press.

Nicholson, J. (1967) 'The distribution of personal income', *Lloyds Bank Review* (January).

Nielsen, J. (1992) 'Islam, Muslims, and British local and central government: structural fluidity', *CSIC Series no. 6*, Birmingham: Selly Oak Colleges.

North West Regional Planning Council (1974) *Strategic Plan for the NW*, London: HMSO.

Offe, C. (1984) *Contradictions of the Welfare State*, London: Hutchinson.

Ohmae, K. (1991) 'The rise of the region state', *Foreign Affairs* 72 (Spring): 78–87.

Olds, K.N. (1988) 'Planning for the housing impacts of a hallmark event: a case study of Expo '86', Unpublished M.A. thesis, The University of British Columbia, Vancouver.

Osborne, D. and Gaebler, T. (1992) *Reinventing Government: How the Entrepreneurial Spirit is Transforming the Public Sector*, Reading, Mass.: Addison-Wesley.

—— (1993) *Reinventing Government*, New York: Plume.

Overbeek, H. (1990) *Global Capitalism and National Decline, the Thatcher Decade in Perspective*, London: Unwin Hyman.

Pacione, M. (1986) 'The changing pattern of deprivation in Glasgow', *Scottish Geographical Magazine* 102: 1499–1520.

—— (1990) 'A tale of two cities: the migration of the urban crisis in Glasgow', *Cities* 7(4): 304–14.

—— (1993) 'The geography of the urban crisis: some evidence from Glasgow', *Scottish Geographical Magazine* 109: 87–95.

Pagelow, M. (1984) *Family Violence*, New York: Praeger.

Painter, K. (1988) *Lighting and Crime: The Edmonton Project*, Middlesex Polytechnic: Centre for Criminology.

Painter, K., Woodhouse, T. and Young, J. (1990) *The Ladywood Crime Survey*, Middlesex Polytechnic: Centre for Criminology.

Parker, T. (1983) *The People of Providence*, London: Hutchinson.

Parker-Jenkins, M. (1991) 'Muslim matters: the educational needs of the Muslim child', *New Community* 17(4): 569–82.

Parry, G., Moyser, G. and Wagstaffe, M. (1987) 'The crowd and the community', in Gaskell, G. and Benewick, R., *The Crowd in Contemporary Britain*, London: Sage.

Parsons, G. (1994) 'There and back again? Religion and the 1944 and 1988 Education Acts', in Parsons, G. (ed.) *The Growth of Religious Diversity. Britain from 1945* (vol. 2), London: Routledge.

Peach, C. and Rossiter, D. (1996) 'Level and nature of spatial concentration and segregation of minority ethnic groups in Great Britain, 1991', in Ratcliffe, P. (ed.) *Social Geography and Ethnicity in Britain: Geographical Spread, Spatial Concentration and Internal Migration*, London: HMSO.

Peach, C. and Byron, M. (1993) 'Caribbean tenants in council housing: "race", class and gender', *New Community*, April: 407–23.

Pearson, G. (1983) *Hooligan: The History of Respectable Fears*, London: Macmillan.

Pearson, J. (1985) *The Profession of Violence: The Rise and Fall of the Kray Twins* (3rd edn), London: Panther.

Pease, K. (1994) 'Crime prevention', in Maguire, M., Morgan, R. and Reiner, R. (eds) *Oxford Handbook of Criminology*, Oxford: Clarendon Press.

Peck, J. (1995) 'Moving and shaking: business élites, state localism and urban privatism', *Progress in Human Geography* 16(2): 16–46.

Peck, J. and Tickell, A. (1995) 'Business goes local', *International Journal of Urban and Regional Research* 19: 55–78.

Peterson, P. (1981) *City Limits*, Chicago: University of Chicago Press.

Phillips, D. (1986) *What Price Equality?*, GLC Housing Policy Report 9, London: GLC.

Pickvance, C. and Preteceille, E. (eds) (1991) *State Restructuring and Local Power: A Comparative Perspective*, London: Pinter.

Pinch, S. (1993) 'Social polarisation: a comparison of the evidence from Britain and the United States', *Environment and Planning A* 25(6): 779–95.

Pitch, T. (1995) *Limited Responsibilites: Social Movements and Criminal Justice*, London: Routledge.

Planning (1991) 'Birmingham takes broader view in regeneration drive', *Planning* 948: 11.

Plymouth 2000 Partnership (1994) *Turning the Tide: Plymouth's Bid for the Single Regeneration Budget*, Plymouth: 2000 Partnership.

Plymouth Health Authority (1992) *Statement of Intent: 1992–93*, Plymouth: Plymouth Health Authority.

Plymouth Task Force (1995) *Action Plan: 1995–96*, Plymouth: Government Office for the South West.

Pollert, A. (ed.) (1991) *Farewell to Flexibility?*, Oxford: Blackwell.

Porter, M.E. (1994) *The Competitive Advantage of the Inner City*, Discussion Paper 6/22/94a, Boston: Harvard Business School.

Poster, M. (1990) *The Mode of Information: Poststructuralism and Social Context*, Cambridge: Polity Press.

Power, A. (1987a) *The PEP Guide to Local Management* (3 vols), London: Department of the Environment.

—— (1987b) *Property Before People: The Management of Twentieth Century Council Housing*, London: Allen & Unwin.

—— (1989) 'Housing, community and crime', in Downes, D. (ed.) *Crime and the City*, London: Macmillan.

Pratt, J. (1989) 'Corporatism: the third model of juvenile justice', *British Journal of Criminology* 29(3): 236–54.

Preteceille, E. (1990) 'Political paradoxes of urban restructuring: globalization of the economy and localization of politics?', in Logan, J.R. and Swanstrom, T. (eds) *Beyond the City Limits*, Philadelphia, Pa.: Temple University Press.

Przeworski, J.F. (1986) 'Changing intergovernmental relations and urban economic development', *Environment and Planning C: Government and Policy* 4: 423–38.

Quilley, S. (1995) 'Globalisation and local economic strategies', BSA Conference Paper, Leicester, April.

Quinton, O. (1990) Interview in the *Magazine* of the Third Poverty Programme, No. 1, July, p. 3.

Radford, J. (1987) 'Policing male violence – policing women', in Hanmer, J. and Maynard, M. (eds) *Women, Violence and Social Control*, London: Macmillan.

Radford, J. and Laffy, C. (1984) 'Violence against women: women speak out', *Critical Social Policy* 11: 111–18.

Ramdin, R. (1987) *The Making of the Black Working Class in Britain*, Aldershot: Gower.

Ratcliffe, P. (1981) *Racism and Reaction: A Profile of Handsworth*, London: Routledge & Kegan Paul.

—— (1986) *Race and Housing in Britain: A Bibliography*, ESRC Centre for Research in Ethnic Relations, University of Warwick.

—— (1992) 'Renewal, regeneration and "race": issues in urban policy', *New Community* 18(3): 387–400.

—— (1994) '"Race", housing and social change in Britain', Paper presented at the 6th International Research Conference on Housing, Global Challenge – Local Challenges in the 21st Century, Beijing, 21–24 September.

—— (forthcoming) '"Race", ethnicity and housing differentials in Britain', in Karn, V. (ed.) *Housing, Education and Employment* (Working Title), London: HMSO.

Ray, L. (1993) *Rethinking Critical Theory: Emancipation in the Age of Global Social Movements*, London: Sage Publications.

Redhead, B. (1993) *Manchester, a Celebration*, London: Deutsch.

Reeves, F. (1989) *Race and Borough Politics*, Aldershot: Avebury.
Reiner, R. (1992) *The Politics of the Police* (2nd edn), Toronto: University of Toronto Press.
—— (1994) 'Policing and the police', in Maguire, M., Morgan, R. and Reiner, R. (eds) *Oxford Handbook of Criminology*, Oxford: Clarendon Press.
Reiner, R. and Spencer, S. (eds) (1993) *Accountable Policing*, London: IPPR.
Reuter, P. (1983) *Disorganized Crime: The Economics of the Visible Hand*, Cambridge, Mass.: MIT Press.
Rex, J. (1991) *Ethnic Identity and Ethnic Mobilisation in Britain*, Monograph in Ethnic Relations no. 5, CRER, University of Warwick.
Rex, J. and Moore, R. (1967) *Race, Community and Conflict: A Study of Sparkbrook*, Oxford: Oxford University Press.
Reynolds, F. (1986) *The Problem Housing Estate*, Aldershot: Gower.
Robbins, D. (1992) *Social Exclusion 1990–1992: The United Kingdom*, Paper for EC Observatory on Policies to Combat Social Exclusion, Brussels: Commission of the European Communities.
Roberts, V., Russell, H., Harding, A. and Parkinson, M. (1995) *Public/Private/Voluntary Partnerships in Local Government*, London and Luton: Local Government Management Board.
Robins, K. (1991) 'Tradition and translation', in Corner, J. and Harvey, S., *Enterprise and Heritage*, London: Routledge.
Robinson, F. and Shaw, K. (1991) 'Urban regeneration and community involvement', *Local Economy* 6(1): 61–73.
Robson, B. (1988) *Those Inner Cities*, Oxford: Clarendon Press.
—— (1989) 'Social and economic futures for the large city', in Herbert, D.T. and Smith, D.M. (eds) *Social Problems and the City: New Perspectives*, Oxford: Oxford University Press.
Robson, B. *et al.* (1994) *Assessing the Impact of Urban Policy*, London: Department of the Environment.
Rodgers, B. (1980) 'Manchester revisited', in White, H.P., *The Continuing Conurbation*, London: Gower Press.
Rogers, R. and Fisher, M. (1992) *A New London*, London: Penguin.
Room, G. (1994) 'Poverty studies in the European Union: retrospect and prospect', Paper to Conference on Understanding Social Exclusion: Lessons from Transnational Research Studies, London: PSI.
Rose, D. (1995) 'Back to jackboot justice', *The Observer*, 12 March.
Rotherham MBC (n.d.) *The Rothercard Discount Scheme*.
Ruggiero, V. (1986) 'The encounter between big business and organized crime', *Capital and Class* 26: 21–7.
Runciman, W. (1965) *Relative Deprivation and Social Justice*, Routledge & Kegan Paul.
Sabel, C.F. (1989) 'Flexible specialisation and the re-emergence of regional economies', in Hirst, P.Q. and Zeitlin, J. (eds) *Reversing Industrial Decline?*, Oxford: Berg.
San Francisco Chronicle (1993) 'Centre to open after 3 decades of controversy', 8 October.
San Francisco Weekly (1989) 'The endless saga of Yerba Buena', 16 August, p. 7.
Sanders, H. and Stone, C. (1987) 'Developmental politics reconsidered', *Urban Affairs Quarterly* 22(4): 521–39.
Sarre, P., Phillips, D. and Skellington, R. (1989) *Ethnic Minority Housing: Explanations and Policies*, Aldershot: Avebury.
Sassen, S. (1988) *The Mobility of Capital and Labour*, New York: Cambridge University Press.
—— (1991) *The Global City: New York, London, Tokyo*, Princeton, N.J.: Princeton University Press.
—— (1994) *Cities in the World Economy*, London: New Pine Press.
Savage, M. and Warde, A. (1993) *Urban Sociology, Capitalism and Modernity*, London: Macmillan.
Savitch, H.V. (1988) *Post Industrial Cities*, Princeton, N.J.: Princeton University Press.
Schinkel, K. (1993) *The English Journey in 1826*, New Haven, Conn.: Yale University Press.
Seeley, J. (1966) 'The slum, its nature, use and users', in Wheaton, W., *Urban Housing*, New York: The Free Press.
Sennett, R. (1986) *The Fall of Public Man*, New York: Knopf.
Sharkansky, I. (1975) *The United States: A Study of a Developing Country*, New York: David McKay.
Shevky, E. (1972) *Social Area Analysis*, Westport, Conn.: Greenwood Press.

Simpson, A. (1981) *Stacking the Decks*, Nottingham: Nottingham Community Relations Council.

Skellington, R. (with P. Morris) (1992) *'Race' in Britain Today*, London: Sage/Open University Press.

Smith, A.D. (1986) *The Ethnic Origins of Nations*, Oxford: Blackwell.

Smith, L. (1989) *Domestic Violence*, London: HMSO.

Smith, S. (1989) *The Politics of 'Race' and Residence*, Cambridge: Polity Press.

—— (1991) ' "Race" and housing in Britain', Paper prepared for the Joseph Rowntree Foundation 'Race' and Housing Workshop, University of York, 4–5 April.

Solomos, J. (1989) *Race and Racism in Contemporary Britain*, London: Macmillan.

Somers, M.R. (1994) 'The narrative construction of identity: a relational and network approach', *Theory and Society* 23(4): 605–49.

Stacey, M. (1969) 'The myth of community studies', *British Journal of Sociology* 20(2): 134–47.

Stanko, E. (1992) 'The image of violence', *Criminal Justice Matters* 8 (Summer): 3.

Steinmetz, S. (1977–8) 'The battered husband syndrome', *Victimology* 2(3–4): 499–509.

Stewart, G. (1992) 'Manchester in 2000: European capital or provincial backwater ?', *City Life* 199: 10–13 (Manchester).

Stewart, J. (1986) *The Future Management of Local Government*, London: Allen & Unwin.

Stewart, J. and Stoker, G. (eds) (1989) *Local Government in Europe: Trends and Developments*, London: Macmillan.

Stewart, M. (1994) 'Between Whitehall and town hall: the realignment of urban regeneration policy in England', *Policy and Politics* 22(2): 133–45.

Stöhr, W.B. (1989) 'Regional policy at the cross-roads: an overview', in Albrechts, L., Moulgert, F., Roberts, P. and Swyngedouw, E. (eds) *Regional Policy at the Cross-Roads: European Perspectives*, London: Jessica Kingsley.

—— (ed.) (1990) *Global Challenge and Local Response: Initiatives for Economic Regeneration in Contemporary Europe*, New York: The United Nations University/Mansell.

Stoker, G. (1996) 'Regime theory and urban politics', in LeGates, R.T. and Stout, F. (eds) *The City Reader*, London: Routledge.

Stoker, G. and Mossberger, K. (1994) 'Urban regime theory in comparative perspective', *Environment and Planning C: Government and Policy* 12: 195–212.

Stone, C. (1984) 'City politics and economic development: political economy perspectives', *Journal of Politics* 46(1): 286–99.

—— (1993) 'Urban regimes and the capacity to govern: a political economy approach', *Journal of Urban Affairs* 15(1): 1–28.

Storch, R. (1976) 'The policeman as domestic missionary; urban discipline and popular culture in northern England 1850–1880', *Journal of Social History* IX(4): 481–509.

Strathclyde Poverty Alliance (1994) *Annual Report 1993–4*, Glasgow: SPA.

Strathclyde Regional Council (1994) *The Social Strategy for the Nineties*, Glasgow: Strathclyde Regional Council.

Straus, M. (1977–8) 'Wife-beating: how common and why?', *Victimology* 2(3–4): 443–58.

—— (1980) 'Victims and aggressors in marital violence', *American Behavioral Scientist*, May/June: 681–704.

—— (1986) 'Domestic violence and homicide antecedents', *Bulletin of the New York Academy of Medicine* 62: 446–65.

Straus, M. and Gelles, R. (1986) 'Societal change and change in family violence from 1975 to 1985 as revealed by two national surveys', *Journal of Marriage and the Family* 48: 465–79.

—— (1988) 'How violent are American families? Estimates from the National Family Violence Resurvey and other studies', in Hotaling, G., Finkelhor, D., Kirkpatrick, J. and Straus, M. (eds) *Family Abuse and its Consequences*, Newbury Park, Calif.: Sage.

Straus, M., Gelles, R. and Steinmetz, S. (1981) *Behind Closed Doors: Violence in the American Family*, New York: Anchor/Doubleday.

Sum, N.L. (1996) 'Strategies for East Asia regionalism and the construction of NIC identities in the post-Cold War era', in Gamble, A. and Payne, A. (eds) *Regionalism and World Order*, Basingstoke: Macmillan.

Swann Committee of Inquiry into the Education of Children from Ethnic Minority Groups (1985) *Education for All*, Cmnd 9453, London: HMSO.

Swanstrom, T. (1988) 'Semisovereign cities: the politics of urban development', *Polity* 21(1): 83–110.

Taylor, A.J.P. (1976) *Essays in English History*, Harmondsworth: Penguin.

Taylor, R. (1996) 'The need for workplace voice', in Radice, G. (ed.) *What Needs to Change: New Visions for Britain*, London: HarperCollins.

Terry, N. (1995) 'From the slums to the stars', *The Lizard* 3 (London).

The Highbury Initiative (1989) *The Highbury Initiative: City Centre Challenge Symposium 1989*, Report of proceedings.

The Planner (1991) 'Award for Planning achievement 1991', 77(40): v–vi.

Tickell, A. and Peck, J. (1992) 'Accumulation, regulation and the geographies of post-Fordism: missing links in regulation research', *Progress in Human Geography* 16(2): 190–218.

Titmuss, R. (1962) *Income Distribution and Social Change*, London: Allen & Unwin.

Tobin, J. (1972) 'Improving the economic status of the negro', quoted by Tabb, W., *The Political Economy of the Black Ghetto*, New York: Norton.

Tömmel, I. (1992) 'System-Entwicklung and Politikgestaltung in der Europäischen Gemeinschaft am Beispiel der Regionalpolitik', in Kreile, M. (ed.) *Die Integration Europas*, Opladen: Westdeutscher Verlag.

Townsend, P. (1979) *Poverty in the United Kingdom*, Harmondsworth: Penguin Books.

—— (1994) 'Think globally, act locally', *European Labour Forum* 13: 2–9.

Troyna, B. (1993) *Racism and Education. Research Perspectives*, Milton Keynes: Open University Press.

Tuck, M. (1991) 'Community and criminal justice system' *Policy Studies* 12: 22–37.

Turner, B.S. (1987) *Medical Power and Social Knowledge*, London: Sage.

Twombly, W. (1975) 'The city needs classy sweat palace', *San Francisco Examiner*, 6 May, p. 45.

Urry, J. (1982) 'Localities, regions and social classes', *International Journal of Urban and Regional Research* 5: 455–74.

Van Kempen, E.T. (1994) 'The dual city and the poor: social polarisation, social segregation and life chances', *Urban Studies* 31(7): 995–1015.

Varelidis, N., Anderson, R. and O'Conghaile, W. (1994) *Consumer-Oriented Action in the Public Services: Overview and Progress Report on a Project*, Dublin: European Foundation for the Improvement of Living and Working Conditions, Working Paper WP/94/01/EN.

Vaz, K. (1993) *The Crisis in Britain's Cities*, London: Cities 2020 (The Campaign to Regenerate Britain's Cities).

Wachtel, E. (1986) 'Expo 86 and the World's Fairs', in Anderson, R. and Wachtel, E. (eds) *The Expo Story*, Madeira Park, B.C.: Harbour Publishing.

Wahlberg, M., Taylor, K. and Geddes, M. (1995) *Enhancing Local Democracy*, London and Luton: Local Government Management Board.

Ward, C. (1988) *Welcome Thinner City*, London: Bedford Square Press.

Weatheritt, M. (1986) *Innovations in Policing*, London: Croom Helm.

Weinstein, H.E. (1970) 'Urban renewal lessons still unlearned', *Wall Street Journal*, 27 May.

Wheeler, R. (1994) 'Campaigning against poverty: the local authority role', *Local Economy* 9(2): 185–91.

Whipp, R. (1990) *Patterns of Labour: Work and Social Change in the Pottery Industry*, London: Routledge.

White, H. (1987) *The Content of the Form*, Baltimore, Md.: Johns Hopkins University Press.

White, J. (1986) *The Worst Street in North London: Campbell Bunk, Islington, Between the Wars*, London: Routledge & Kegan Paul.

Wilkinson, R.G. (1994) *Unfair Shares: The Effects of Widening Income Differences on the Welfare of the Young*, London: Barnardo's.

Willmott, P. (1986) *Social Networks, Informal Care and Public Policy*, London: Policy Studies Institute.

Wilpert, C. (1988) 'Religion and ethnicity: orientations, perceptions and strategies among Turkish Alevi and Sunni migrants in Berlin', in Gerholm, T. and Lithman, Y.G. (eds) *The New Islamic Presence in Western Europe*, London: Mansell.

Wilson, E. (1991) *The Sphinx in the City*, London: Virago.

Wilson, W.J. (1987) *The Truly Disadvantaged*, Chicago: University of Chicago Press.

—— (1991) 'Studying inner city dislocations', *American Sociological Review* 56: 1–14.

—— (1993) *The Ghetto Underclass*, New York: Sage.

Winchester, H.P.M. and White, P.E. (1988) 'The location of marginalised groups in the inner city', *Environment and Planning D: Society and Space* 6: 37–54.

Wood, D. (1991) *The Regional Financial and Professional Structure of the UK*, Manchester: Manchester Business School.

Woodward, R. (1995) 'Approaches towards the study of social polarization in the UK', *Progress in Human Geography* 19(1): 75–89.

Wootton, B. (1959) *Social Science and Social Pathology*, London: Allen & Unwin.

Wright, G. (1994) 'Giving the streets back to the people', Paper presented at the Local Authorities Pedestrian Planning Group Conference, Birmingham.

Wynne, D. and O'Connor, J. (1995) 'City cultures and "new cultural intermediaries"', BSA Conference Paper, Leicester.

Young, I. (1990) 'The ideal of community and the politics of difference', in Nicholson, L. (ed.) *Feminism/Postmodernism*, New York: Routledge.

Young, J. (1988) 'Risk of crime and fear of crime: a realist critique of survey-based assumptions', in Maguire, M. and Pointing, J. (eds) *Victims of Crime: A New Deal?*, Milton Keynes: Open University Press.

—— (1992) 'Ten points of realism', in Young, J. and Matthews, R. (eds) *Rethinking Criminology: The Realist Debate*, London: Sage.

Young, M. and Willmott, P. (1957) *Family and Kinship in East London*, London: Routledge & Kegan Paul.

Zukin, S. (1988) *Loft Living*, London: Hutchinson.

—— (1991) *Landscapes of Power: From Detroit to Disney World*, Berkeley, Calif.: University of California Press.

INDEX

Abbott, P. 145
Abrams, P. 117, 150, 152
actuarial criminal justice 52, 53
Addams, Jane 20
agencies 13, 58, 135–6, 138, 170; *see also* quangos
Aglietta, M. 49
Allen, G. 120
Almond, G. 47
Althusser, L. 130
Altvater, E. 32
Anderson, B. 41n7
Anwar, M. 194
Ashton, J. 141, 143, 144
Association of Metropolitan Authorities 212; Anti-Poverty Network 167
Atkinson, R. 211
Augur, D.A. 75

Bailey, N. 8, 9
Bakshi, P. 32
Ball, W. 14, 198, 200, 202
Ballard, C. 88, 89
Ballard, R. 88, 89
Balloch, S. 167
Barnekov, T. 181
Barnes, J. 212
Barnes, W.R. 29
Bartley, M. 149
Barton, S.E. 188
Batey, P. 167
Beattie, A. 143–4, 149
Beauregard, R.A. 85
Beazley, M. 14
Beckford, J. 14
Bell, D. 34
Ben-Tovim, G. 200, 201
Benington, J. 213
Benko, G. 29
Best, M. 29
Beynon, H. 32
Beynon, J. 206
Bhachu, P. 90
Bianchini, F. 3, 5, 66
Birmingham: community resistance to redevelopment 14, 182, 188–91, 192; Muslims 200; urban governance 13 (form

and direction of urban governance 138–9; hegemony and regime theory applied to urban governance 135–8)
Bishop, P. 145
Blair, Tony 144
Blaxter, M. 141
Boisier, S. 36
Bonefeld, W. 138
Booth, Charles 20
Bottoms, A. 44, 45, 52, 117, 159
bourgeoisie 20
Boyle, R. 78
Braham, P. 198
Bramley, G. 215
Breines, W. 103
Brenner, R. 48, 49
Bristol, anti-poverty initiative 213–14
British Sociological Association Annual Conference (1995) 1
Brogden, M. 43
Brown, C. 92, 94
Brownill, S. 169
Brownlow (N.I.) partnership programme 171–2, 213, 214
Brush, L. 103
Bulmer, M. 87
Bunton, R. 143, 144
Burrows, J. 42
Burrows, R. 144
business tourism 136, 137, 188
Butler, E. 169
Byron, M. 93, 94

Campbell, B. 205, 209
capitalism 2, 11, 20, 41, 54
capitalist city 49–50
Carley, M. 135, 137, 189
Carpenter, M. 144
Castells, M. 29, 49, 51, 56, 61, 66, 73, 74, 84, 85, 142, 150
centralisation 169–70, 207
Chalkley, B. 145
Champion, S. 65
Charteris, S. 216
Chaston, I. 149
Cheetham, J. 198
Cherry, G. 137